WordPerfect® Office 2000 for Linux®

fast&easy®

Send Us Your Comments:
To comment on this book or any other PRIMA TECH title, visit our reader response page on the Web at **www.prima-tech.com/comments**.

How to Order:
For information on quantity discounts, contact the publisher: Prima Publishing, P.O. Box 1260BK, Rocklin, CA 95677-1260; (916) 787-7000. On your letterhead, include information concerning the intended use of the books and the number of books you want to purchase. For individual orders, turn to the back of this book for more information.

WordPerfect® Office 2000 for Linux®
fast&easy®

Brian Proffitt

A Division of Prima Publishing

© 2000 by Prima Publishing. All rights reserved. No part of this book may be reproduced or transmitted in any form or by any means, electronic or mechanical, including photocopying, recording, or by any information storage or retrieval system without written permission from Prima Publishing, except for the inclusion of brief quotations in a review.

A Division of Prima Publishing

Prima Publishing and colophon and Fast and Easy® are registered trademarks of Prima Communications, Inc. PRIMA TECH is a trademark of Prima Communications, Inc., Roseville, California 95661.

Publisher: Stacy L. Hiquet

Marketing Manager: Judi Taylor

Associate Marketing Manager: Heather Buzzingham

Managing Editor: Sandy Doell

Acquisitions Editor: Kim Spilker

Technical Reviewer: Van R. Hendrickson

Book Production and Editorial: Argosy/West Newton, MA

Cover Design: Prima Design Team

Corel® and WordPerfect® are registered trademarks of Corel Corporation or Corel Corporation Limited in Canada, the United States and/or other countries. All other trademarks are the property of their respective owners.

Important: Prima Publishing cannot provide software support. Please contact the appropriate software manufacturer's technical support line or Web site for assistance.

Prima Publishing and the author have attempted throughout this book to distinguish proprietary trademarks from descriptive terms by following the capitalization style used by the manufacturer.

Information contained in this book has been obtained by Prima Publishing from sources believed to be reliable. However, because of the possibility of human or mechanical error by our sources, Prima Publishing, or others, the Publisher does not guarantee the accuracy, adequacy, or completeness of any information and is not responsible for any errors or omissions or the results obtained from use of such information. Readers should be particularly aware of the fact that the Internet is an ever-changing entity. Some facts may have changed since this book went to press.

ISBN: 0-7615-2857-1

Library of Congress Catalog Card Number: 00-106646

Printed in the United States of America

00 01 02 03 04 DD 10 9 8 7 6 5 4 3 2 1

To my wife, my best friend

Contents at a Glance

Introduction xxi

PART I
GETTING STARTED 1

Chapter 1   Welcome to WordPerfect Office 2000 3
Chapter 2   Working with Files 9
Chapter 3   Getting Help with WordPerfect Office 2000 27

PART II
WORKING WITH WORDS 35

Chapter 4   Learning WordPerfect Basics 37
Chapter 5   Formatting a WordPerfect Document 47
Chapter 6   Improving Your Writing 71
Chapter 7   Building with Tables and Columns 83
Chapter 8   Adding Style to Your Document 99
Chapter 9   Managing Longer Documents 111

PART III
WORKING WITH DATA 133

Chapter 10   Learning Quattro Pro Basics 135
Chapter 11   Editing a Spreadsheet 147
Chapter 12   Working with Functions and Formulas 159

Chapter 13	Formatting Notebooks	169
Chapter 14	Completing Your Spreadsheet	181
Chapter 15	Manipulating Data	189
Chapter 16	Charting Data	203

PART IV
WORKING WITH ADVANCED DATA 217

| Chapter 17 | Learning Paradox Basics | 219 |
| Chapter 18 | Working with Paradox | 243 |

PART V
WORKING WITH IDEAS 259

Chapter 19	Learning Presentations Basics	261
Chapter 20	Editing a Slide Show	271
Chapter 21	Working with Presentations Special Effects	285
Chapter 22	Drawing with Presentations	297

PART VI
WORKING WITH TIME AND PEOPLE 315

Chapter 23	Learning the CorelCENTRAL Calendar	317
Chapter 24	Using CorelCENTRAL Calendar to Keep Organized	331
Chapter 25	Using CorelCENTRAL Memo to Keep Informed	339
Chapter 26	Using CorelCENTRAL Address Book to Keep in Touch	343

PART VII
APPENDIXES 355

| Appendix A | WordPerfect Office 2000 for Linux Installation | 357 |
| Appendix B | Using Shortcut Keys | 367 |

Glossary 375
Index 381

Contents

Introduction xxi

PART I
GETTING STARTED 1

Chapter 1 **Welcome to WordPerfect Office 2000** 3
Starting WordPerfect Office 2000 4
    Starting WordPerfect within X Window 4
    Starting WordPerfect from the Command Line 5
Exploring WordPerfect Office 2000 6
Exiting WordPerfect Office 2000 7

Chapter 2 **Working with Files** 9
Starting a New Document 10
    Making an Empty Document 10
    Using PerfectExpert 10
Opening Documents 18
    Opening an Existing Document 18
    Opening a Recently Edited Document 19
    Opening a "Foreign" Document 20
    Opening Multiple Documents 21
Saving Your Document 22
    Saving a Document 22

CONTENTS

Resaving a Document 24
Printing a Document 24
Closing a Document 25

Chapter 3 Getting Help with WordPerfect Office 2000 27
Starting Online Help 28
Searching for Answers in Help 30
Using PerfectExpert 31
Getting Assistance as You Go 31
Stopping PerfectExpert 33

PART II
WORKING WITH WORDS 35

Chapter 4 Learning WordPerfect Basics 37
Typing Text 38
Editing Text 38
Inserting Text 38
Selecting Text 40
Deleting Text 41
Correcting Your Mistakes 41
Navigating within a Document 43
Using Shadow Cursor 43
Using the Scroll Bars 45
Using the Keyboard 46

Chapter 5 Formatting a WordPerfect Document 47
Enhancing Text 48
Changing the Font 48
Changing the Font Size 49
Using QuickFonts 49
Applying Bold, Italic, or Underline 50
Changing Text Case 52

Inserting Special Characters and Symbols 52
Moving or Copying Text 54
   Moving Text 54
   Copying Text 56
   Using Click and Drag 58
Working with Bulleted or Numbered Lists 59
Arranging Text on a Page 61
   Aligning Text 61
   Changing Line Spacing 62
   Indenting Text 63
Working with Tabs 65
   Setting Tabs 65
   Moving Tabs 67
   Deleting Tabs 69

Chapter 6   **Improving Your Writing** **71**
Using Find and Replace 72
   Finding Terms 72
   Replacing Terms 74
Correcting Spelling Errors 75
   Using Spell-As-You-Go 75
   Running a Spell Check 77
Working with Grammar-As-You-Go 78
Working with QuickCorrect 79
   Adding QuickCorrect Entries 79
   Deleting QuickCorrect Entries 81
Working with Prompt-As-You-Go 82

Chapter 7   **Building with Tables and Columns** **83**
Organizing with Tables 84
   Creating Tables 84
   Editing Tables 89

CONTENTS

    Formatting Tables 92
  Creating Multi-Column Documents 95
    Creating Columns 95
    Formatting Columns 96

Chapter 8   **Adding Style to Your Document........................ 99**
  Using Artwork 100
    Inserting a Graphic 100
    Editing a Graphic 102
    Wrapping Text around a Graphic 105
  Using Make It Fit 106
  Using Text Boxes 107
    Making a Text Box 107
    Making a Multi-Column Text Box 108
  Inserting Another Document 109

Chapter 9   **Managing Longer Documents........................ 111**
  Setting Page Options 112
    Changing Margins 112
    Setting Paper Orientation 113
    Selecting a Paper Size 114
  Inserting a Page Break Manually 115
    Inserting a Page Break 115
    Deleting a Page Break 116
  Working with Headers and Footers 117
    Creating a Header or Footer 117
    Adding Date and Time 118
    Page Numbering 119
  Creating Footnotes and Endnotes 121
  Building a Table of Contents 124
  Creating an Index 127

PART III
WORKING WITH DATA 133

Chapter 10 Learning Quattro Pro Basics 135
Exploring the Spreadsheet 136
Moving around the Spreadsheet 137
Entering Data 138
    Entering Text 138
    Entering Numeric Data 139
    Entering Cell Addresses 140
Editing Data 141
    Replacing the Contents of a Cell 141
    Editing the Contents of a Cell 142
Using Multiple Sheets 143
    Navigating to Multiple Sheets 143
    Building Multi-Sheet Addresses 144

Chapter 11 Editing a Spreadsheet 147
Selecting Data 148
Inserting Rows and Columns 150
    Inserting Rows 150
    Inserting Columns 152
Deleting Rows and Columns 153
Moving Data 155
    Copying and Pasting Cells 155
    Using Click and Drag to Move Data 157

Chapter 12 Working with Functions and Formulas 159
Creating Formulas 160
    Creating a Simple Formula 160
    Creating a Complex Formula 161
Using Addresses in a Formula 162
    Using Relative Addresses 162

CONTENTS xiii

Inserting Relative Addresses Automatically	163
Using Absolute Addresses	165
Using Functions	166

Chapter 13 Formatting Notebooks 169

Formatting Numbers	170
Changing the Decimal Point Places	170
Applying New Data Formats	171
Applying New Formats with QuickFormat	172
Adjusting Column Widths	173
Setting Cell Alignment	175
Adjusting Cell Alignment	175
Aligning across Multiple Cells	176
Formatting with Fonts	176
Changing a Font	177
Changing a Font Size	177
Applying a Font Attribute	178
Adding Borders	178
Customizing Your Workspace	180

Chapter 14 Completing Your Spreadsheet 181

Preparing to Print	182
Setting Up Margins	182
Setting Page Orientation and Size	183
Getting It All on One Page	184
Printing a Spreadsheet	186
Using Print Preview	186
Printing Your Work	187

Chapter 15 Manipulating Data 189

Entering Data Faster	190
Using QuickType	190
Using QuickFill	191

Filtering Data 193
    Using the QuickFilter to Filter Data 193
    Using the Custom Filter 195
Sort Data with Multiple Criteria 198
Grouping Your Data 200

Chapter 16   Charting Data 203

Creating a Chart 204
    Making a Chart with Chart Expert 204
    Making a Chart with QuickChart 208
Modifying a Chart 209
    Resizing a Chart 209
    Moving a Chart 211
    Changing a Chart Style 212
    Modifying Chart Data 213
Deleting a Chart 215

PART IV
WORKING WITH ADVANCED DATA 217

Chapter 17   Learning Paradox Basics 219

Database Concepts 220
Examining the Paradox Environment 222
Creating a Database 222
    Creating a Table with Table Expert 222
    Creating a Form with Form Expert 229
    Creating a Query with Query Expert 233
    Creating a Report with Report Expert 238

Chapter 18   Working with Paradox 243

Creating Mailing Labels 244
Publishing Data to a Web Page 249
Using Data in a Quattro Pro Spreadsheet 252

Importing and Exporting Data 253
    Importing Data 253
    Exporting Data 256

PART V
WORKING WITH IDEAS 259

Chapter 19   Learning Presentations Basics 261
Starting Presentations 262
Creating a Basic Slide Show 264
Switching Views 265
    Viewing with the Slide Editor 265
    Using Slide Outliner 267
    Using Slide Sorter 268
    QuickPlay a Slide Show 269

Chapter 20   Editing a Slide Show 271
Working with Slides 272
    Adding Slides 272
    Deleting Slides 273
    Rearrange Slides 274
Manipulating Text 276
    Adding Text to a New Slide 276
    Editing Text 277
    Changing the Font 278
    Deleting a Text Object 279
Changing Slide Designs 280
Changing Slide Show Designs 280
Making Speaker Notes 282
Printing in Presentations 283
    Printing a Slide Show 283
    Printing Speaker and Audience Notes 284

Chapter 21   Working with Presentations Special Effects 285
Adding Tables 286
Inserting Charts 289
Adding Transitions 293
Applying Sound Effects 295

Chapter 22   Drawing with Presentations 297
Exploring the Drawing Tools 298
Creating Shapes 300
Creating Filled Shapes 304
Creating Lines and Curves 307
Creating Action Shapes 310
Integrating the Bitmap Editor 311

PART VI
WORKING WITH TIME AND PEOPLE 315

Chapter 23   Learning the CorelCENTRAL Calendar 317
Viewing CorelCENTRAL Calendar 318
Changing the Calendar's View 319
Creating an Event 320
Creating Recurring Events 323
Editing an Event 326
    Moving to a Different Time 326
    Moving to a Different Date 328
Deleting an Event 329

Chapter 24   Using CorelCENTRAL Calendar to Keep Organized 331
Creating a Task 332
Completing a Task 334
Assigning a Task to an Event 335
Deleting a Task 337

Chapter 25	**Using CorelCENTRAL Memo to Keep Informed**	**339**
	Creating a Memo	340
	Organizing Memos	341
Chapter 26	**Using CorelCENTRAL Address Book to Keep in Touch**	**343**
	Creating an Address	344
	Editing Addresses	346
	Importing Addresses	347
	Searching for Addresses	350
	Creating New Address Books	351
	Managing Address Books	352

PART VII
APPENDIXES 355

Appendix A	**WordPerfect Office 2000 for Linux Installation**	**357**
	Installing the Software	358
	Registering the Software	361
	Setting Up a Printer	363
Appendix B	**Using Shortcut Keys**	**367**
	Using Common WordPerfect Office 2000 Shortcut Keys	368
	Using WordPerfect Shortcut Keys	370
	Using Quattro Pro Shortcut Keys	371
	Using Presentations Shortcut Keys	372
	Using CorelCENTRAL Shortcut Keys	372
	Using Paradox Shortcut Keys	373

Glossary **375**

Index **381**

Acknowledgments

You cannot imagine the hard work done by so many people to put a book together. The editors, the layout technicians, and the proofreaders all did a wonderful job in making the book you now hold in your hands. I thank them profusely for their efforts.

I also am blessed on a personal level with the support and love of my wife and two daughters, without whom I could never accomplish anything.

About the Author

The author is not world-renowned but he gets by. In his disguise as mild-mannered **Brian Proffitt**, he lives in Indianapolis, Indiana, with his gorgeous wife and two beautiful daughters.

The author of *Install, Configure, and Customize Red Hat Linux 6.1* (Prima, 1999) and *Sun Install, Configure, and Customize Corel Linux* (Prima, 2000), Brian spends his copious free time (ha!) taking flying lessons, waving his arms around in conversation, and generally just confusing the heck out of his friends.

Introduction

This *Fast & Easy* series guide from Prima Tech is an excellent introduction to one of the hottest office suite applications on the market today—WordPerfect Office 2000—running on one of the fastest-growing operating systems—Linux.

Linux and WordPerfect are a good match in today's software world. Corel invested a great amount of time in a new Linux distribution, so it stands to reason that it should bring its powerful office suite over to the Linux platform.

The makers of WordPerfect Office 2000 did an interesting thing when they migrated their product to the side of penguins. Instead of directly translating their software into Motif, the usual Linux environment, Corel instead opted to port the entire suite using WINE. WINE, for those of you who haven't heard, is a Windows emulator that runs on top of Linux and allows (with some special tweaking) Windows applications to run within Linux.

The upshot of all this technical gobbledygook is that WordPerfect Office 2000 for Linux has much the same look, feel, and functionality of its Windows counterpart. Thus, you have an enormously powerful and quite popular set of office applications available for Linux.

As more applications arrive on the Linux platform, it might soon become a reality that Linux as a desktop platform can actively compete with Windows. Finally, users have a choice in what they can use.

Who Should Read This Book?

This book is perfect for the first-time WordPerfect user. Even if you have a passing familiarity with other office suites, the sheer functionality of the WordPerfect suite means you need to learn quite a few new things.

This book also serves as an excellent reference resource. Whenever you venture into new WordPerfect territory, you can take a quick look and see how to perform the new task.

Added Advice to Make You a Pro

The book contains other helpful elements, as well, that offer insight and key information related to the topic being discussed.

- **Tips** tell you about new and faster ways to accomplish a goal.
- **Notes** delve into background information regarding a given topic.

The appendixes show you how to obtain and install WordPerfect Office 2000 for Linux from the Internet. You also learn the key combinations used in all the WordPerfect Office 2000 components.

PART I
Getting Started

Chapter 1
   Welcome to WordPerfect Office 2000..... 3

Chapter 2
   Working with Files.................... 9

Chapter 3
   Getting Help with WordPerfect
   Office 2000......................... 27

1
Welcome to WordPerfect Office 2000

WordPerfect has long been a favorite word processor among Linux users. Now that Corel has made the entire WordPerfect Office 2000 suite available on the Linux platform, users can enjoy the full functionality of all the applications in the WordPerfect family. This family consists of no less than five applications: a word processor, a spreadsheet application, a slide show creator, a database tool, and a personal information manager. Despite the wide range of functionality, there are similarities throughout the WordPerfect Office 2000 interface. In this chapter, you'll learn how to:

- Start and exit WordPerfect component applications
- Recognize the common screen elements of WordPerfect Office 2000

Starting WordPerfect Office 2000

When you want to start any application in the WordPerfect Office 2000 suite, there are generally two methods to accomplish this: using the menus within your graphic interface, or typing the appropriate command directly into the Linux command line.

Starting WordPerfect within X Window

In this example, we use the KDE desktop environment in Corel Linux 1.1. Your screen might look slightly different on your Linux machine, particularly if you are using a different desktop environment. But the basic principles still apply across most forms of Linux and their desktops.

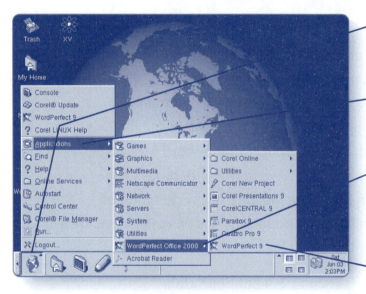

1. **Click** on the **Application Starter**. The main menu will appear.

2. **Move** the **mouse pointer** to Applications. The Applications menu will appear.

3. **Move** the **mouse pointer** to WordPerfect Office 2000. The WordPerfect Office 2000 menu will appear.

4. **Click** on **WordPerfect 9**. WordPerfect will start.

STARTING WORDPERFECT OFFICE 2000

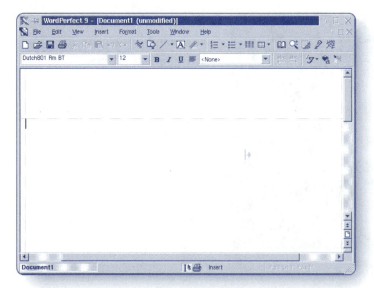

You can use this method with any of the WordPerfect Office 2000 applications.

NOTE

The first time you start an application in the Office 2000 suite, you see a License message box that displays the License Agreement. Simply read the agreement and click on the Accept button to proceed to the application.

Starting WordPerfect from the Command Line

If you are a Linux user who prefers to start applications from the command line, your needs are accommodated as well.

1. Click on the **Console icon** on the Panel. The Console window will appear.

NOTE

Every graphic interface in Linux has some kind of console or command-line application, such as the one shown here. If you start yours slightly differently, that's fine. After starting the console application, command-line windows are pretty much the same.

2. Type the **wordperfect command** in the window. WordPerfect will start.

You can use this method with any of the WordPerfect Office 2000 applications. Table 1-1 lists the commands you need for each application.

Table 1-1 Console Commands to Start WordPerfect Applications

Application	Command
WordPerfect	wordperfect
Quattro Pro	quattropro
Paradox	paradox
Presentations	presentations
CorelCENTRAL Address Book	ccaddressbook
CorelCENTRAL Calendar	cccalendar
CorelCENTRAL Memos	ccmemo

Exploring WordPerfect Office 2000

Even though there is more than one application in the WordPerfect Office 2000 suite, each application shares a number of common interface features, such as the ones illustrated in this Quattro Pro screen.

EXITING WORDPERFECT OFFICE 2000   7

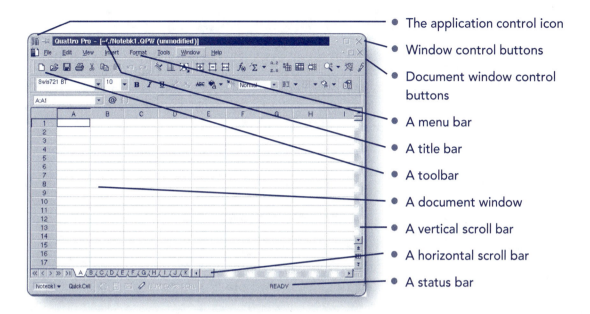

- The application control icon
- Window control buttons
- Document window control buttons
- A menu bar
- A title bar
- A toolbar
- A document window
- A vertical scroll bar
- A horizontal scroll bar
- A status bar

Exiting WordPerfect Office 2000

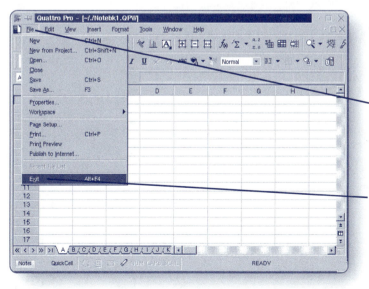

Exiting any of the Office 2000 applications is simplicity itself, as you will see in the following steps.

1. Click on **File** in any WordPerfect Office 2000 application. The File menu will appear.

2. Click on **Exit**. The application will close.

> **TIP**
>
> Other methods of exiting an application include clicking on the Close button (☒) (which looks like an X) in the upper-right corner of the screen. You can also press Alt+F4 on your keyboard simultaneously.

> **NOTE**
>
> If you have not saved any of your work when you exit an application, the Office 2000 application asks whether you want to save it. You can review saving files in Chapter 2, "Working with Files."

2

Working with Files

Whatever you do in WordPerfect Office 2000, you work with a document. Although people tend to think documents are only created by word processor applications, the truth is that a document is any kind of file—not just a WordPerfect file. How you manage these documents gives you a critical edge in using WordPerfect Office 2000. In this chapter, you'll learn how to:

- Create a new empty Office 2000 document or use PerfectExpert to make a document from a template
- Save your document
- Open a document, including those outside of Office 2000's formats
- Print a document
- Close a document

Starting a New Document

When you create documents in WordPerfect Office 2000, you have the choice of creating a new, empty document or a document patterned after one of the dozens of available templates.

Making an Empty Document

Within any WordPerfect Office 2000 application, you can start a new, empty document at any time.

1. Click on **File** in any WordPerfect 2000 application. The File menu will appear.

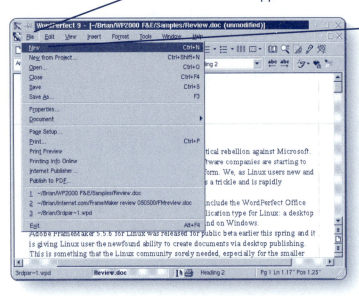

2. Click on **New**. A new document will appear.

> **TIP**
> You can press Ctrl+N to start a new empty document.

Using PerfectExpert

WordPerfect Office 2000 provides a lot of built-in creativity for users with the help of the PerfectExpert tool. PerfectExpert enables users to create new documents using several templates as a guide.

Opening an Installed Template

During the installation of WordPerfect Office 2000, dozens of sample templates were installed for your use. Here's how to access them.

STARTING A NEW DOCUMENT 11

1. Click on **File** in any WordPerfect 2000 application. The File menu will appear.

2. Click on **New from Project**. The PerfectExpert dialog box will appear.

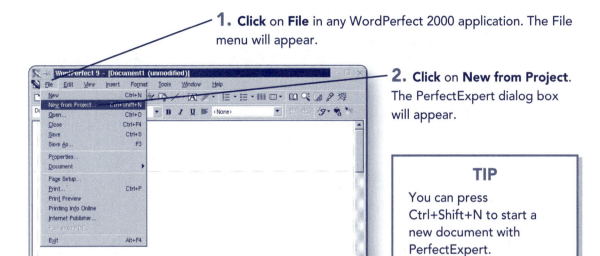

TIP

You can press Ctrl+Shift+N to start a new document with PerfectExpert.

3. Click on the **project** you want to use. The project is highlighted.

4. Click on **Create**. The PerfectExpert dialog box will close and a warning dialog box will appear the first time you use a project.

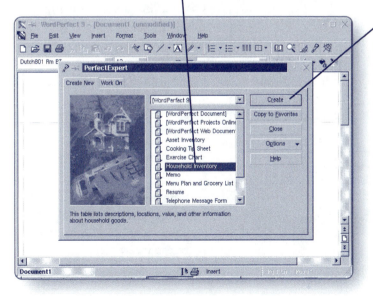

12 CHAPTER 2: WORKING WITH FILES

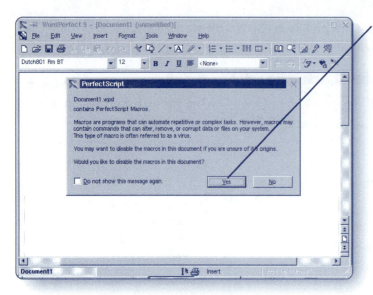

5. Click on **Yes** because we know this is a valid source document. The dialog box will close and the new document template will appear.

Opening an Online Template

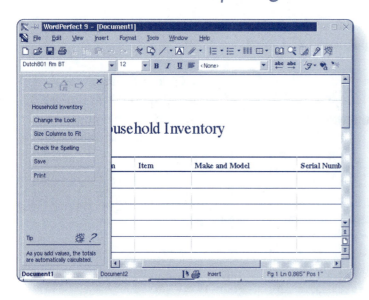

Besides the several templates installed with WordPerfect Office 2000, there are many others available for you to use on the Internet. With PerfectExpert, getting and installing these templates is a snap!

TIP
Before beginning this series of steps, it is helpful if you connect your system to the Internet.

STARTING A NEW DOCUMENT   13

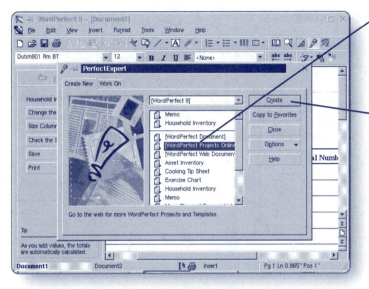

1. In PerfectExpert, **click** on **WordPerfect Projects Online**. The WordPerfect Projects Online line will be highlighted.

2. Click on **Create**. The default Web browser on your system will open itself to the WordPerfect Projects page at OfficeCommunity.com.

3. Click the **SmartTools – Projects & Templates link**. The SmartTools page will appear.

14 CHAPTER 2: WORKING WITH FILES

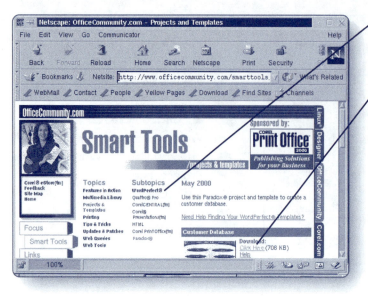

4. **Click** the **appropriate application link**. That month's template page will appear.

5. **Click** the **Click Here link** for the project you want. The Save As dialog will appear.

6. **Click** on **OK**. The file will be saved and the Save As dialog box will close.

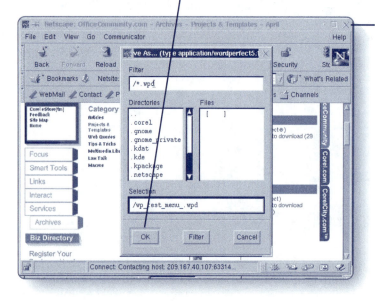

7. **Click** the **Close button** (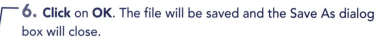). Netscape will be halted.

STARTING A NEW DOCUMENT   15

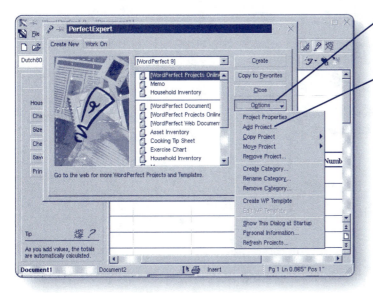

8. Click on **Options**. The Options menu will appear.

9. Click on **Add Project**. The Add Project Wizard will open.

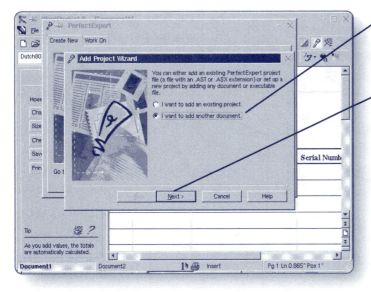

10. Click the **I want to add another document option**. The option will be selected.

11. Click on **Next**. The next screen of the wizard will appear.

16   CHAPTER 2: WORKING WITH FILES

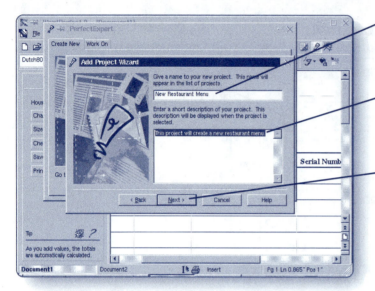

12. **Type** a **name** for the project. The name will be displayed.

13. **Type** a brief **description** for the project. The description will be displayed.

14. **Click** on **Next**. The next screen of the wizard will appear.

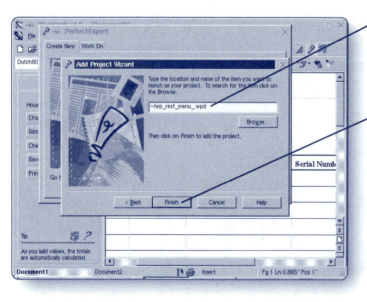

15. **Type** the **full path and file name** for your project document. The name will be displayed.

16. **Click** on **Finish**. A dialog box will appear.

STARTING A NEW DOCUMENT   17

17. **Click** on **OK**. The dialog box will close.

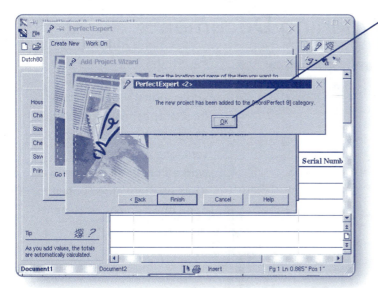

18. Click on the **new project**. The project will be selected.

19. Click on **Create**. The PerfectExpert dialog box will close and the new document template will appear.

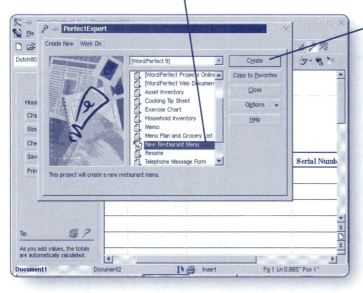

Opening Documents

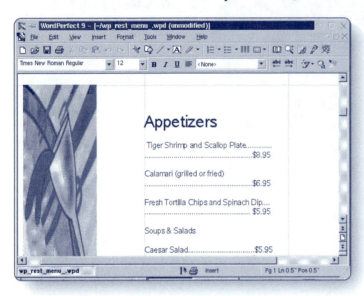

As you get started with the WordPerfect Office 2000 applications, sooner or later (probably sooner) you will need to open a document that you or someone else has already worked on. In this section we examine the methods used to open one or many documents.

Opening an Existing Document

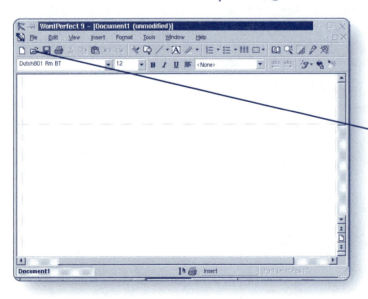

If you need to work on a document that has been worked on before, it's a simple matter to bring it back up for additional editing.

1. Click on the **Open button**. The Open File dialog box will appear.

> **TIP**
> You can press Ctrl+O to start the Open File dialog box.

OPENING DOCUMENTS

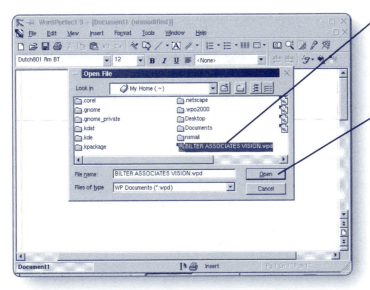

2. **Click** on the **file you want to open**. The file will be highlighted and will appear in the box next to File name.

3. **Click** on **Open**. The Open File dialog box will close and the desired file will appear in the document window.

Opening a Recently Edited Document

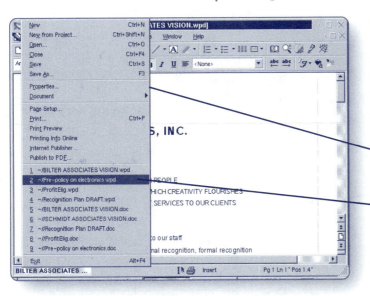

Should you need to open a document you recently worked on, WordPerfect Office 2000 applications make it even easier to find and open those documents.

1. **Click** on **File**. The File menu will appear.

2. **Click** on **one of the eight most-recently edited files**. The desired file will appear in the document window.

CHAPTER 2: WORKING WITH FILES

Opening a "Foreign" Document

Not only can you open any WordPerfect application file, you can also open a large variety of files with formats other than WordPerfect Office 2000's. This simple function increases your sharing connectivity with Linux and Windows users alike!

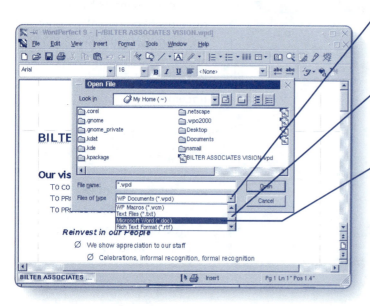

1. **Click** on the **Open button**. The Open File dialog box will appear.

2. **Click** on the **down arrow (↓)** next to the Files of type box. A drop-down list will appear.

3. **Scroll** down the **drop-down list**. The file type you need will be highlighted.

4. **Click** on the **file type** you want. That file type will replace the drop-down list and the files window now will display only files of that type.

OPENING DOCUMENTS

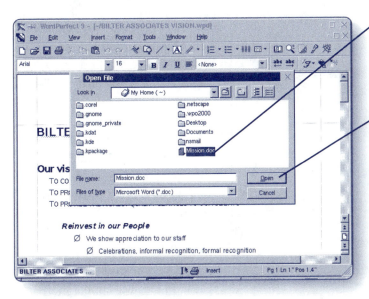

5. **Click** on the **file you want to open**. The file will be highlighted and will appear in the box next to File name.

6. **Click** on **Open**. The Open File dialog box will close and the desired file will appear in the document window.

Opening Multiple Documents

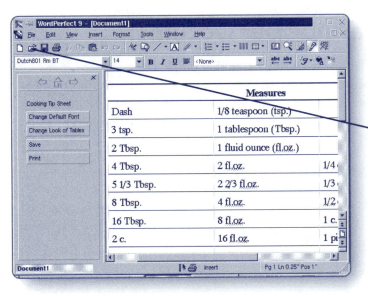

You are not limited to opening just one document at a time. The WordPerfect applications allow you to open as many documents as you'd like at the same time.

1. Click on the **Open button**. The Open File dialog box will appear.

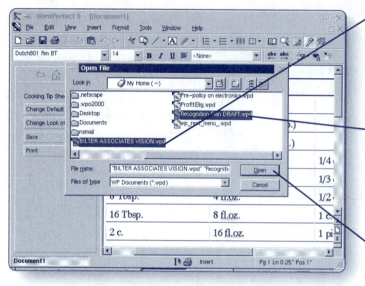

2. **Press** the **Ctrl key** and **click** on a **file you want to open**. The file will be highlighted and will appear in the box next to File name.

3. **Click** on another **file** while still holding the Ctrl key. The file will be highlighted and will also appear in the box next to File name.

4. **Click** on **Open**. The Open File dialog box will close and the desired files will appear in the document window.

Saving Your Document

After you have finished working with your document, it is necessary for you to save your work. Saving a document is not hard and you should do it often while working with documents, in case there's a power failure or some other calamity.

Saving a Document

The first time you work with a document and save it, you need to give it a new file name and choose where to save the file on your Linux file system.

SAVING YOUR DOCUMENT   23

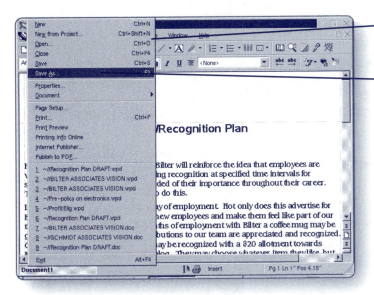

1. Click on **File**. The File menu will appear.

2. Click on **Save As**. The Save As dialog box will appear.

TIP
You can press F3 to start the Save As dialog box.

3. Click on the **down arrow** (↓) next to Save in to select a new drive location in which to save the file. The directories in that section of the drive will be displayed in the file window.

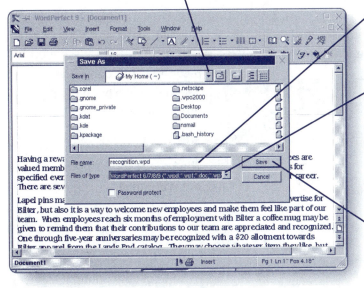

4. Type a **file name** in the box next to File name. The file name will be displayed in the box.

5. Click on the **down arrow** (↓) next to Files of type to select a new file type to save the file as. The file name's extension will change to reflect that of the file type.

6. Click on **Save**. The Save As dialog box will close and the file will be stored in the appropriate location.

Resaving a Document

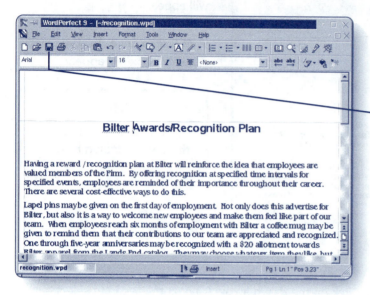

After the initial "save as" routine, you can resave a document as often as you'd like with a minimum of effort.

1. Click on the **Save button**. The file will be saved, and the "unmodified" status will appear next to the file name in the title bar.

TIP
You can also press Ctrl+S to quickly save the file.

Printing a Document

Even though we have the ability to create and use fully electronic documents, there is still the overwhelming urge to get a document printed on paper. WordPerfect Office 2000 recognizes this deep-seated need and enables you to print documents easily.

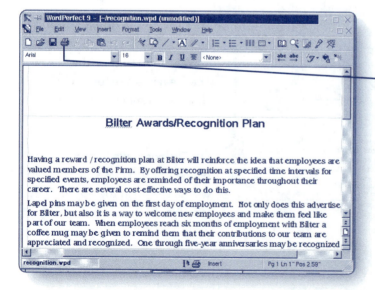

1. Click on the **Print button**. The Print to lp, WINEPS dialog box will appear.

TIP
You can also press Ctrl+P to begin the printing process.

CLOSING A DOCUMENT

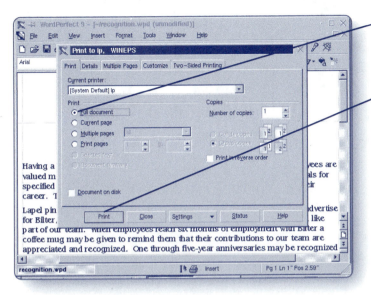

2. Click the **Full document option**. The option will be selected.

3. Click on **Print**. The Print to lp, WINEPS dialog box will close and the document will be printed.

Closing a Document

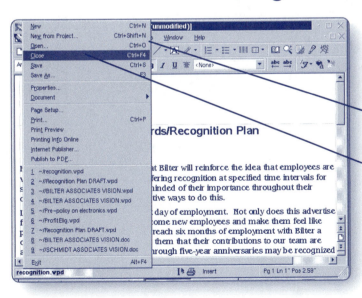

When you are finished working in a particular document, you can close the document without closing the entire application.

1. Click on **File**. The File menu will appear.

2. Click on **Close**. The currently open document will close.

TIP

You can also press Ctrl+F4 to close an open document.

3

Getting Help with WordPerfect Office 2000

No matter how intuitive designers try to make them, computers are not easy to use—unless you are under the age of 16. Many software designers recognize this fact and try to implement online help. WordPerfect Office 2000 has this traditional online help for you to use, but it does not stop there. You also can get help from the Internet and use a tool that can guide you through a task as you are doing it! In this chapter, you'll learn how to:

- Master the online help in Office 2000
- Let PerfectExpert guide you through tasks

Starting Online Help

When you can't find an answer to a problem, you might consult a reference. The reference might be your friend, a lifeline, or just a book like this one. In WordPerfect, the fastest place to check is the online help files.

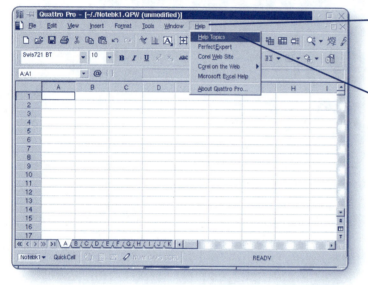

1. Click on **Help** in any WordPerfect 2000 application. The Help menu will appear.

2. Click on **Help Topics**. Your default Web browser will appear, opened to the help files for that particular Office 2000 application.

STARTING ONLINE HELP   29

3. Click on the **expansion control** for the desired topic. The list of subtopics will appear.

4. Click on the desired **topic**. The topic will be highlighted and the content of the topic will appear in the content frame of the browser.

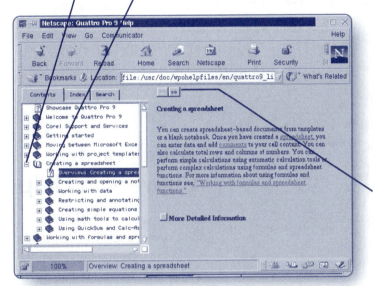

NOTE
The small plus signs in the topic area are expansion controls and will "open" the subtopics within a given topic.

5. Click on the **Next Page control**. The next help topic will be displayed in the content frame.

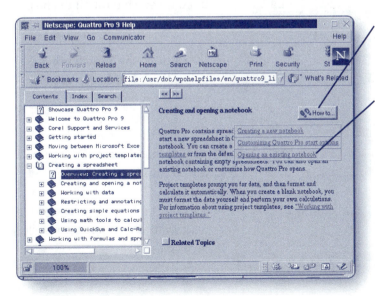

6. Click on **How To**. A list of specific topic-related tasks will appear.

7. Click on a **task**. The task will be displayed in the content frame.

8. Click on the **box** next to Related Topics at the bottom of the topic page. A list of topic-related links will appear.

9. Click on a **topic link**. The content frame will display the new topic.

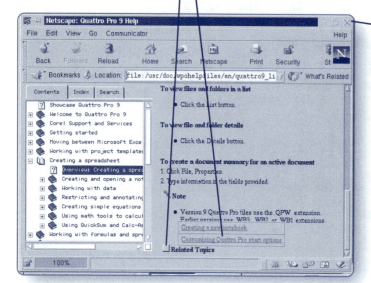

10. Click the **Close button** (❌). The Web browser will close.

Searching for Answers in Help

Sometimes the topic headings don't reveal exactly what you are looking for. Or you might simply not have time to skim the headings. Luckily, you can directly search through the help topics.

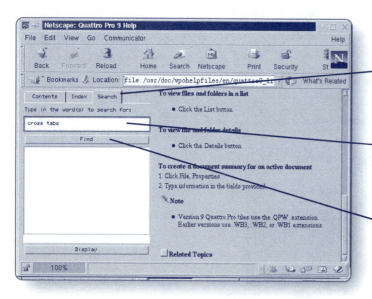

1. Click on the **Search tab** in online help. The Search tab will come to the front.

2. Type the **keyword(s)** you want to learn about. The terms will be displayed.

3. Click on **Find**. Any related topics with the search terms will be displayed.

USING PERFECTEXPERT   31

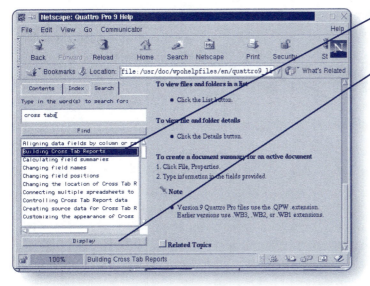

4. Click on the **desired topic**. The topic will be highlighted.

5. Click on **Display**. The content frame will display the topic.

Using PerfectExpert

If you get stuck on how to do something, you might not need to leave the application in which your are working. With the help of PerfectExpert, you can get hints right as you are working.

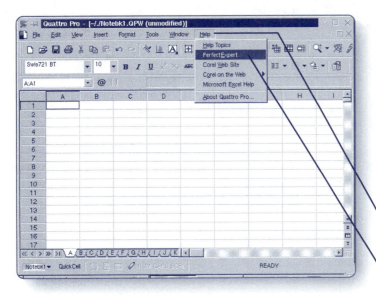

Getting Assistance as You Go

Not only does PerfectExpert help you start up a new document, it also can assist you with the document you are working in.

1. Click on **Help**. The Help menu will appear.

2. Click on **PerfectExpert**. The PerfectExpert pane will open adjacent to the document window.

32   CHAPTER 3: GETTING HELP WITH WORDPERFECT OFFICE 2000

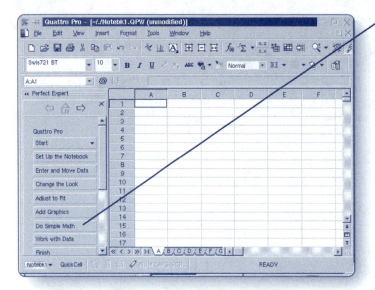

3. Click on the **desired topic**. The content of the topic will fill the PerfectExpert pane.

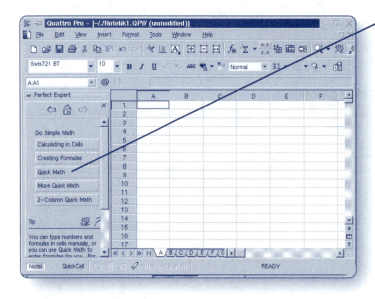

4. Click on the **desired subtopic**. The tool to accomplish the task will open.

NOTE

If there is no specific tool to accomplish the task, then a detailed set of instructions will appear in the PerfectExpert pane.

Stopping PerfectExpert

After you are finished with PerfectExpert, you need to close it to regain your document window space.

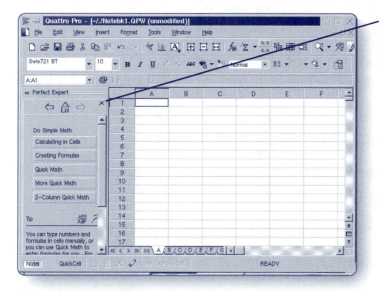

1. Click the **Close button** (☒) in the PerfectExpert pane. The pane will close.

Part I Review Questions

1. How do you start a WordPerfect program? See *"Starting WordPerfect within X Window"* in Chapter 1.

2. How many applications are in the WordPerfect Office 2000 suite? See *"Exploring WordPerfect Office 2000"* in Chapter 1.

3. How do you exit a WordPerfect program? *See "Exiting WordPerfect Office 2000"* in Chapter 1.

4. How do you create a new empty document? See *"Making an Empty Document"* in Chapter 2.

5. What is PerfectExpert? See *"Using PerfectExpert"* in Chapter 2.

6. How do you use templates? See *"Opening an Installed Template"* in Chapter 2.

7. How can you open a Microsoft Office document in WordPerfect Office 2000? See *"Opening a 'Foreign' Document"* in Chapter 2.

8. Where can you print a document? See *"Printing a Document"* in Chapter 2.

9. How do you search the help files? See *"Searching for Answers in Help"* in Chapter 3.

10. How do you get help as you work in WordPerfect Office 2000? See *"Getting Assistance as You Go"* in Chapter 3.

PART II
Working with Words

Chapter 4
  Learning WordPerfect Basics **37**

Chapter 5
  Formatting a WordPerfect Document . . . **47**

Chapter 6
  Improving Your Writing **71**

Chapter 7
  Building with Tables and Columns **83**

Chapter 8
  Adding Style to Your Document **99**

Chapter 9
  Managing Longer Documents **111**

4

Learning WordPerfect Basics

The word processor component of WordPerfect Office 2000 is called, appropriately enough, WordPerfect. WordPerfect's main job is to get your words down on paper, be it real or electronic. In this chapter, you'll learn how to:

- Create text in your document
- Edit a document by inserting, selecting, and deleting text
- Correct mistakes using the Undo and Redo functions
- Navigate within your document

Typing Text

We have come a long way since the days of the Gutenberg press, where small pieces of movable type were painstakingly arranged to create a single page of a book. Now, creating letters, reports, and even books is as easy as twiddling your fingers.

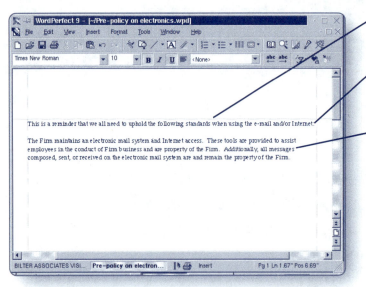

1. **Type** some **text**. The text will appear onscreen.

2. **Press** the **Enter key**. A new line will be started.

3. **Type** a **paragraph**. The text will wrap automatically, so you need only press the Enter key at the end of the paragraph.

Editing Text

It is not often that you can enter all your text exactly right the first time. As you create documents, you often think of a better way to say something after typing it. This is when it's useful to know how to edit text in WordPerfect.

Inserting Text

Inserting text within a WordPerfect document is simple. You can even type text over existing text, as you learn in this section.

EDITING TEXT 39

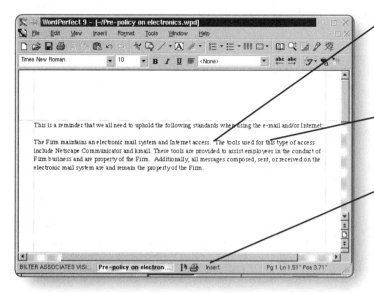

1. **Click** the **mouse pointer** within your document. The insertion point will appear where you click.

2. **Type** some **text**. The text will appear onscreen, pushing the existing text aside.

3. **Click** on **Insert** in the status bar. The status will change to Typeover.

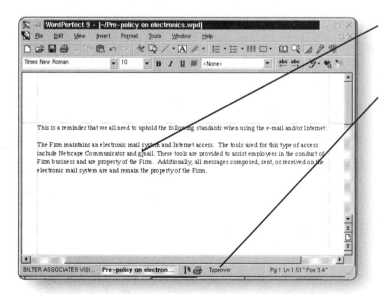

4. **Type** some **text**. The text will appear onscreen, overwriting the existing text.

5. **Click** on **Typeover** in the status bar. The status will return to Insert.

Selecting Text

When dealing with blocks of text, a useful technique is to select the text first. Once the text is selected, any changes made to the selection affect all of the text within.

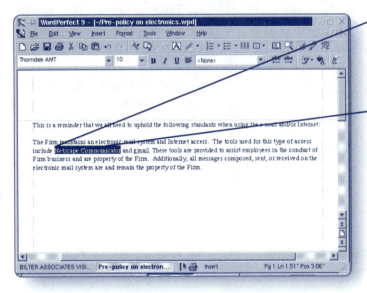

1. **Click** the **mouse pointer** within your document. The insertion point will appear where you click.

2. **Drag** the **mouse pointer** across the line of text. The text will be highlighted as you move the mouse.

3. **Release** the **mouse pointer**. The selected text will be highlighted on the screen.

NOTE

To remove the selection highlight from the document, simply click the mouse pointer anywhere within the document.

TIP

Double-click on a word to select the entire word. To select an entire paragraph, triple-click on the text within that paragraph.

CORRECTING YOUR MISTAKES

Deleting Text

When pruning roses, you have to get tough with them to bring out the best blossoms. And sometimes, you have to cut some text to bring out the best writing.

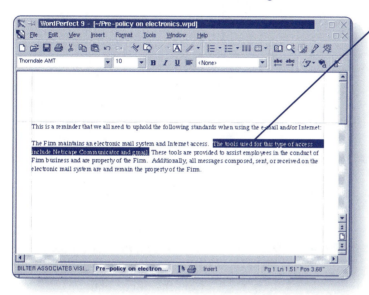

1. Select some **text** within your document. The text will be highlighted onscreen.

2. Press the **Delete key**. The text will be deleted from the document.

Correcting Your Mistakes

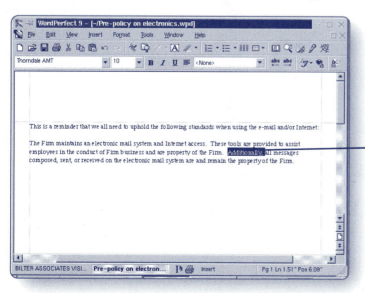

If you make a change you did not want to make after all, has WordPerfect got the tools for you! Undo and Redo help you reverse any errors you might have made.

1. Select some **text** within your document. The text will appear highlighted onscreen.

2. Press the **Delete key**. The text will be deleted from the document.

42　CHAPTER 4: LEARNING WORDPERFECT BASICS

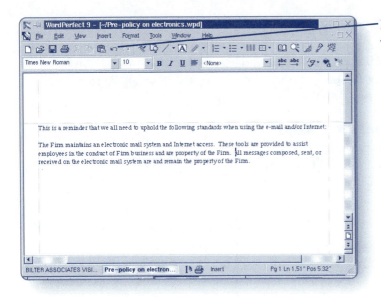

3. Click on the **Undo button**. The selected text will reappear.

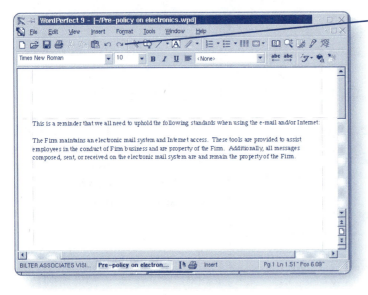

4. Click on the **Redo button**. The text will again be deleted from the document.

Navigating within a Document

Moving around from word to word in a document can be rather tedious and slow using only the arrow keys. There are better and faster ways to navigate a WordPerfect document.

Using Shadow Cursor

The Shadow Cursor allows you to place your mouse pointer anywhere on the screen, regardless of whether text is there already. This feature is a great advantage that gives you excellent control over the placement of text.

1. **Click** on **View**. The View menu will appear.

2. **Click** on **Shadow Cursor**. The Shadow Cursor mouse pointer will appear.

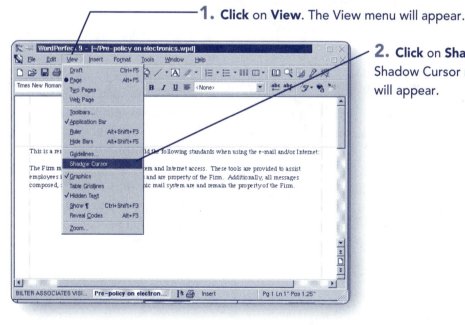

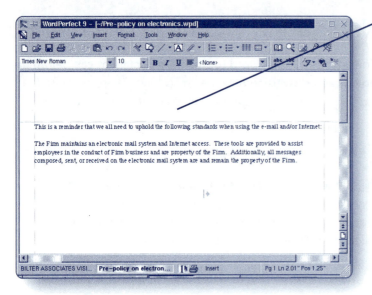

3. Move the **Shadow Cursor mouse pointer** to a blank section of your document. The pointer's "shadow" will appear at the location of the insertion point.

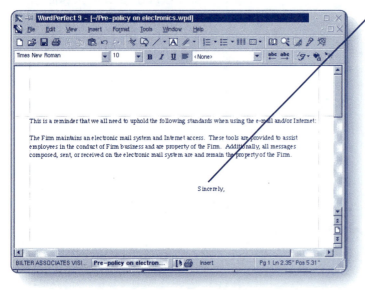

4. Click the **Shadow Cursor mouse pointer** in the blank area. The insertion point will be placed independently of other text.

5. Type additional **text**. The text will appear starting at the new insertion point.

NAVIGATING WITHIN A DOCUMENT

Using the Scroll Bars

To really move quickly around a document, use the scroll bars. These devices get you where you are going in a hurry.

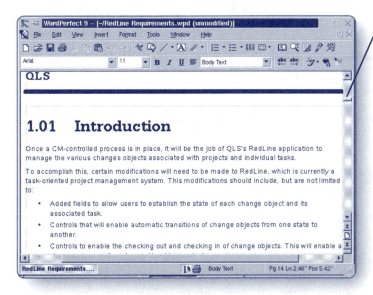

1. Click and **hold** the **scroll bar slide** in the vertical scroll bar. The tool will be selected.

2. Move the **slide** up or down the scroll bar. The document will shift with the movement.

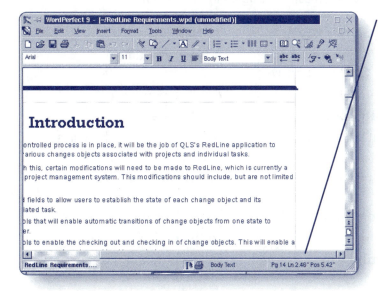

3. Click on the **scroll bar slide** in the horizontal scroll bar.

4. Move the **slide** left or right in the scroll bar. The document will shift with the movement.

CHAPTER 4: LEARNING WORDPERFECT BASICS

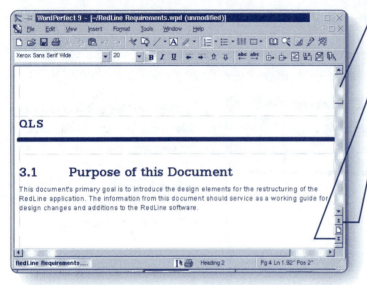

5. **Click** on the **vertical scroll bar**. The document will move up or down a full screen.

6. **Click** on the **Next Page browse control**. The document will move down a page.

7. **Click** on the **Previous Page browse control**. The document will move up a page.

Using the Keyboard

If you need to move around the document and you are not comfortable with the mouse, you can use the keyboard for more than just the left, right, up, and down arrow keys. The following table lists the various WordPerfect key combinations that you can use to navigate in a document.

Type This Key	*To Navigate*
Ctrl+left arrow or Ctrl+right arrow	A word at a time
Page Up	A full screen up
Page Down	A full screen down
Alt+Page Up	To the header of the current page
Alt+Page Down	To the footer of the current page
Home	To the beginning of a line
End	To the end of a line
Ctrl+Home	To the beginning of a document
Ctrl+End	To the end of a document

5
Formatting a WordPerfect Document

WordPerfect can do more for your documents than behave as a glorified typewriter. You can apply wonderful effects to your text, resize text, and move text around your document, for starters. In this chapter, you'll learn how to:

- Make changes to text, such as changing its font, size, and attributes
- Insert special characters
- Move or copy text within a document
- Change text spacing in a document
- Set, move, and delete tabs

Enhancing Text

You have seen all the fancy documents that word processors can create. Now, it's your turn to start applying attractive effects to your text.

Changing the Font

The *font* of a text character is the appearance of the text. Some fonts lend themselves to more legibility, and others call attention to themselves. With WordPerfect's RealTime Preview, you can see the effect of a font change before you make it.

1. Select the **text** you want to affect. The text will be highlighted.

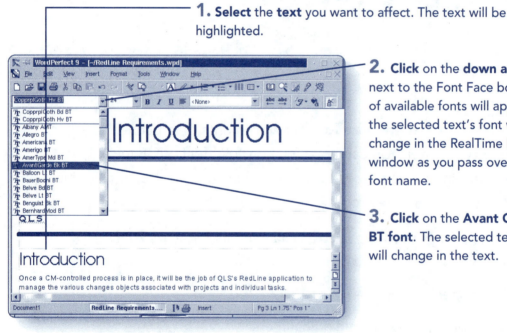

2. Click on the **down arrow (↓)** next to the Font Face box. A list of available fonts will appear and the selected text's font will change in the RealTime Preview window as you pass over each font name.

3. Click on the **Avant Garde Bk BT font**. The selected text's font will change in the text.

ENHANCING TEXT

Changing the Font Size

Not only do fonts come in all shapes, but they also come in a variety of sizes. Font sizes are measured in *points*. There are 72 points to an inch.

1. **Select** the **text** you want to affect. The text will be highlighted.

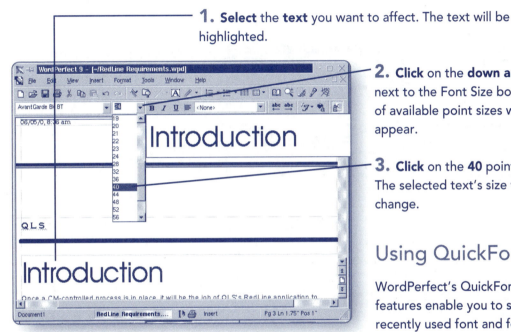

2. **Click** on the **down arrow (↓)** next to the Font Size box. A list of available point sizes will appear.

3. **Click** on the **40** point size. The selected text's size will change.

Using QuickFonts

WordPerfect's QuickFonts features enable you to select a recently used font and font size combination in your document.

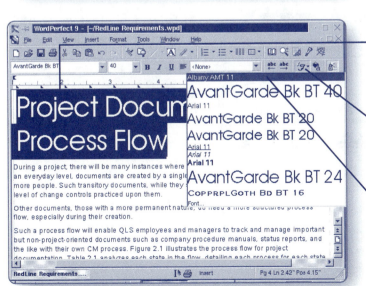

1. **Select** the **text** you want to affect. The text will be highlighted.

2. **Click** on the **QuickFonts button**. A list of recent font and font attributes will appear.

3. **Click** on a **font**. The selected text's font and size will change to the new attributes.

Applying Bold, Italic, or Underline

Beyond changing the font of text, you can apply attributes to the text. Attributes are bold, italic, or underline.

1. Select the **text** you want to affect. The text will be highlighted.

2. Click on the **Bold button**. The text will become bold.

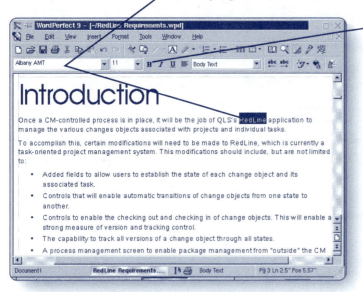

3. Select more **text** you want to affect. The text will be highlighted.

4. Click on the **Italic button**. The text will become italicized.

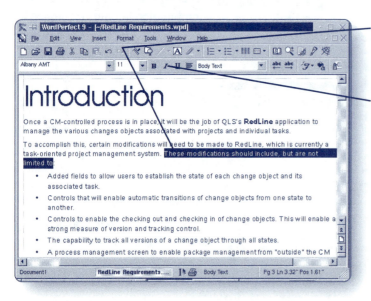

ENHANCING TEXT 51

5. Select more **text** you want to affect. The text will be highlighted.

6. Click on the **Underline button**. The text will be underlined.

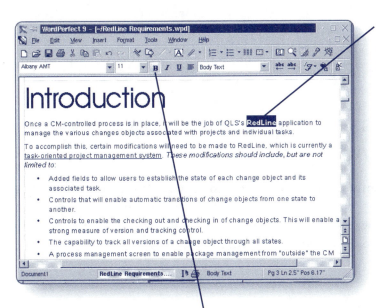

7. Select the **bold text** created earlier. The text will be highlighted.

8. Click on the **Bold button**. The bold attribute will be removed from the text.

Changing Text Case

The way text is capitalized (or not) is referred to as its *case*. A regular sentence, with only the first letter capitalized, is normal sentence case. A passage of text WITH ALL OF THE LETTERS CAPITALIZED is in uppercase.

1. Select the **text** you want to affect. The text will be highlighted.

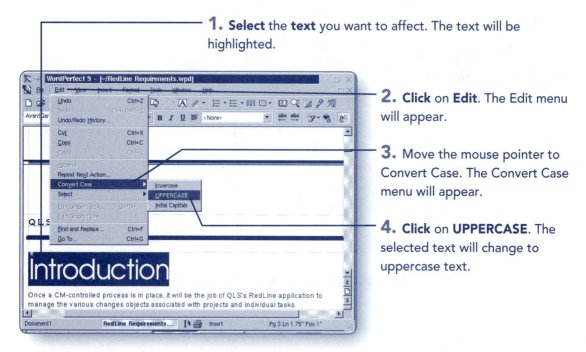

2. Click on **Edit**. The Edit menu will appear.

3. Move the mouse pointer to Convert Case. The Convert Case menu will appear.

4. Click on **UPPERCASE**. The selected text will change to uppercase text.

Inserting Special Characters and Symbols

Umlauts, grave marks, and iconic symbols—terms that sound as though they belong in a dark, spooky cemetery. Believe it or not, these are descriptions of special characters and symbols WordPerfect can place in your document.

INSERTING SPECIAL CHARACTERS AND SYMBOLS 53

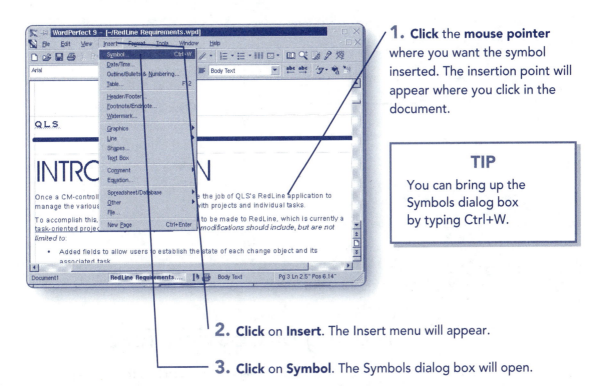

1. Click the **mouse pointer** where you want the symbol inserted. The insertion point will appear where you click in the document.

TIP
You can bring up the Symbols dialog box by typing Ctrl+W.

2. Click on **Insert**. The Insert menu will appear.

3. Click on **Symbol**. The Symbols dialog box will open.

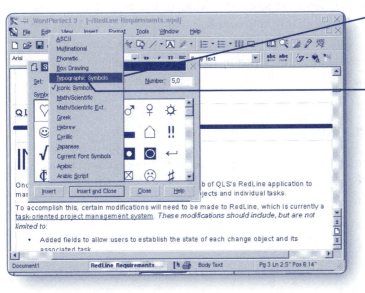

4. Click on the **list arrow** next to the Set list. A list of available font sets will appear.

5. Click on **Typographic Symbols** in the Set list. The typographic symbol set will appear.

CHAPTER 5: FORMATTING A WORDPERFECT DOCUMENT

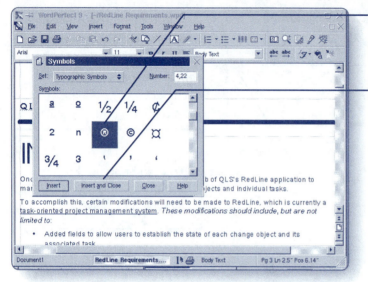

6. **Click** on a **character**. A symbol will be highlighted with a blinking box.

7. **Click** on **Insert and Close**. The character will be placed where the insertion point appears in the document.

Moving or Copying Text

In the olden days (five years ago), if you had to move a passage of text, you used an editor's knife to literally cut the text off the layout sheet, whereupon you then physically pasted the text with wax onto another part of the page. Today, you can achieve the same effect in seconds without all the sticky wax. The process is still called cutting and pasting, however.

Moving Text

Moving text around a document with the keyboard is a simple process. Using the key combinations for Cut (Ctrl+X) and Paste (Ctrl+V) speeds you along.

MOVING OR COPYING TEXT 55

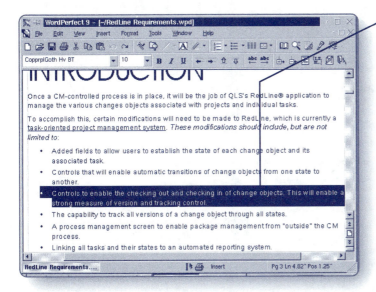

1. Select the **text** you want to move. The text will be highlighted.

2. Type Ctrl+X. The selected text will disappear.

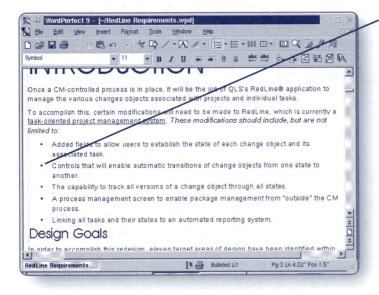

3. Move the **mouse pointer** to the new location for the text.

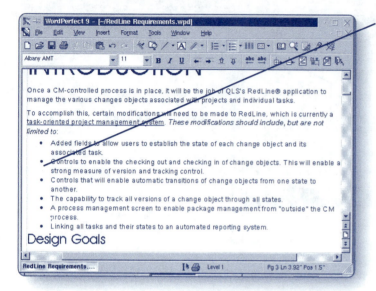

4. Type Ctrl+V. The cut text will appear at the new location.

Copying Text

Copying text no longer has to involve retyping it. Use the key combination for Copy (Ctrl+C) to make copying a snap.

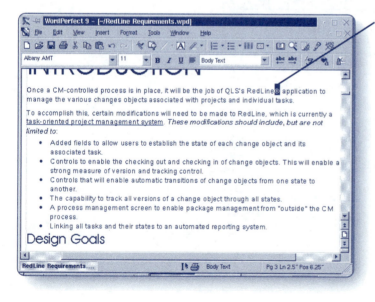

1. Select the **text** you want to copy. The text will be highlighted.

2. Type Ctrl+C. Although nothing visible occurs, the selected text will be placed in WordPerfect's internal *clipboard* for pasting later.

MOVING OR COPYING TEXT 57

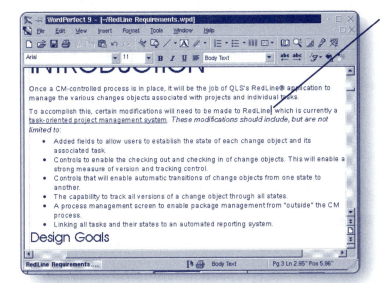

3. Move the **mouse pointer** to the new location for the text.

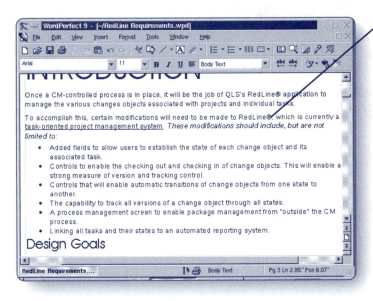

4. Type Ctrl+V. The copied text will appear at the new location.

Using Click and Drag

In WordPerfect you can move text using only the mouse.

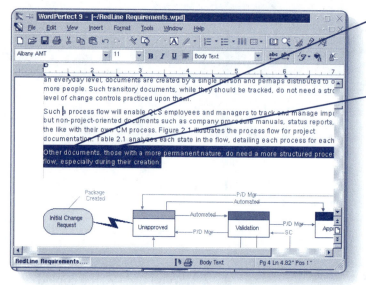

1. Select the **text** you want to move. The text will be highlighted.

2. Click on the **selected text**. The mouse pointer will change to the drag pointer.

3. Drag the **selected text** to another location in the document. The drag pointer will be moved to the new location.

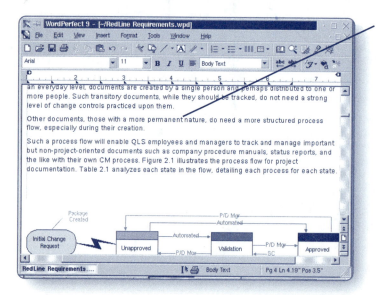

4. Release the **mouse button**. The selected text will appear at the new location.

Working with Bulleted or Numbered Lists

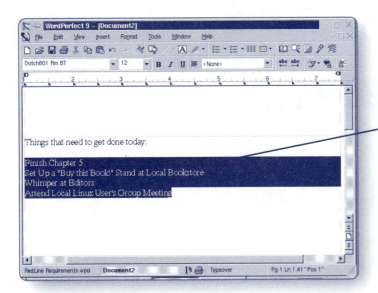

Lists are helpful when you want to make points or organize thoughts. WordPerfect lets you create nice-looking lists in moments!

1. Select the **text** to become a bulleted list. The text will be highlighted.

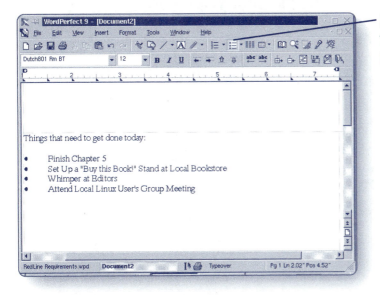

2. Click on the **Bullets button**. The text will become a bulleted list.

60 CHAPTER 5: FORMATTING A WORDPERFECT DOCUMENT

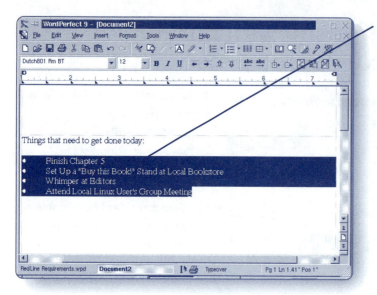

3. Select the **text** to become a numbered list. The text will be highlighted.

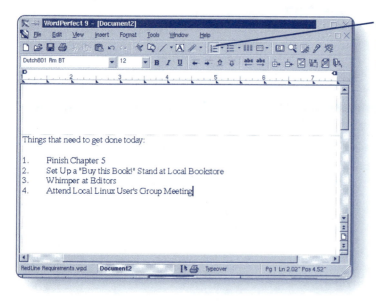

4. Click on the **Numbering button**. The text will become a numbered list.

Arranging Text on a Page

Most text is automatically aligned to the left margin of a page and single-spaced. Sometimes, however, you want to make changes to this norm.

Aligning Text

You can align text in four ways in WordPerfect: left, center, right, and justified.

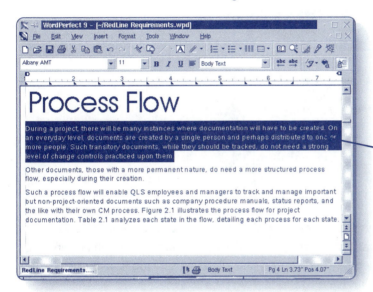

1. Select the **text** to realign. The text will be highlighted.

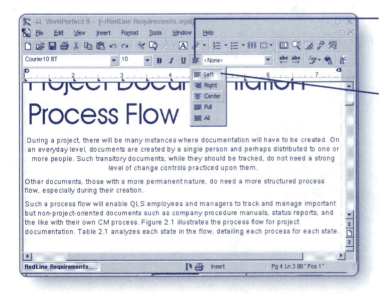

2. Click the **Justification button**. The list of alignments will appear.

3. Move the **mouse pointer** along the list. As each alignment is highlighted, a RealTime Preview of the alignment setting will appear in the document.

62 CHAPTER 5: FORMATTING A WORDPERFECT DOCUMENT

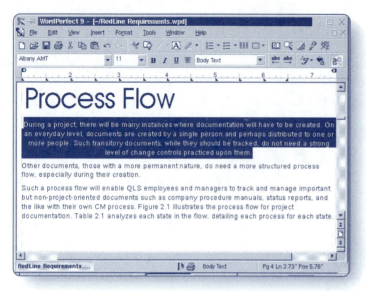

4. Click on **Center**. The selected text will be centered between the left and right margins of the page.

Changing Line Spacing

If you are over a certain age, you might remember double-spacing reports in typing class in school. Although not an everyday occurrence, changing line spacing is something you might want to tackle from time to time.

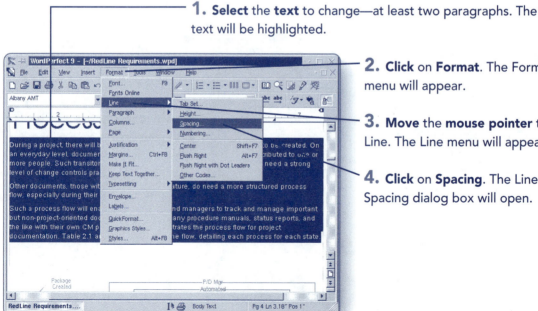

1. Select the **text** to change—at least two paragraphs. The text will be highlighted.

2. Click on **Format**. The Format menu will appear.

3. Move the **mouse pointer** to Line. The Line menu will appear.

4. Click on **Spacing**. The Line Spacing dialog box will open.

ARRANGING TEXT ON A PAGE

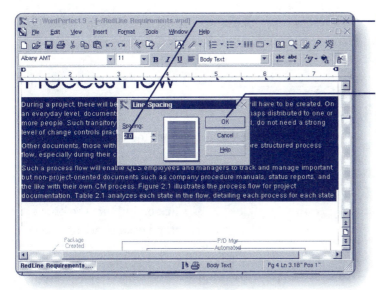

5. Type the value **2.0** in the Spacing field. The value will be changed.

6. Click on **OK**. The Line Spacing dialog box will close.

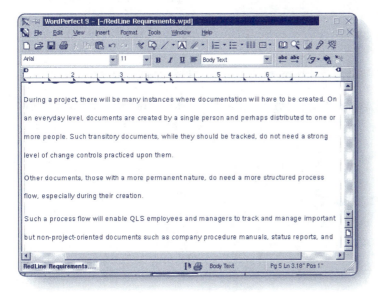

The selected text changes to double-line spacing.

Indenting Text

In a WordPerfect document, you can create three kinds of indents: regular, hanging, and double.

CHAPTER 5: FORMATTING A WORDPERFECT DOCUMENT

1. Click the **mouse pointer** on the beginning of the paragraph to indent. The insertion point will appear in the paragraph.

2. Click on **Format**. The Format menu will appear.

3. Move the **mouse pointer** to Paragraph. The Paragraph menu will appear.

4. Click on **Indent**. The entire paragraph will be indented one inch.

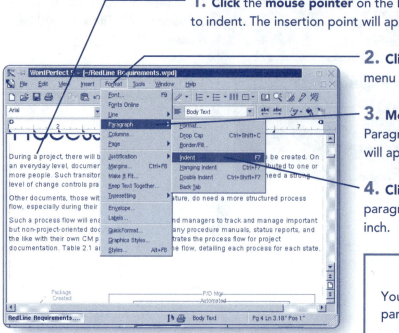

TIP
You can indent a paragraph by pressing F7.

5. Click on **Format**. The Format menu will appear.

6. Move the **mouse pointer** to Paragraph. The Paragraph menu will appear.

7. Click on **Hanging Indent**. The entire paragraph will be indented one inch except for the first line.

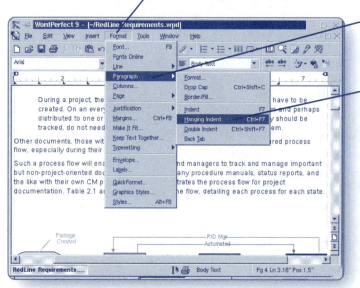

TIP
You can create a hanging indent of a paragraph by pressing Ctrl+F7.

ARRANGING TEXT ON A PAGE

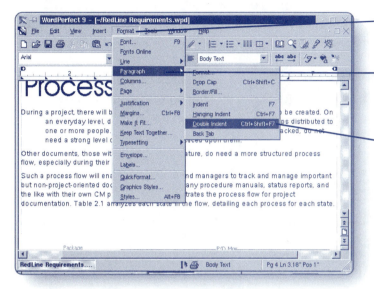

8. **Click** on **Format**. The Format menu will appear.

9. **Move** the **mouse pointer** to Paragraph. The Paragraph menu will appear.

10. **Click** on **Double Indent**. The entire paragraph will be indented one inch on both sides.

TIP
You can create a double indent of a paragraph by pressing Ctrl+Shift+F7.

TIP
You can change the indentation of multiple paragraphs at once by selecting them first and then making indent changes in the Format menu.

Working with Tabs

Setting and inserting tabs is the best way to separate text uniformly. Tabs provide precision to the placement of text in a document.

Setting Tabs

You can set tab stops differently for any paragraph.

TIP
The Ruler is made visible by pressing Alt+Shift+F3.

1. Right click the **bottom of the Ruler**. The Tab Control menu will appear.

2. Click on **Clear All Tabs**. All of the preset tabs in the ruler will disappear.

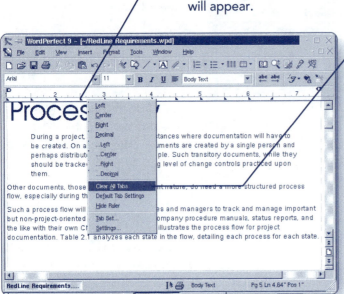

3. Click the **mouse pointer** in the paragraph to change the tab settings. The text insertion point appears in the paragraph.

4. Click on the **ruler** at the spot where you want the first tab stop to be. A tab stop marker will appear on the ruler.

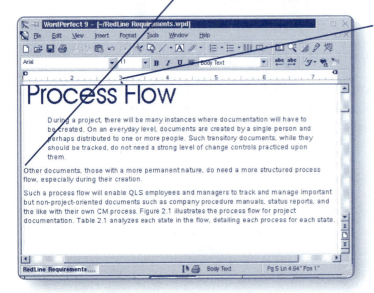

WORKING WITH TABS   67

5. Type a **Tab** at the beginning of the paragraph. The first character of the paragraph will move to the location of the tab stop. The tab length is equal to the length of the first tab stop.

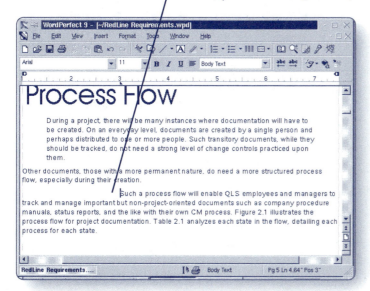

TIP
You can add more tab settings by clicking on multiple locations on the ruler.

TIP
You can change the tab settings of multiple paragraphs at once by selecting them first and then making tab changes on the ruler.

Moving Tabs

After you place tabs on the ruler, you can move them quickly.

CHAPTER 5: FORMATTING A WORDPERFECT DOCUMENT

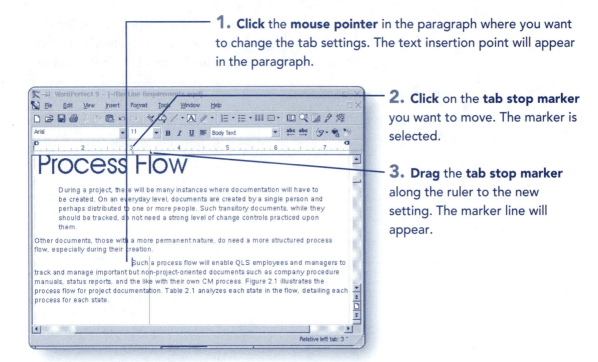

1. Click the **mouse pointer** in the paragraph where you want to change the tab settings. The text insertion point will appear in the paragraph.

2. Click on the **tab stop marker** you want to move. The marker is selected.

3. Drag the **tab stop marker** along the ruler to the new setting. The marker line will appear.

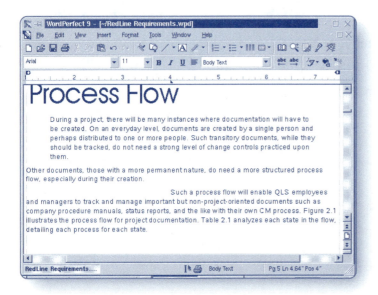

4. Release the **mouse button**. The tab stop will appear in its new location, and the paragraph's tabs will adjust accordingly.

Deleting Tabs

When you need to remove a tab setting, you can do so without even pressing the Delete key.

1. Click the **mouse pointer** in the paragraph to change the tab settings. The text insertion point will appear in the paragraph.

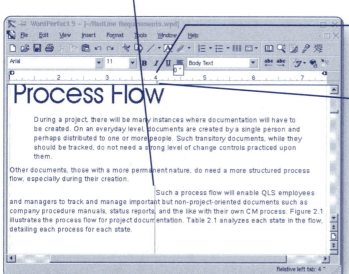

2. Click on the **tab stop marker** you want to delete. The marker is selected.

3. Drag the **tab stop marker** down from the ruler. The tab stop marker will disappear from the ruler.

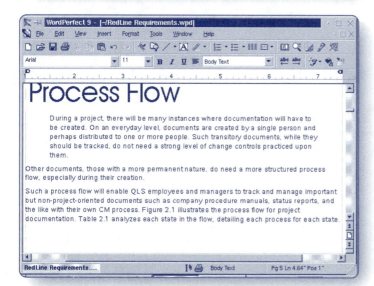

4. Release the **mouse button**. The tab stop will be deleted.

6

Improving Your Writing

If you think WordPerfect does nothing more than get your words down on paper, think again. WordPerfect can take an active role in helping you write *better*. In this chapter, you'll learn how to:

- Search for and replace text
- Perform a spelling check on your document
- Have WordPerfect automatically check your spelling and correct misspelled words
- Allow WordPerfect to check your document's grammar
- Use Prompt-As-You-Go as a shortcut to type commonly used terms

Using Find and Replace

Finding a particular word or phrase in a document longer than a page can be tedious. WordPerfect's Find and Replace tool does the hard work for you, and can change the found text into whatever you need.

Finding Terms

The Find component of the Find and Replace tool tracks down any character, word, or phrase in a WordPerfect document.

1. **Click** on **Edit**. The Edit menu will open.

2. **Click** on **Find and Replace**. The Find and Replace dialog box will open.

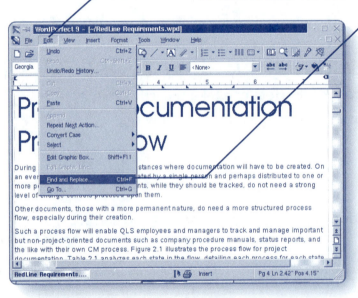

TIP
You can start the Find and Replace dialog box by pressing Ctrl+F.

USING FIND AND REPLACE

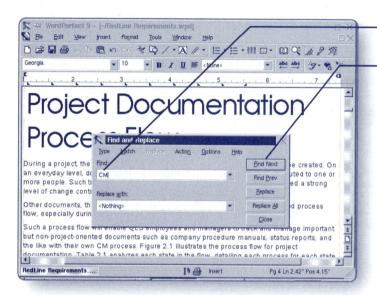

3. Type a **term** in the Find box.

4. Click on **Find Next** to begin the search for the target term. WordPerfect will highlight the first occurrence of the term it discovers.

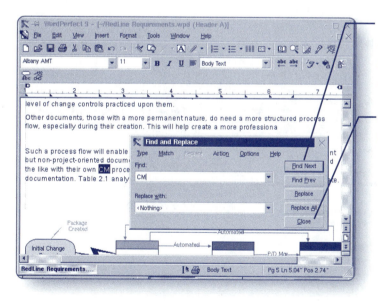

5. Click on **Find Next** again to continue the search. The next instance of the item will be displayed.

6. Click on **Close**. The Find and Replace dialog box will close.

Replacing Terms

You can replace multiple instances of a word or phrase in your document.

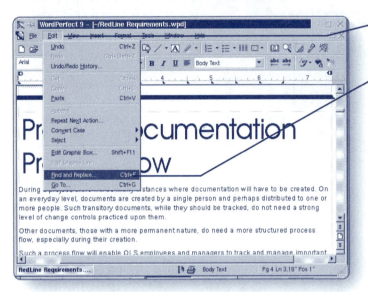

1. Click on **Edit**. The Edit menu will open.

2. Click on **Find and Replace**. The Find and Replace dialog box will open.

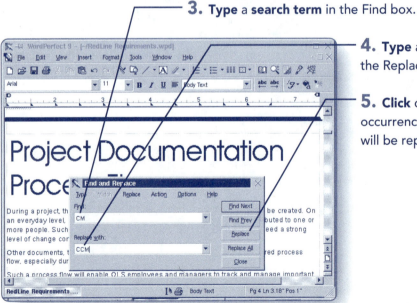

3. Type a **search term** in the Find box.

4. Type a **replacement term** in the Replace with box.

5. Click on **Replace**. The first occurrence of the search term will be replaced.

CORRECTING SPELLING ERRORS

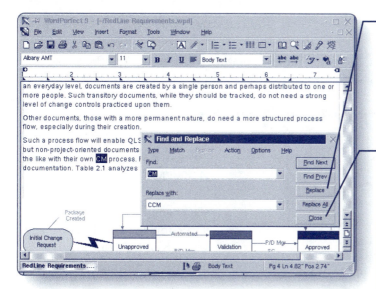

6. Click on **Replace** again. The next instance of the phrase will be highlighted, and you can decide whether to replace the phrase or skip it to search for another instance.

7. Click on **Close**. The Find and Replace dialog box will close.

> **TIP**
> You might be tempted to just click on the Replace All button. You can, but be cautious because you might end up replacing words or parts of words you don't want to change.

Correcting Spelling Errors

The winner of the 2000 Scripps Howard National Spelling Bee won the contest for correctly spelling *demarche* (which is a diplomatic or political maneuver). For those of us who have trouble spelling ordinary words, WordPerfect gives us hope.

Using Spell-As-You-Go

WordPerfect can check your spelling as you type, alerting you to misspelled words.

1. Click on **Tools**. The Tools menu will appear.

2. Move the **mouse pointer** to Proofread. The Proofread menu will appear.

3. Click on **Spell-As-You-Go**. Unrecognized words in the document will be immediately underlined.

4. Examine the **misspelled or unrecognized words**. See if any words have been incorrectly marked.

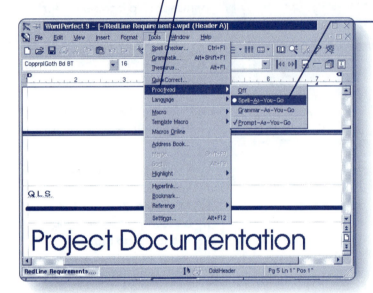

5. Press the **right mouse button** *(right-click)* on an underlined word. A context menu will appear, listing a number of alternative spellings for the word.

6a. Click on the **correct spelling** of the word. The word will be corrected.

OR

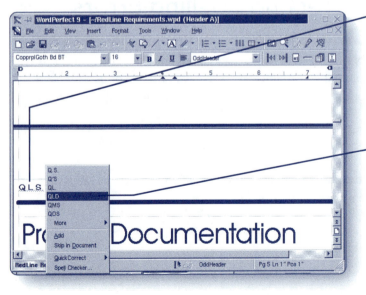

CORRECTING SPELLING ERRORS

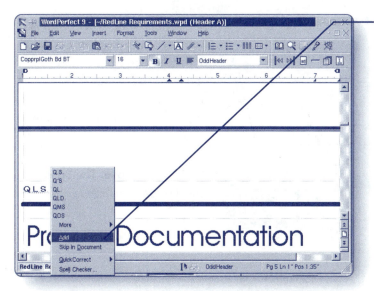

6b. Click on **Add** if the word is correctly spelled and WordPerfect does not recognize it. The word will be added to WordPerfect's dictionary and all other occurrences of the word will no longer be underlined.

Running a Spell Check

If you do not have time to individually check all of the underlined words, you can run a comprehensive search for misspelled words using the Spell Checker tool.

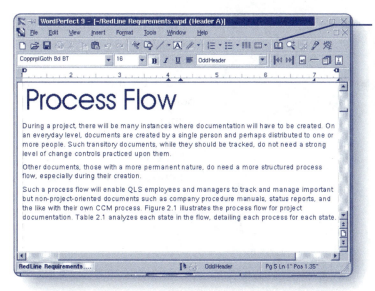

1. Click on the **Spell Checker button**. The Spell Checker pane will open.

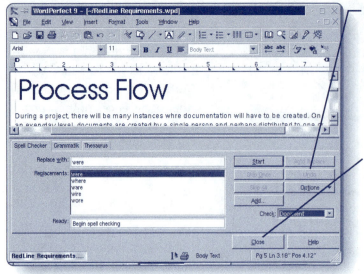

2. Click on **Skip Once**, **Skip All**, **Replace**, **Auto Replace**, or **Add**, depending on what action you want to take for each unrecognized word. The action you select will be applied to the word.

3. Click on **Close**. The Spell Checker pane will close.

Working with Grammar-As-You-Go

WordPerfect can check your grammar as you type, alerting you to any questionable grammar usage.

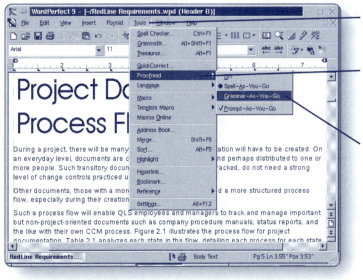

1. Click on **Tools**. The Tools menu will appear.

2. Move the **mouse pointer** to Proofread. The Proofread menu will appear.

3. Click on **Grammar-As-You-Go**. Phrases and words in the document with poor grammar will be immediately underlined.

WORKING WITH QUICKCORRECT

4. Right-click on an **underlined word** or **phrase**. A context menu will appear, listing a correction for the term.

5. Click on the **corrected term** of the word. The term will be replaced.

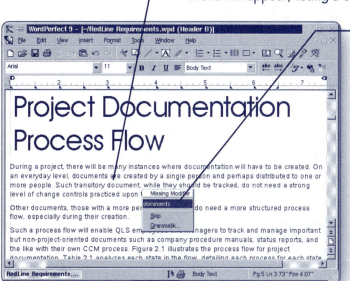

Working with QuickCorrect

Ever have a word that you always misspell? QuickCorrect can silently watch out for these foibles and correct them as you type them.

Adding QuickCorrect Entries

Although WordPerfect already defines a lot of QuickCorrect terms, you have your own idiosyncratic spelling problems. Add them to the QuickCorrect listing, so WordPerfect can catch them too.

1. Click on **Tools**. The Tools menu will appear.

2. Click on **QuickCorrect**. The QuickCorrect dialog box will open.

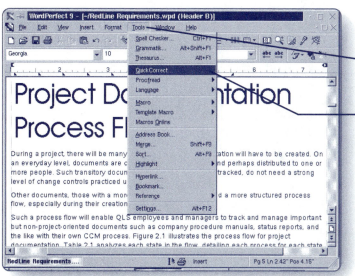

CHAPTER 6: IMPROVING YOUR WRITING

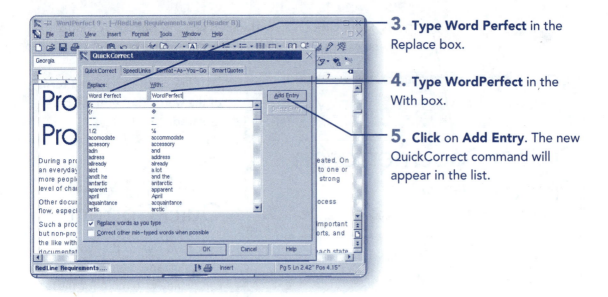

3. **Type Word Perfect** in the Replace box.

4. **Type WordPerfect** in the With box.

5. **Click** on **Add Entry**. The new QuickCorrect command will appear in the list.

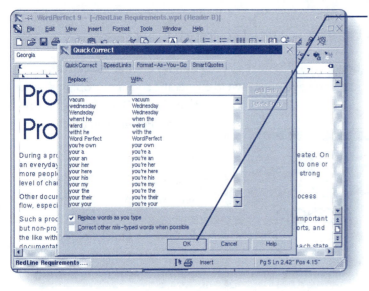

6. **Click** on **OK**. The QuickCorrect dialog box will close.

Deleting QuickCorrect Entries

If you ever need to delete a QuickCorrect entry, here's how you do it.

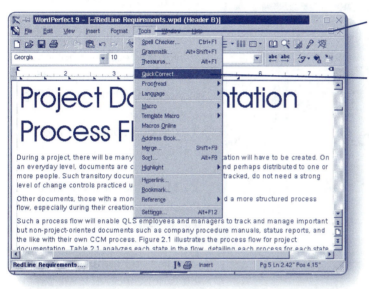

1. Click on **Tools**. The Tools menu will appear.

2. Click on **QuickCorrect**. The QuickCorrect dialog box will open.

3. Click on the **listing** to be removed. The listing will be highlighted.

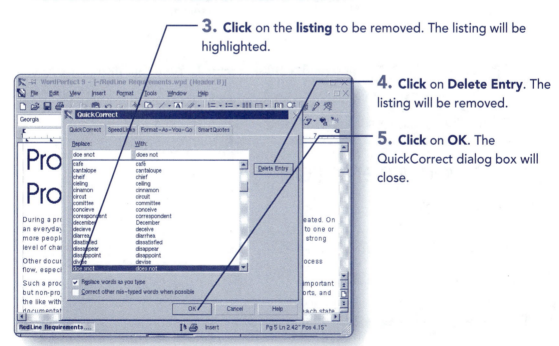

4. Click on **Delete Entry**. The listing will be removed.

5. Click on **OK**. The QuickCorrect dialog box will close.

Working with Prompt-As-You-Go

Sometimes you might start writing a word and then completely blank on how to spell it. WordPerfect's Prompt-As-You-Go gives the proper amount of nudging to keep you writing.

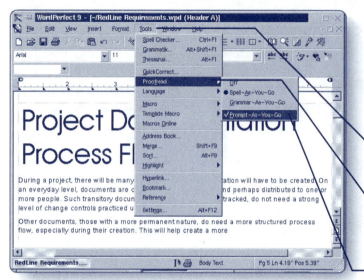

1. Click on **Tools**. The Tools menu will appear.

2. Move the **mouse pointer** to Proofread. The Proofread menu will appear.

3. Click on **Prompt-As-You-Go** if it is not checked. It will be selected.

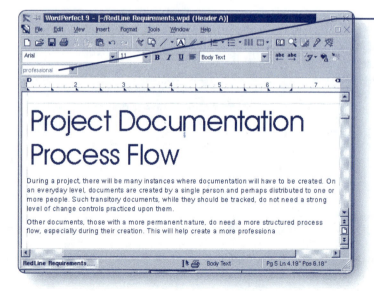

4. Type your **document**. As you type, spelling suggestions will appear in the Property Bar for the word you are typing.

7

Building with Tables and Columns

More and more in these modern times, people are going into business for themselves. Whether it's the average-paid grunt working in the corporate cubicle or the high-paid entrepreneur, these people are discovering that they need to be not only in the business of their work but also in selling themselves. They want to get the job done, but they also want to be noticed doing it. WordPerfect's tables and columns features enable you to create documents that get you and your work noticed. In this chapter, you'll learn how to:

- Make and edit tables for data and page layout
- Create stunning documents and newsletters using multi-column layout

Organizing with Tables

Creating a table in your document need not be like jumping into a teacup from 100 feet up. WordPerfect makes it as easy as stepping into a nice relaxing bath.

Creating Tables

Tables are used to organize your data into a compact form. Now if only they could do that for our waistlines.

Using the Create Table Tool

The more controlled way of creating a table is to use the Create Table tool.

1. Click the **mouse pointer** where you want to insert the table. The insertion point will appear where you click.

2. Click on **Insert**. The Insert menu will open.

3. Click on **Table**. The Create Table dialog box will open.

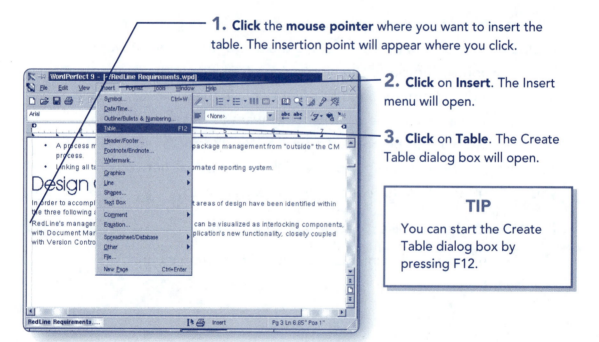

TIP

You can start the Create Table dialog box by pressing F12.

ORGANIZING WITH TABLES

4. Type the **number of columns** for your table. The value will appear in the Columns field.

5. Press the **Tab key**. The insertion point will move to the Rows field.

6. Type the **number of rows** for your table. The value will appear in the Rows field.

7. Click on **Create**. The Create Table dialog box will close and the table with the correct specifications will appear at the insertion point in the text.

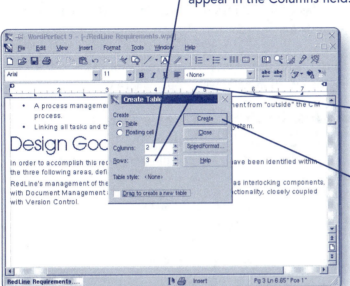

8. Type the **data** into the table. The data will appear in the table's cells.

TIP

Press the Tab key to move the insertion point between table cells.

Using Table QuickCreate

An even faster way of making a table in your document is to use QuickCreate.

1. Click the **mouse pointer** where you want to insert the table. The insertion point will appear where you click.

2. Click the **Table QuickCreate button**. The Table row and column grid will appear.

3. Drag the **mouse pointer** down and across the grid until you reach the table size you want. The grid will be highlighted to show your selection.

ORGANIZING WITH TABLES

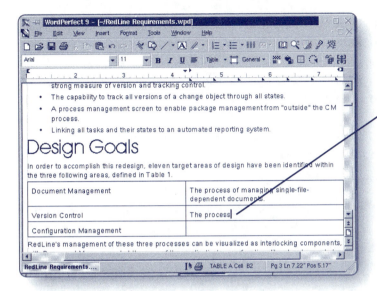

4. Release the **mouse button**. A table with the correct specifications will appear at the insertion point in the text.

5. Type the **data** into the table. The data will appear in the table's cells.

Dragging a Table

There are a variety of ways a table can be created. One variant is to drag-and-drop a table into being as a graphic object. This is a fast method, but be aware that as a graphic object, the table is essentially a picture and will not have some of the inherent features of a table—such as the ability to span across pages.

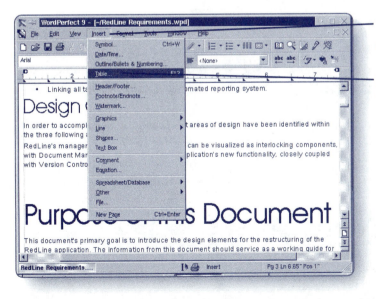

1. Click on **Insert**. The Insert menu will open.

2. Click on **Table**. The Create Table dialog box will open.

CHAPTER 7: BUILDING WITH TABLES AND COLUMNS

3. Type the **number of columns** for your table. The value will appear in the Columns field.

4. Press the **Tab key**. The insertion point will move to the Rows field.

5. Type the **number of rows** for your table. The value will appear in the Rows field.

6. Click the **box** next to Drag to create a new table. A check (√) will be placed in the check box.

7. Click on **Create**. The Create Table dialog box will close and the table pointer will appear in the document window.

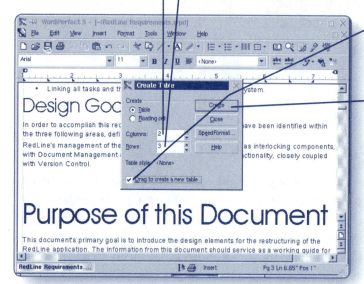

8. Click and drag the **table cursor** across your document. A dashed-line representation of the table's size will appear.

9. Release the **mouse button**. A graphic object containing a table with the correct specifications and defined size will appear in the text.

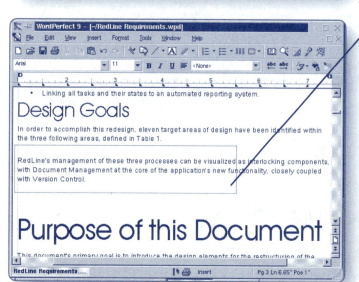

ORGANIZING WITH TABLES

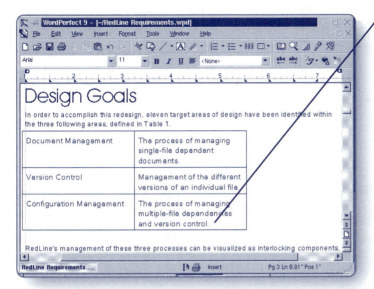

10. **Type** the **data** into the table. The data will appear in the table's cells.

Editing Tables

Once a table is created and data is entered, you can still add and delete to the structure of the table if need be.

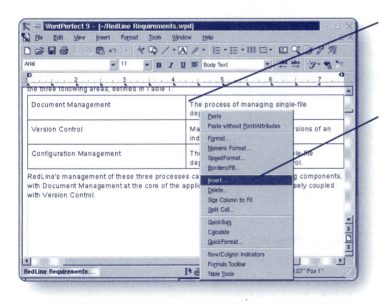

1. **Press** the **right mouse button** (*right-click*) on a data cell. The Table Configuration menu will appear.

2. **Click** on **Insert**. The Insert Columns/Rows dialog box will open.

3. **Click** the **Rows option**. The Rows option will be highlighted.

4. **Type** a **number of rows** to insert. The value is displayed in the Rows field.

5. **Click** the **Before option**. The Before option is selected.

6. **Click** on **OK**. The Insert Columns/Rows dialog box will close and the new rows will appear in the table.

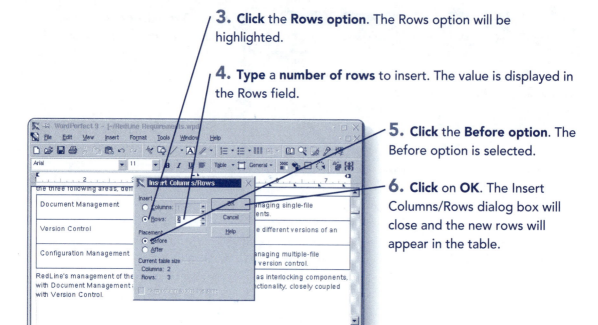

7. **Right-click** on a **data cell** in one of the new rows. The Table Configuration menu will appear.

8. **Click** on **Delete**. The Delete Structure/Content dialog box will open.

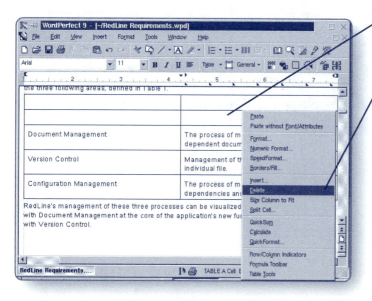

ORGANIZING WITH TABLES

9. Click the **Rows option**. The Rows option will be highlighted.

10. Type a **number of rows** to delete. The value will be displayed in the Rows field.

11. Click on **OK**. The Delete Structure/Content dialog box will close and the specified number of rows will disappear from the table.

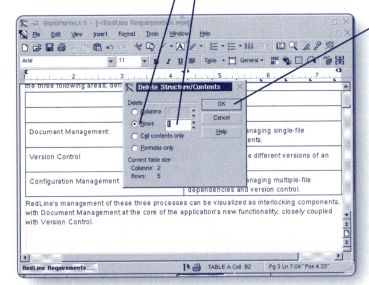

12. Type data in the new row. The data will appear in the appropriate cells.

13. Move the **mouse pointer** over the dividing line between the columns. The pointer will change to a line moving pointer.

14. Click and drag the **line moving pointer** to the left. The line indicator will also move to the left.

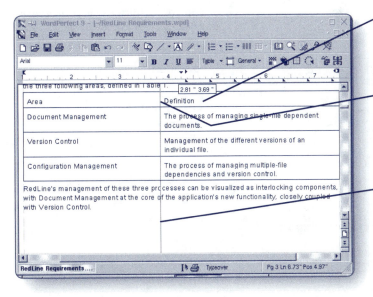

CHAPTER 7: BUILDING WITH TABLES AND COLUMNS

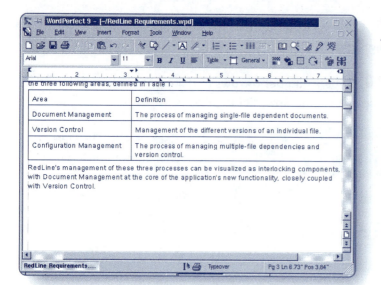

15. Release the **mouse button**. The columns will be resized.

Formatting Tables

A table is, essentially, just a collection of data in rows and columns. But who wants just essentially in this day and age?

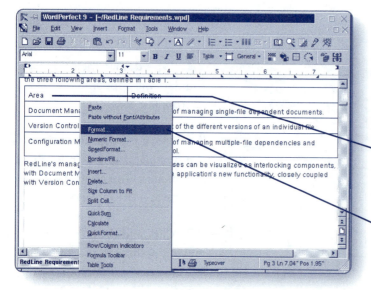

Using the Format Tool

You can configure virtually every property a table might have. You can even lock cells so they can't be edited.

1. Right-click on a **data cell**. The Table Configuration menu will appear.

2. Click on **Format**. The Properties for Table Format dialog box will open.

ORGANIZING WITH TABLES

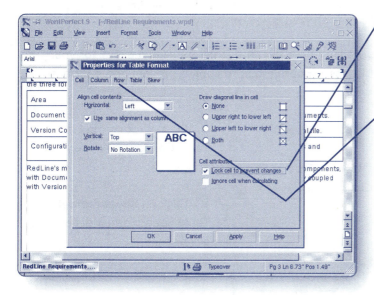

3. Click on the **box** next to Lock cell to prevent changes. A √ will be placed in the check box.

4. Click on the **Row tab**. The Row pane will appear.

5. Click on the **Fixed option**. The option will be highlighted.

6. Type a **value** for row height. The value (in inches) will appear in the Fixed field.

7. Click on **OK**. The Properties for Table Format dialog box will close and the table will reflect the changes.

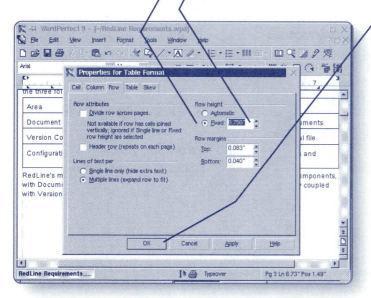

Using SpeedFormat

If you don't have the time to create a unique look for your tables, use SpeedFormat to apply a preconfigured format for you.

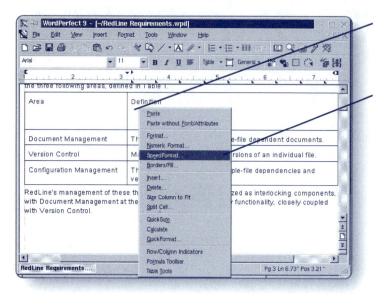

1. Right-click on the **table**. The Table Configuration menu will appear.

2. Click on **SpeedFormat**. The Table SpeedFormat dialog box will open.

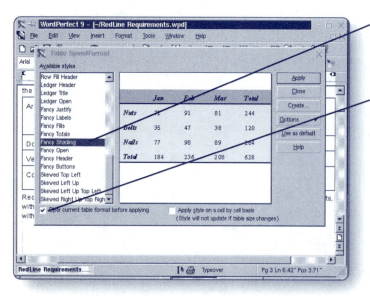

3. Click on a **format**. A preview of the format will appear in the preview window.

4. Click on the **box** next to Clear current table format before applying. A √ will be placed in the check box.

CREATING MULTI-COLUMN DOCUMENTS

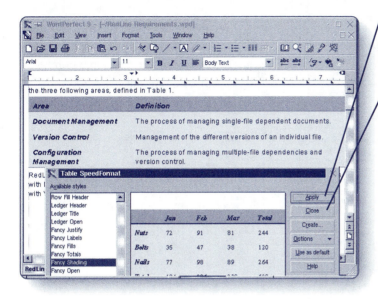

5. Click on **Apply**. The selected format will be applied to the table.

6. Click on **Close**. The Table SpeedFormat dialog box will close.

Creating Multi-Column Documents

If you want to make a newsletter or magazine-style document, then you need to manipulate the amount of columns a document contains. The default number of columns, of course, is the one great-big column most documents have. Changing and manipulating this number is simplicity itself.

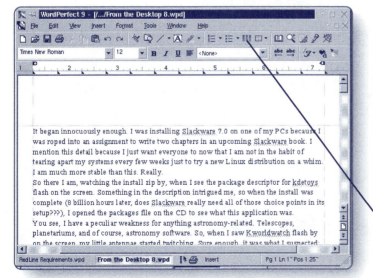

Creating Columns

Creating additional columns in WordPerfect is not too hard. In fact, it's remarkably easy.

1. Click on the **Columns button.** The Column menu will appear.

CHAPTER 7: BUILDING WITH TABLES AND COLUMNS

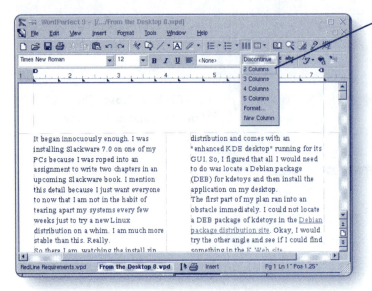

2. Click on the **desired number of columns**. The Column menu will close and the same number of columns will appear in the document.

Formatting Columns

Once you have a multi-column document, you can easily format the columns as well.

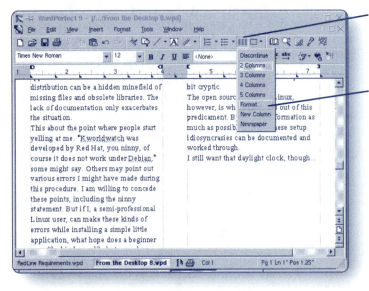

1. Click on the **Columns button**. The Column menu will appear.

2. Click on **Format**. The Column menu will close and the Columns dialog box will appear.

CREATING MULTI-COLUMN DOCUMENTS

3. Click on **Balanced Newspaper option**. The option will be selected.

4. Click on the **spin controls** of the Space between field to **adjust** the **setting** to .300 inches. The values in the Columns Widths area of the dialog box will be changed to reflect this new setting.

5. Click on **OK**. The Columns dialog box will close and the document will reflect your changes.

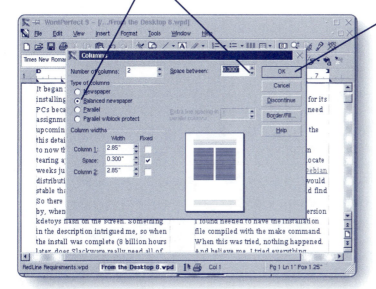

8

Adding Style to Your Document

These days, it takes more than snappy prose to make a document stand out. Sharp-looking documents are becoming the norm. WordPerfect has the tools to take your documents to this new visual level. In this chapter, you'll learn how to:

- Insert artwork into your document
- Wrap text around artwork in your document
- Make your text meet exacting space requirements
- Use text boxes for great layout effects
- Place objects from other documents within your document

Using Artwork

A picture is worth...well, you know the rest. People in many societies put a lot of effort into using graphics to get their point across. Just think how boring (and short) this book would be without pictures!

Inserting a Graphic

When you create a document, the use of graphics will assist in getting your point across. Don't get carried away however—too much artwork will drown out the text!

1. Click the **mouse pointer** where you want to insert the graphic. The insertion point will appear where you click.

2. Click on **Insert**. The Insert menu will open.

3. Move the **mouse pointer** to Graphics. The Graphics menu will open.

4. Click on **From File**. The Insert Image dialog box will open.

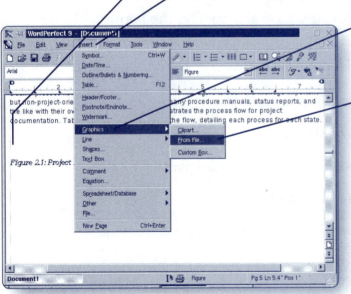

USING ARTWORK 101

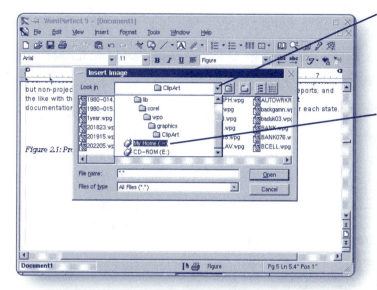

5. **Click** the **down arrow** (↓) next to the Look in box. A list of common file system points will appear.

6. **Click** on **My Home**. The file list will now display the contents of your home directory.

> **NOTE**
> In Linux, every user is given his or her own home directory under /home/username. This is a good spot to keep your personal files.

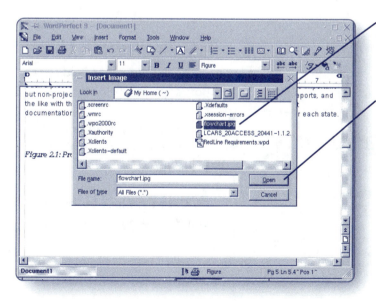

7. **Click** the **graphic file** you want to insert. The file will be highlighted.

8. **Click** on **Open**. The Insert Image dialog box will close and the selected artwork will appear in the text.

Editing a Graphic

Once you have a graphic in place, you can edit it to further help it match your document's style.

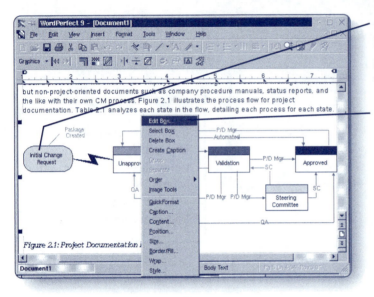

1. Press the **right mouse button** (*right-click*) on the graphic. The Image Editing menu will appear.

2. Click on **Edit Box**. The Edit Box dialog box will open.

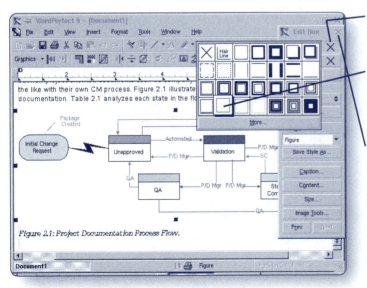

3. Click the **Border field**. The Border palette will open.

4. Click a **preferred border**. The border will appear around the image.

5. Click the **Close button**. The Edit Box dialog box will close.

USING ARTWORK   103

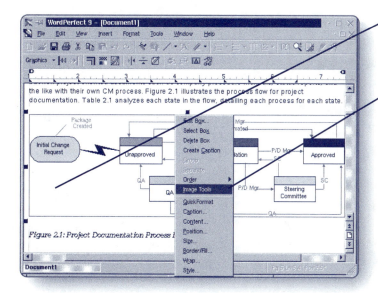

6. Right-click the **mouse pointer** on the graphic. The Image Editing menu will appear.

7. Click on **Image Tools**. The Image Tools dialog box will open.

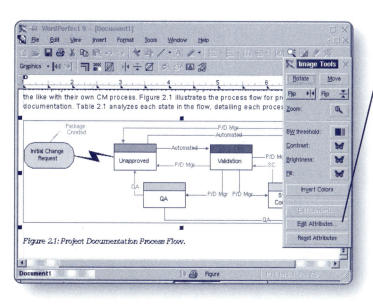

8. Click on **Edit Attributes**. The Image Settings dialog box will appear.

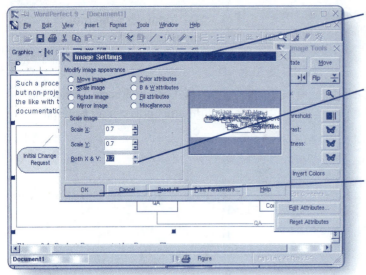

9. **Click** on **Scale Image**. The Scale Image parameters will appear.

10. **Click** the **Both X & Y spin control** to change the value to .7. The value will be changed in all three scale fields.

11. **Click** on **OK**. The Image Settings dialog box will close and the image (but not the box) will be scaled to the specified size.

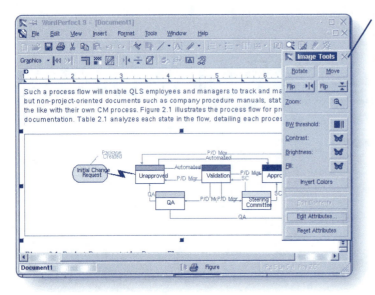

12. **Click** the **Close button**. The Image Tools dialog box will close.

USING ARTWORK

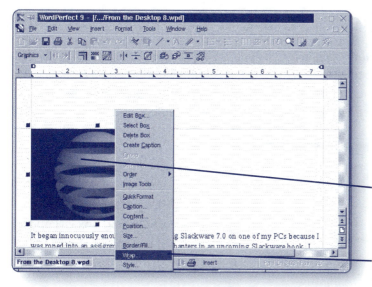

Wrapping Text around a Graphic

Graphics, without meaning to, can hog a lot of space in your document. You can circumvent this limitation by wrapping text around the image.

1. Right-click the **mouse pointer** on the graphic. The Image Editing menu will appear.

2. Click on **Wrap**. The Wrap Text dialog box will open.

3. Click on the **Square option**. The Square option will be selected and the Wrap text around options will be activated.

4. Click on the **Largest side option**. The option will be selected.

5. Click on **OK**. The Wrap Text dialog box will close and the text will be wrapped around the graphic.

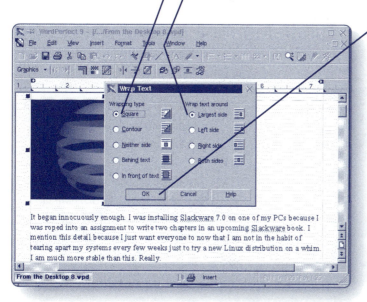

TIP

You can create a nifty effect by selecting the Behind text option for the graphic. Then simply select and apply a new color to the text on the graphic for better contrast.

Using Make It Fit

Every once in a while you are given a requirement to make a document exactly a certain length. In this age of electronic documents, this is not such a common requirement, but it's nice to know you can still do it if need be.

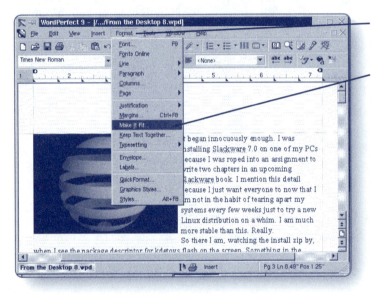

1. **Click** on **Format**. The Format menu will appear.

2. **Click** on **Make It Fit**. The Make It Fit dialog box will open.

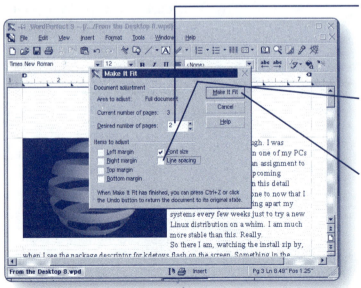

3. **Type** a **new value** in the Desired number of pages field. The value will appear in the field.

4. **Click** on the **box** next to Line spacing. The Line spacing box will be unchecked.

5. **Click** on **Make It Fit**. The Make It Fit dialog box will close and the document will be altered to the new specifications.

Using Text Boxes

You use text boxes to create interesting layout effects. By placing some text within a text box, you can make that text behave independently of other text on the same page.

Making a Text Box

Text boxes are objects that act just like graphics, in terms of layout. They are simply boxes that contain text, rather than a picture, and can either anchor to the page or float in the document.

1. Click the **mouse pointer** where you want to insert the text box. The insertion point will appear where you click.

2. Click on **Insert**. The Insert menu will appear.

3. Click on **Text Box**. A text box will appear in the document at the insertion point.

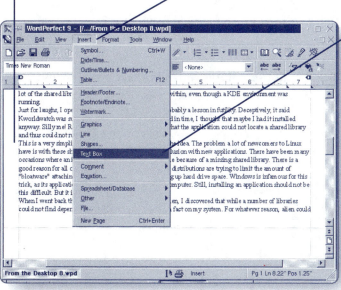

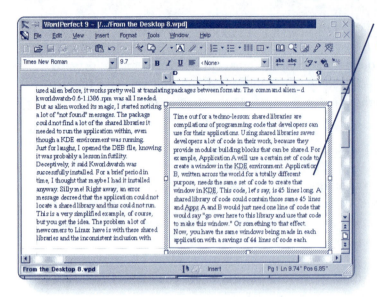

4. Type text in the text box. The box will grow to accommodate the text within.

Making a Multi-Column Text Box

Creating text boxes with multiple columns is a useful feature of WordPerfect.

1. Click the **mouse pointer** within the text box. The insertion point will appear where you click.

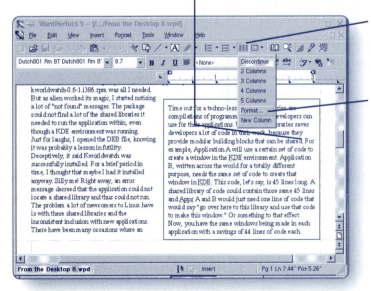

2. Click on the **Columns button**. The Columns menu will appear.

3. Click on **Format**. The Columns dialog box will appear.

INSERTING ANOTHER DOCUMENT 109

4. Click on the **Balanced Newspaper option**. The option will be selected.

5. Reduce the **Space value** to .100. The value will be displayed in the Space field.

6. Click on **OK**. The Columns dialog box will close and the text box contents will reflect the new values.

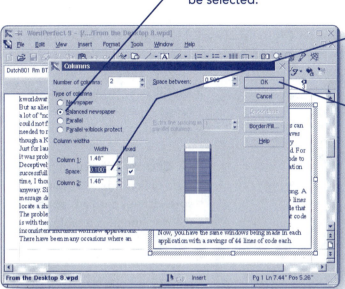

Inserting Another Document

Not only can you make great stuff in WordPerfect, you can also import material from other documents created in the WordPerfect 2000 office suite!

1. Click the **mouse pointer** where you want to insert the graphic. The insertion point will appear where you click.

2. Click on **Insert**. The Insert menu will open.

3. Move the **mouse pointer** to Spreadsheet/Database. The Spreadsheet/Database menu will open.

4. Click on **Import**. The Import Data dialog box will open.

5. Type the **path and name of the file** in the Filename field. The file name and path will be displayed.

6. Click on **OK**. A list of available ranges in the spreadsheet will be displayed.

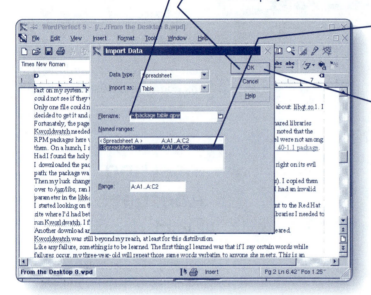

7. Click on the **appropriate range**. The range will be selected.

8. Click on **OK**. The Import Data dialog box will close and spreadsheet data will appear in the document as a table.

9
Managing Longer Documents

WordPerfect makes it easy to create documents of any size. It includes several tools to give your documents a professional typeset look. In this chapter, you'll learn how to:

- Configure the page
- Create page breaks
- Build page headers and footers
- Create a table of contents
- Make an index

Setting Page Options

Not all pages fit 8½" × 11" sheets. For off-sized pages with differing margins, you can quickly configure WordPerfect to conform.

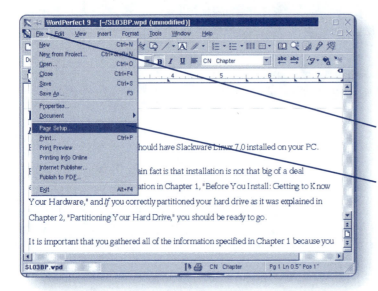

Changing Margins

Changing the margins of a page is a simple operation in WordPerfect.

1. Click on **File**. The File menu will appear.

2. Click on **Page Setup**. The Page Setup dialog box will open.

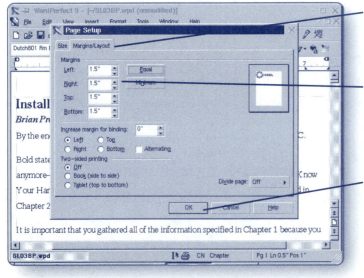

3. Click on the **Margins/Layout tab**. The Margins/Layout tab will come to the front.

4. Change the **Left**, **Right**, **Top**, and **Bottom fields** to 1.5". The values will be displayed in those fields.

5. Click on **OK**. The Page Layout dialog box will close and the margins of the document will be changed.

SETTING PAGE OPTIONS 113

Setting Paper Orientation

When paper is held as a tall sheet, it is in portrait orientation. When it is short and wide, it is in landscape orientation. You can change this electronically in WordPerfect.

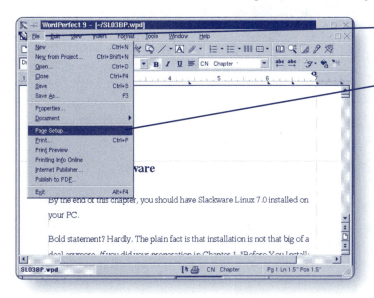

1. Click on **File**. The File menu will appear.

2. Click on **Page Setup**. The Page Setup dialog box will open.

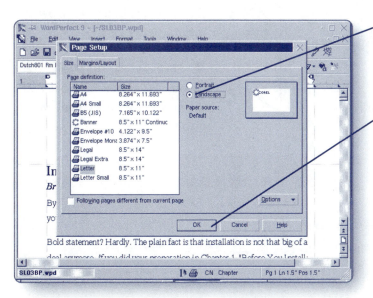

3. Click on the **Landscape option**. The option is selected and the preview display will show the result.

4. Click on **OK**. The Page Layout dialog box will close and the orientation of the document will be changed.

Selecting a Paper Size

Besides letter-size paper, you can use many other paper sizes.

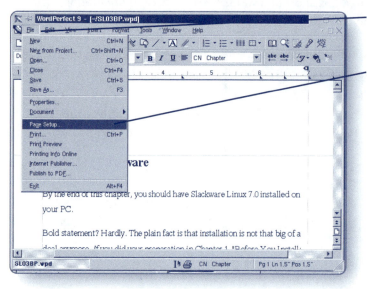

1. Click on **File**. The File menu will appear.

2. Click on **Page Setup**. The Page Setup dialog box will open.

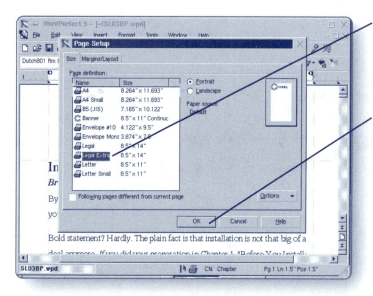

3. Click on a **paper size**. The paper size will be selected and the preview display will show the result.

4. Click on **OK**. The Page Layout dialog box will close and the newly sized document will be displayed.

Inserting a Page Break Manually

When you create documents in WordPerfect, new pages are generated as text overflows from one page to the next. You can, however, dictate where one page stops and where a new one begins.

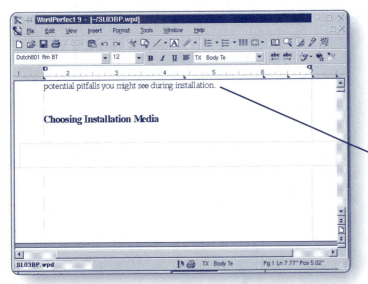

Inserting a Page Break

Stopping a page at a certain point is the job of the page break.

1. Click the **mouse pointer** where you want the page break. The insertion point will appear where you click.

2. Press Ctrl+Enter. The page break will appear at the insertion point.

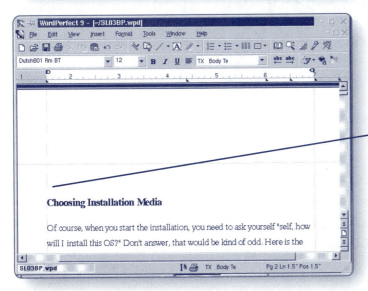

The new page begins.

Deleting a Page Break

If you want to remove a page break that was manually inserted, follow these short steps.

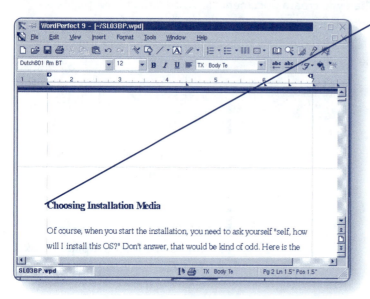

1. Click the **mouse pointer** on the first line just after the page break. The insertion point will appear where you click.

2. Press the **Backspace** key. The page break will be removed.

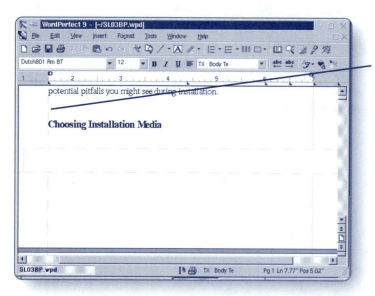

The page break disappears.

Working with Headers and Footers

In most professional publications, you see headers and footers. It is here that page numbers, dates, and other pertinent information can appear.

Creating a Header or Footer

Making a simple header or footer is a quick process.

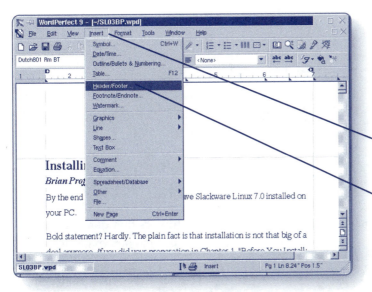

1. **Click** on **Insert**. The Insert menu will appear.

2. **Click** on **Header/Footer**. The Headers/Footers dialog box will appear.

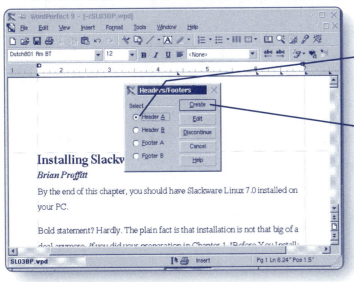

3. **Click** on the **Header A option**. The option will be selected.

4. **Click** on **Create**. The Headers/Footers dialog box will close and the new header will appear in the document.

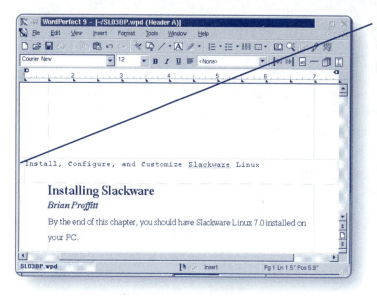

5. Type text. Text will appear in the new header on every page.

Adding Date and Time

You can add fields to headers and footers that generate the date or time automatically.

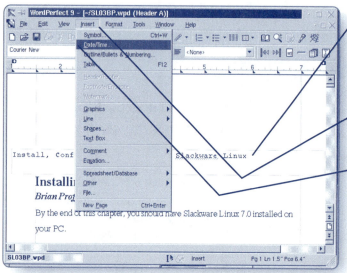

1. Click the **mouse pointer** in the header or footer you want to edit. The insertion point will appear where you click.

2. Click on **Insert**. The Insert menu will appear.

3. Click on **Date/Time**. The Date/Time dialog box will appear.

WORKING WITH HEADERS AND FOOTERS

4. Click the **date/time format** you want. The format will be selected.

5. Click on the **box** next to Keep the inserted date current. A check (√) will be placed in the check box.

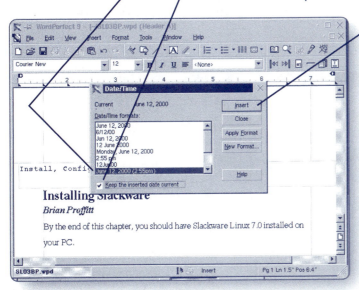

6. Click on **Insert**. The Date/Time dialog box will close and the date/time will appear at the insertion point.

Page Numbering

When your documents get big, you need to number the pages to keep them straight. You don't have to type them all in yourself—WordPerfect will handle it for you.

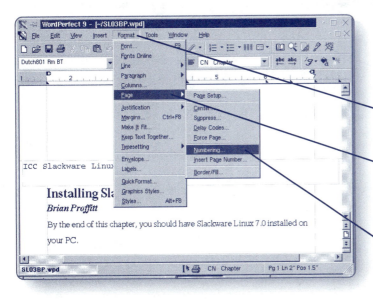

1. Click on **Format**. The Format menu will open.

2. Move the **mouse pointer** to Page. The Page menu will appear.

3. Click on **Numbering**. The Select Page Numbering Format dialog box will appear.

120 CHAPTER 9: MANAGING LONGER DOCUMENTS

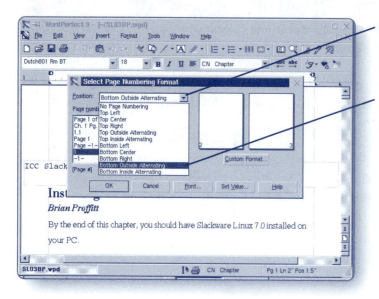

4. **Click** on the **down arrow (↓)** next to the Position box. The Position list will be displayed.

5. **Click** on a **position**. The position will be selected.

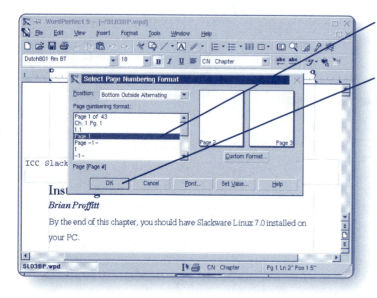

6. **Click** on a **format**. The format will be selected.

7. **Click** on **OK**. The Select Page Numbering Format dialog box will close and the page numbers will appear at the appropriate positions on the pages.

Creating Footnotes and Endnotes

When creating more technical documents, you might need to insert footnotes or endnotes.

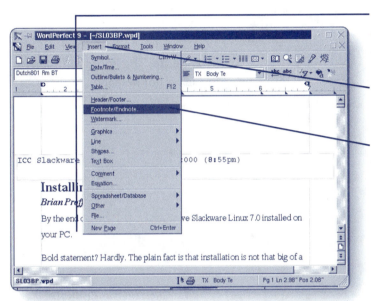

1. **Click** the **mouse pointer** at the footnote. The insertion point will appear where you click.

2. **Click** on **Insert**. The Insert menu will appear.

3. **Click** on **Footnote/Endnote**. The Footnote/Endnote dialog box will open.

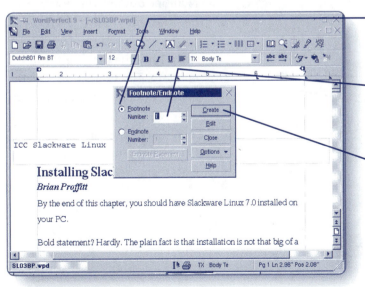

4. **Click** on the **Footnote Number option**. The option will be selected.

5. **Type** the **number** for the footnote. The value is displayed in the Footnote Number box.

6. **Click** on **Create**. The Footnote/Endnote dialog box will close and a footnote marker will appear in the text at the text insertion point, and a new footer will appear on the same page.

7. **Type text** in the footnote.

8. **Click** the **mouse pointer** at the endnote. The insertion point will appear where you click.

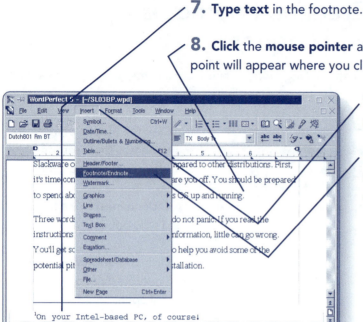

9. **Click** on **Insert**. The Insert menu will appear.

10. **Click** on **Footnote/ Endnote**. The Footnote/Endnote dialog box will open.

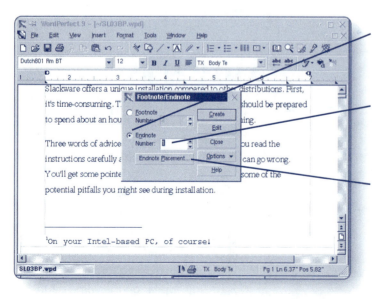

11. **Click** on the **Endnote Number option**. The option will be selected.

12. **Type** the **number** for the endnote. The value is displayed in the Endnote Number box.

13. **Click** on **Endnote Placement**. The Endnote Placement dialog box will open.

CREATING FOOTNOTES AND ENDNOTES 123

14. Click on the **Insert endnotes at insertion point option**. The option will be selected.

15. Click on **OK**. The Endnote Placement dialog box will close.

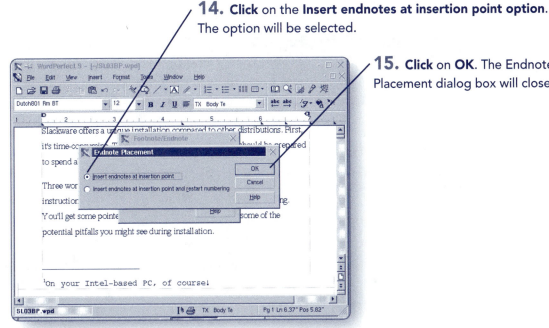

16. Click on **Create**. The Footnote/Endnote dialog box will close and an endnote marker will appear in the text at the text insertion point, and a new footer with the endnote will appear on the last page of the document.

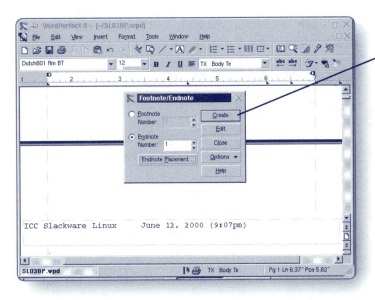

124 CHAPTER 9: MANAGING LONGER DOCUMENTS

17. **Type text** in the endnote.

18. Click outside the **endnote footer** to resume document editing. The insertion point will appear where you click.

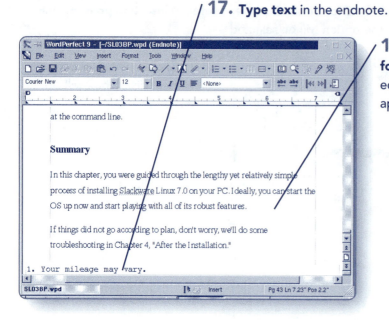

Building a Table of Contents

One feature of longer documents is a table of contents. WordPerfect can make one for you with ease.

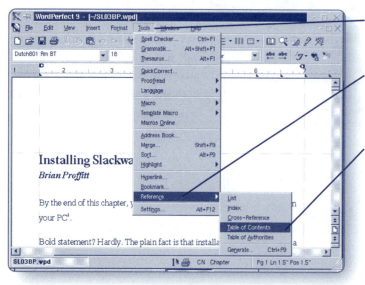

1. Click on **Tools**. The Tools menu will open.

2. Move the **mouse pointer** to Reference. The Reference menu will appear.

3. Click on **Table of Contents**. The Table of Contents toolbar will appear.

BUILDING A TABLE OF CONTENTS   125

4. Select the **text** to use in the Table of Contents. The text is highlighted.

5. Click the **Mark 1 button**. The selected heading is marked as a first-level heading for the table of contents.

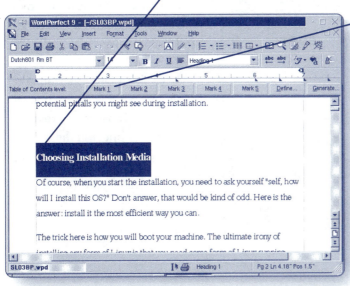

6. Repeat steps 4 and 5 for all other headings in the document. Second-level headings are Mark 2, third-level Mark 3, and so on.

7. Click the **mouse pointer** on a blank line in the document. The insertion point will appear where you click.

8. Click the **Define button**. The Define Table of Contents dialog box will open.

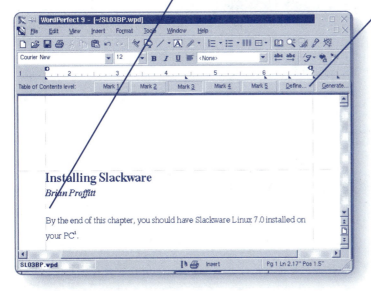

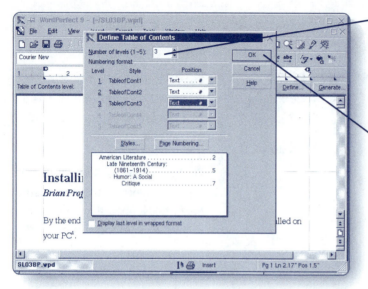

9. Type 3 in the Number of levels box. The value will be displayed and the position boxes will be activated for the second and third levels.

10. Click on **OK**. The Define Table of Contents dialog box will close and a Table of Contents marker will appear in the document.

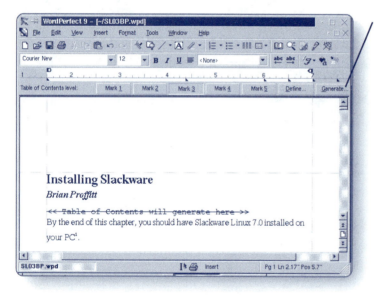

11. Click the **Generate button**. The Generate dialog box will open.

CREATING AN INDEX

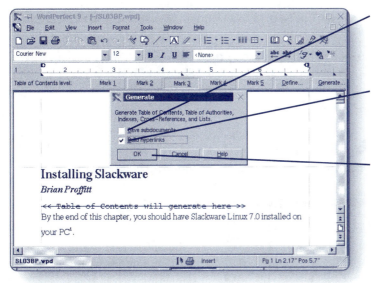

12. **Click** on the **box** next to Save subdocuments. The box will be unchecked.

13. **Click** on the **box** next to Build hyperlinks. A √ will be placed in the check box.

14. **Click** on **OK**. The Generate dialog box will close and the Table of Contents will be created.

Creating an Index

Like creating a table of contents, creating an index in WordPerfect is an automated process. Indexes are especially useful in larger documents, where finding a subject may not be as straightforward. But you have to do some work in advance.

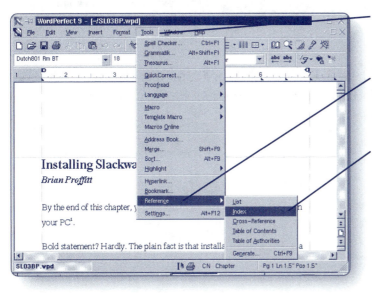

1. **Click** on **Tools**. The Tools menu will open.

2. **Move** the **mouse pointer** to **Reference**. The Reference menu will appear.

3. **Click** on **Index**. The Index toolbar will appear.

4. Select the **text** to use in the index. The text is highlighted.

5a. Click in the **Heading box**. The selected text is placed in the Heading box as a first-level heading for the index.

OR

5b. Click in the **Subheading** box. The selected text is placed in the Subheading box as a second-level heading for the index.

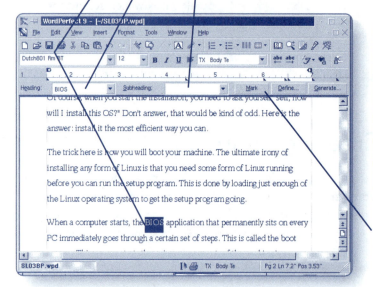

> **NOTE**
>
> If you use text in the Subheading box, there must be text in the Heading box to tie the subheading. Use the drop-down list to keep your headings consistent.

6. Click on the **Mark button**. The text in the fields will be marked for later display in the index.

7. Repeat steps 4 through 6 for all other indexed text in the document. The index entries will be created as you continue.

CREATING AN INDEX 129

8. Click the **mouse pointer** on a blank line in the document where you want to insert the index. The insertion point will appear where you click.

9. Click the **Define button**. The Define Index dialog box will open.

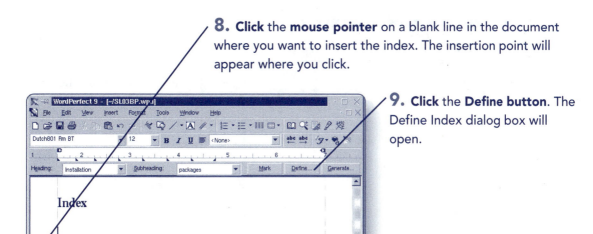

10. Click the **down arrow (↓)** next to the **Position box**. The Position list will appear.

11. Click on a **position**. The position will be selected.

12. Click on **OK**. The Define Index dialog box will close and an Index marker will appear in the document.

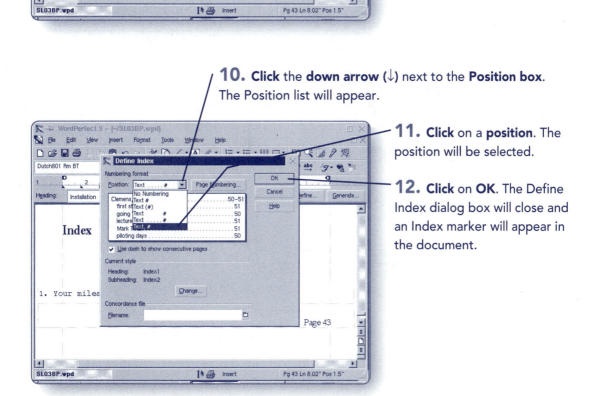

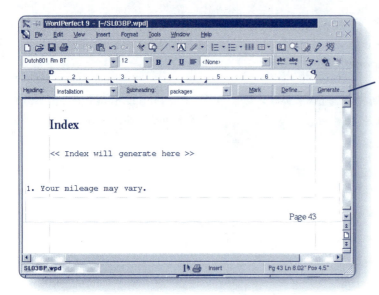

13. **Click** the **Generate button**. The Generate dialog box will open.

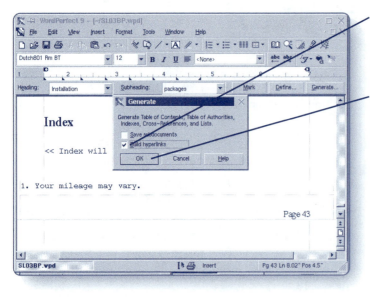

14. **Click** on the **box** next to Build hyperlinks. A √ will be placed in the check box.

15. **Click** on **OK**. The Generate dialog box will close and the Index will be created.

Part II Review Questions

1. What are the two editing modes in WordPerfect? See *"Inserting Text"* in Chapter 4.

2. How do you place text exactly where you want it? See *"Using Shadow Cursor"* in Chapter 4.

3. How do you use characters that are not on the keyboard? See *"Inserting Special Characters and Symbols"* in Chapter 5.

4. What are the two tools you use to check your spelling? See *"Correcting Spelling Errors"* in Chapter 6.

5. How can you avoid typing common phrases over and over again? See *"Working with Prompt-As-You-Go"* in Chapter 6.

6. How do you create tables in WordPerfect? See *"Creating Tables"* in Chapter 7.

7. How do you insert a graphic? See *"Inserting a Graphic"* in Chapter 8.

8. How do you make a document a specific length? See *"Using Make It Fit"* in Chapter 8.

9. How do you change your page settings? See *"Setting Page Options"* in Chapter 9.

10. How can you number pages in your document? See *"Page Numbering"* in Chapter 9.

PART III

Working with Data

Chapter 10
  Learning Quattro Pro Basics **135**

Chapter 11
  Editing a Spreadsheet **147**

Chapter 12
  Working with Functions and Formulas . . . **159**

Chapter 13
  Formatting Notebooks **169**

Chapter 14
  Completing Your Spreadsheet **181**

Chapter 15
  Manipulating Data **189**

Chapter 16
  Charting Data. **203**

10
Learning Quattro Pro Basics

Spreadsheets got their start when accountants used to create large, table-sized sheets of paper to handwrite their numbers and calculations. This tedious and often frustrating practice has translated well into software form, particularly with Quattro Pro. In this chapter, you'll learn how to:

- Identify spreadsheet and Quattro Pro elements
- Enter data into a spreadsheet
- Edit spreadsheet data
- Work with multiple spreadsheets

Exploring the Spreadsheet

Quattro Pro's interface contains several elements common to most spreadsheet programs, so there won't be much to throw you.

- **Cell.** Contains the data values of the spreadsheet. The intersection of a row and a column form a cell.
- **Sheet coordinates.** Displays the row-and-column coordinates of a selected cell or cell range.
- **Input line.** Inputs data into the selected cell.
- **Column heading.** Indicates the column of a selected cell when bold.
- **Row heading.** Indicates the row of a selected cell when bold.
- **Sheet tab.** Accesses other sheets within the spreadsheet file.
- **Status indicator.** Displays the status of your work.
- **Pane splitter.** Controls division of the sheet window.

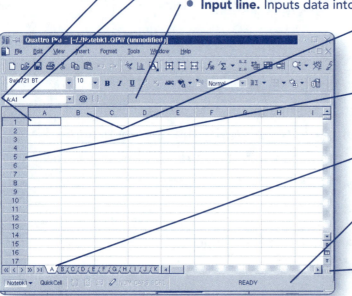

Moving around the Spreadsheet

Getting around a spreadsheet file is like moving around on a big map: Knowing where you are is half the challenge.

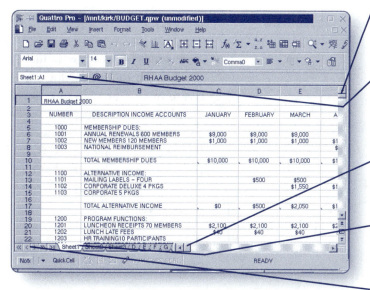

- **Vertical scroll bar.** Click and drag this bar to move up and down the spreadsheet.

- **Sheet coordinates box.** Type cell coordinates or range names here to directly access a cell or range.

- **Horizontal scroll bar.** Click and drag this bar to move left and right in the spreadsheet.

- **Sheet tab.** Click on a tab to open other sheets within the spreadsheet file.

- **Navigation buttons.** Use these to move between the sheets of your notebook.

Entering Data

You can place various kinds of data in a cell: text, numbers, cell references, and formulas. Formulas are examined in Chapter 12, "Working with Functions and Formulas." In the meantime, you can explore how you enter the other three data types.

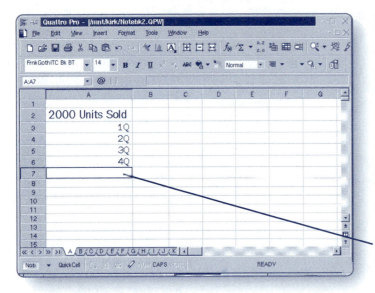

Entering Text

Text is defined as any data that Quattro Pro cannot manipulate in a formula. Generally, text is alphanumeric in nature, although you can use pure numbers as text and not numeric data. The year 2000, for example, is often a proper name instead of a numeric value.

1. Click on a **cell**. The cell will be highlighted.

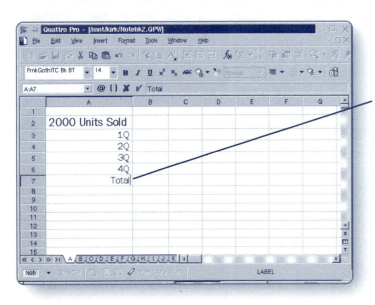

2. Type some **text**. The text will appear in the cell and on the input line.

3. Press the **Enter key**. The text will be entered into the cell.

Entering Numeric Data

Quattro Pro can use numeric data when it calculates values in formulas. Again, it should be noted that all numbers qualify as numeric data.

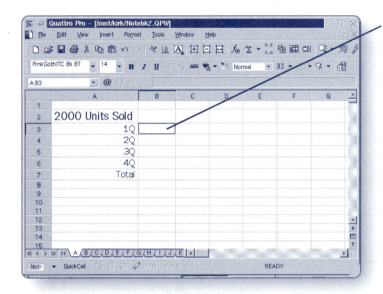

1. Click on a **cell**. The cell will be highlighted.

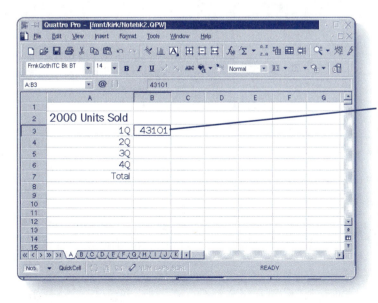

2. Type a **numeric value**. The value will appear in the cell and on the input line.

3. Press the **Enter key**. The value will be entered into the cell.

Entering Cell Addresses

Part of the beauty of a spreadsheet is the ability of one cell to reference the values (text or numeric) of another cell. Addresses can reflect a single cell or a range of cells. You can even incorporate references into formulas, as is shown in Chapter 12.

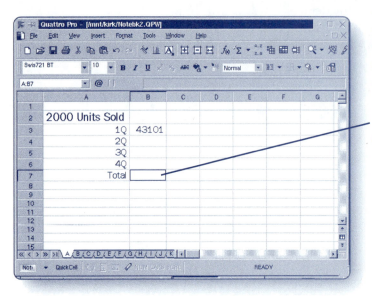

1. Click on a **cell**. The cell will be highlighted.

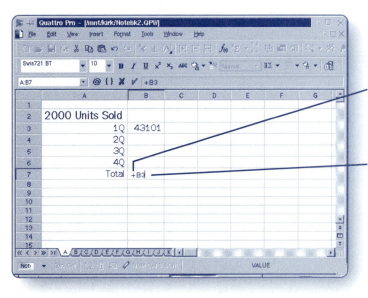

2. Type a **plus sign (+)**. The sign will appear in the cell and on the input line.

3. Type the **cell coordinates** of a cell containing data. The cell coordinates will appear in the input line.

4. Press the **Enter key**. The value of the addressed cell will appear in the addressing cell.

Editing Data

Changing the contents of a cell is simple, but you need to know where to start. One method allows you to easily change a portion of a cell's contents, and another tends to replace all of a cell's contents.

Replacing the Contents of a Cell

If you need to replace the contents of a cell all at once, try this method.

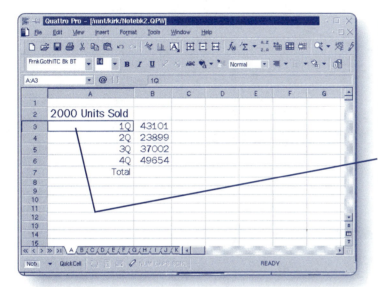

1. Click on a **cell**. The cell will be highlighted.

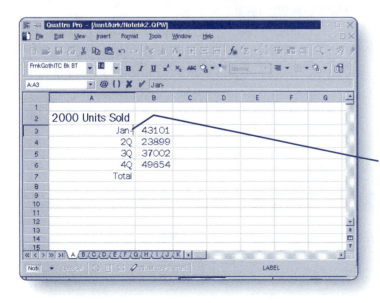

2. Type a new **value**. The value will appear in the cell and on the input line.

3. Press the **Enter key**. The value is entered into the cell.

142 CHAPTER 10: LEARNING QUATTRO PRO BASICS

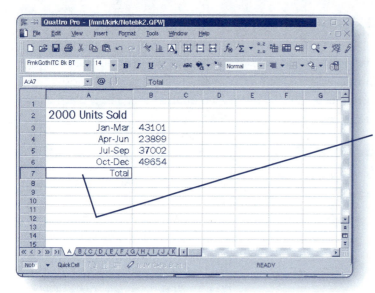

Editing the Contents of a Cell

To change only some of a cell's contents, start in the input line.

1. Click on a **cell**. The cell will be highlighted.

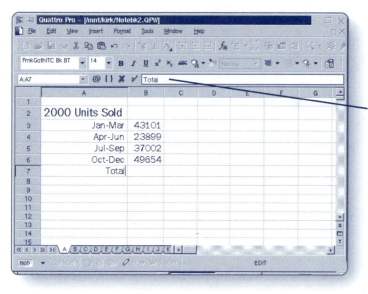

2. Click the **mouse pointer** at the proper place on the input line. The insertion point will appear where you click.

USING MULTIPLE SHEETS 143

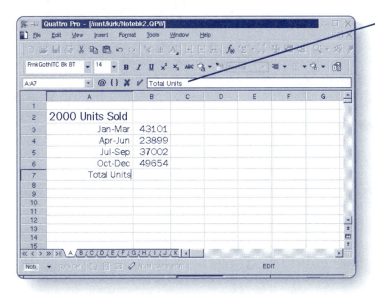

3. Edit the **value** on the input line. The value will be changed.

4. Press the **Enter key**. The new value will be entered into the cell.

TIP
You can also click on the Accept button to enter data into a cell.

Using Multiple Sheets

Like the spreadsheets of old, spreadsheet files contain many sheets to fill with data, like the pages of a book. Quattro Pro notebooks begin with three sheets, which you can access and reference with ease.

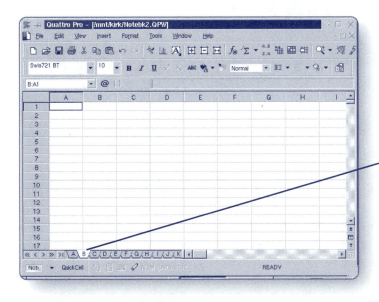

Navigating to Multiple Sheets

Getting to another sheet is as easy as turning a page, without those pesky paper cuts.

1. Click on a **sheet tab**. The sheet will come to the front.

Building Multi-Sheet Addresses

Not only can you reference cells in a spreadsheet, you can reference any cell in the spreadsheet, regardless of what sheet it's on.

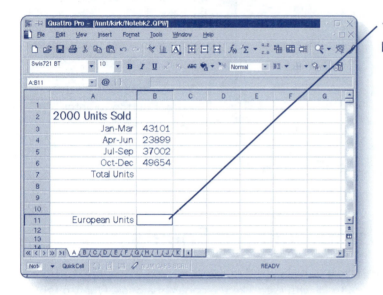

1. Click on a **cell**. The cell will be highlighted.

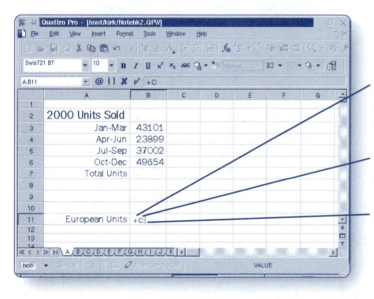

2. Type a **plus sign (+)**. The sign will appear in the cell and on the input line.

3. Type the **sheet name** of the target cell.

4. Type a **colon (:)** in the cell.

USING MULTIPLE SHEETS   145

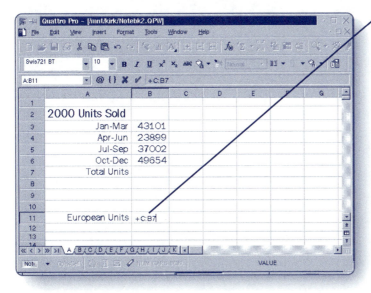

5. **Type** the **cell coordinates** of the target cell.

6. **Press** the **Enter key**. The value will be entered into the cell.

11

Editing a Spreadsheet

Although a spreadsheet might look rather inflexible with its rows and columns, it is not by any means a fixed document. You can add or subtract rows and columns and move your data as needed. In this chapter, you'll learn how to:

- Select data in one or more cells
- Insert rows and columns
- Remove rows and columns
- Shift data around the spreadsheet

Selecting Data

To change data within a cell or cells, they must be selected. You have already learned in Chapter 10, "Learning Quattro Pro Basics," how to select a single cell by clicking on it. Now, see how you can select multiple cells.

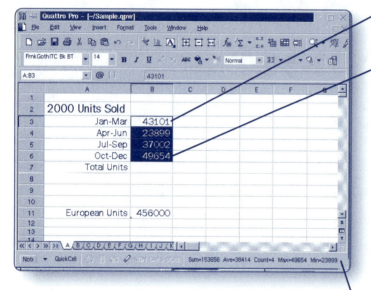

1. **Click** on a **cell**. The cell will be highlighted.

2. **Press** the **Shift key** and **click** on another **cell**. The second cell will be highlighted, as will all of the cells in between.

TIP
Notice the status indicator when you select a range of cells. If numeric data is present, the indicator will display a wealth of data, including sum, average, cell count, maximum value, and minimum value.

SELECTING DATA 149

3. Click on a **cell**. The cell will be highlighted.

4. Click and **drag** the **mouse pointer** to a destination cell. The destination cell will be highlighted, as will all of the cells in between.

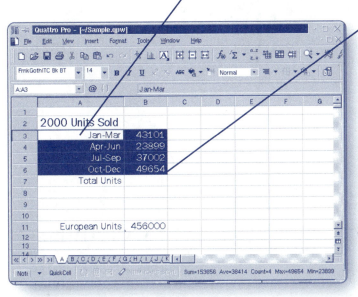

5. Click on a **row heading**. The entire row will be highlighted.

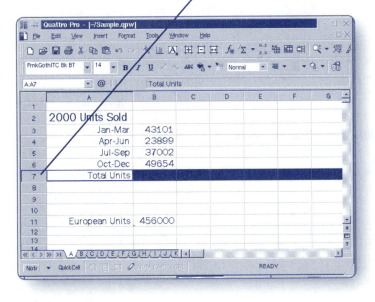

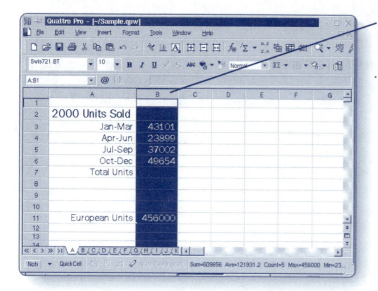

6. Click on a **column heading**. The entire column will be highlighted.

Inserting Rows and Columns

Sometimes, you might find you have to insert additional rows and columns in a Quattro Pro spreadsheet.

Inserting Rows

Inserting a row into a spreadsheet is not difficult if you use the row headings. Just remember: Rows will be inserted above the current row.

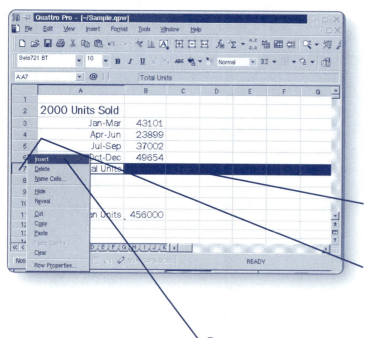

1. Select a **cell** in the row where you want to insert another row. The cell will be highlighted.

2. Right-click on the **row heading**. The row's Context menu will appear.

3. Click on **Insert**. A new row will appear above the current one.

INSERTING ROWS AND COLUMNS   151

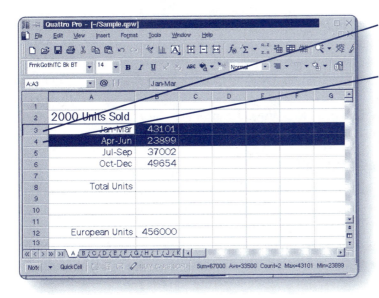

4. Click on a **row heading**. The row will be highlighted.

5. Hold the **Shift key** and **click** on another **row heading**. A second row and all rows in between will be highlighted.

6. Right-click on a selected **row heading**. The rows' Context menu will appear.

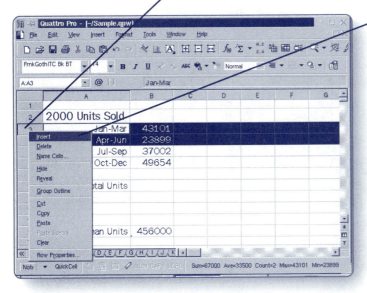

7. Click on **Insert**. New rows equal to the number of selected rows will appear above the selected rows.

Inserting Columns

Inserting a column is exactly like inserting rows. One thing to note: Columns are inserted to the left of the current column.

1. **Select** a **cell** in the column where you want to insert another column. The cell will be highlighted.

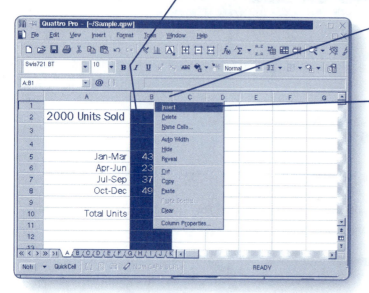

2. **Right-click** on a **column heading**. The column's Context menu will appear.

3. **Click** on **Insert**. A new column will appear to the left of the current one.

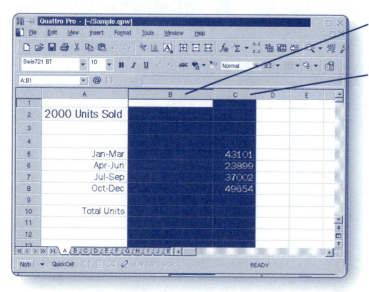

4. **Click** on a **column heading**. The column will be highlighted.

5. **Hold** the **Shift key** and **click** on another **column heading**. A second column and all columns in between will be highlighted.

DELETING ROWS AND COLUMNS   153

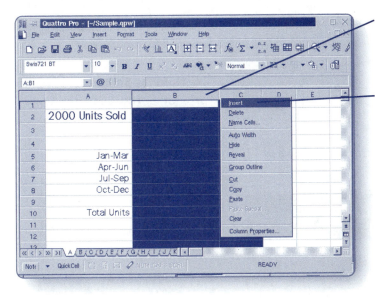

6. **Right-click** on a selected **column heading**. The columns' Context menu will appear.

7. **Click** on **Insert**. New columns equal to the number of selected columns will appear to the left of the selected columns.

Deleting Rows and Columns

When deleting columns and rows, it is important to distinguish between deleting the row or the row's data. Selecting a row or column and just pressing the Delete key empties that row or column's cells of data. You must use the headings to remove the row or column entirely. This example deletes single and multiple rows and works the same way for columns.

1. **Select** a **cell** in the row you want to remove. The cell will be highlighted.

2. **Right-click** on the **row heading**. The row's Context menu will appear.

3. **Click** on **Delete**. The row will be deleted.

154 CHAPTER 11: EDITING A SPREADSHEET

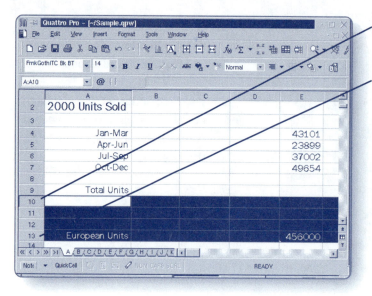

4. Click on a **row heading**. The row will be highlighted.

5. Hold the **Shift key** and **click** on another **row heading**. A second row and all rows in between will be highlighted.

6. Right-click on a selected **row heading**. The rows' Context menu will appear.

7. Click on **Delete**. The selected rows will be removed.

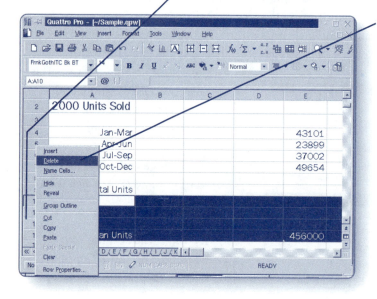

MOVING DATA 155

Moving Data

When you initially create a spreadsheet, you might give little thought to where data is placed on a sheet. If you have to share the file with someone else, you might need to organize the cells in a way that makes sense to other people.

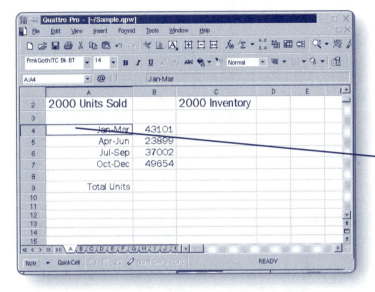

Copying and Pasting Cells

Moving cells around in Quattro Pro is a lot like moving text around in WordPerfect.

1. Select a **cell** to copy. The cell will be highlighted.

2. Press Ctrl+C. The cell's contents will be copied.

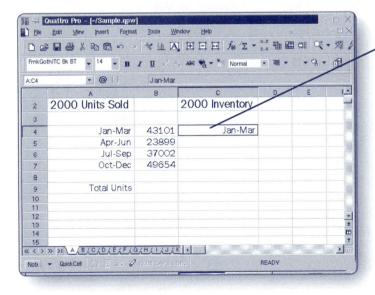

3. Click on the destination **cell**. The cell will be highlighted.

4. Press Ctrl+V. The copied cell will appear in the new destination cell.

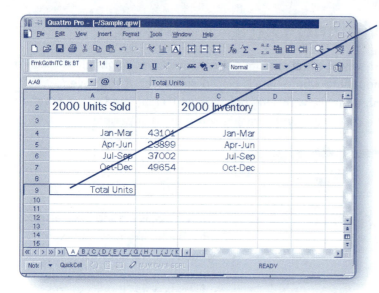

5. Select a **cell** to move. The cell will be highlighted.

6. Press Ctrl+X. The cell's contents will be removed.

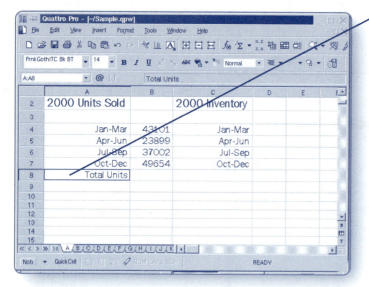

7. Click on the destination **cell**. The cell will be highlighted.

8. Press Ctrl+V. The cut cell will appear in the new destination cell.

Using Click and Drag to Move Data

You can move selected cells around a spreadsheet using only the mouse.

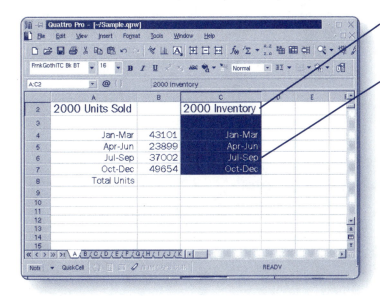

1. Select a **cell range** to move. The range will be highlighted.

2. Click on the **edge** of the selected cell range. The range will be ready to move.

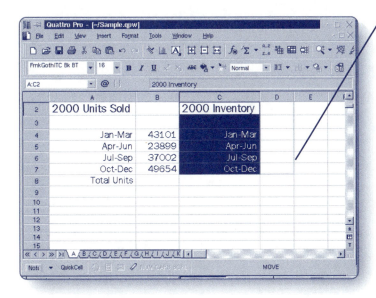

3. Drag the **cell range** to its new destination. The outline of the cell range will appear in another color as you drag it across the screen.

158 CHAPTER 11: EDITING A SPREADSHEET

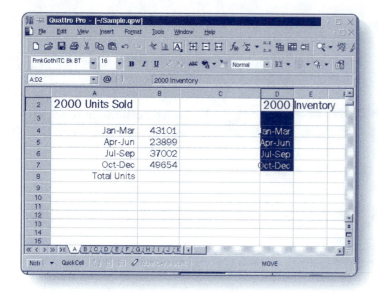

4. Release the **mouse button**. The cell range will be placed in the new location.

12

Working with Functions and Formulas

Putting all these numbers and values into the spreadsheet does you little good if they're just sitting there. The power of a spreadsheet application such as Quattro Pro is how it can work with those numbers to discover new values. In this chapter, you'll learn how to:

- Write formulas, both simple and complex
- Use cell references within a formula
- Copy and move formulas
- Build functions using Quattro Pro's function tools

Creating Formulas

A formula compares two or more values in a certain way and then uses the comparison as a new value. In other words, the value of 1 is compared to another value of 1 in such a way that they are combined. Together, their new value is 2. Formulas compare values using operators and functions. Operators are the action symbols you already know, such as + and −. Functions are less common, but more powerful, and will be examined later in this chapter.

Creating a Simple Formula

A simple formula uses one kind of operator at a time. Values in the formula can be numeric data or references. Table 12.1 shows the operators Quattro Pro uses and how they differ from everyday use.

Table 12.1 Traditional versus Quattro Pro Operators

Formula	Quattro Pro Formula
2+2=4	2+2=4
2−2=0	2−2=0
2×2=4	2*2=4
4÷2=2	4/2=2
$2^2=4$	2^2=4

CREATING FORMULAS 161

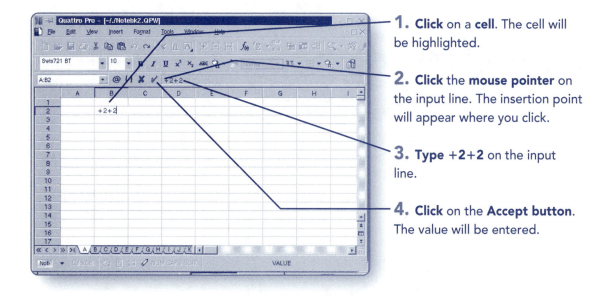

1. **Click** on a **cell**. The cell will be highlighted.

2. **Click** the **mouse pointer** on the input line. The insertion point will appear where you click.

3. **Type** **+2+2** on the input line.

4. **Click** on the **Accept button**. The value will be entered.

Creating a Complex Formula

A complex formula contains more than one operator type, such as 3×3 + 4÷2. When Quattro Pro makes calculations in complex formulas, it performs multiplication and division operators first and then addition and subtraction.

TIP
To keep things less confusing, use parentheses in complex formulas whenever possible.

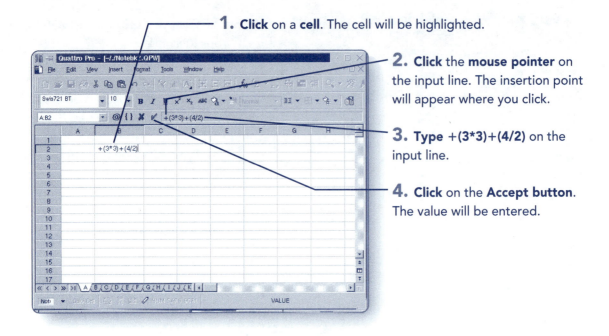

1. Click on a **cell**. The cell will be highlighted.

2. Click the **mouse pointer** on the input line. The insertion point will appear where you click.

3. Type **+(3*3)+(4/2)** on the input line.

4. Click on the **Accept button**. The value will be entered.

Using Addresses in a Formula

Using addresses in a formula is an important part of tapping into Quattro Pro's power.

Using Relative Addresses

A *relative address* is a cell reference that maintains the link between the referenced and referencing cell even if one of the cells is moved. These are great to use if you expect future redesigns of your spreadsheet.

USING ADDRESSES IN A FORMULA   163

1. Click on a **cell**. The cell will be highlighted.

2. Click the **mouse pointer** on the input line. The insertion point will appear where you click.

3. Type +D4+D5 on the input line.

4. Click on the **Accept button**. The value will be entered.

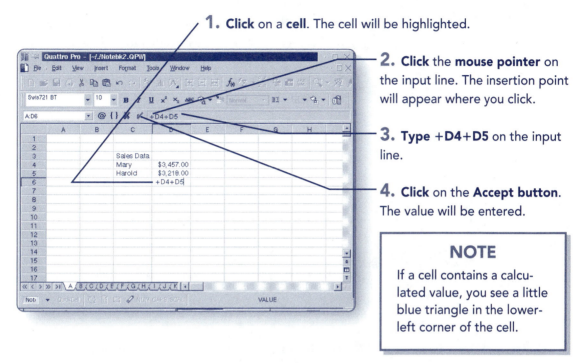

NOTE
If a cell contains a calculated value, you see a little blue triangle in the lower-left corner of the cell.

Inserting Relative Addresses Automatically

Quattro Pro can automatically create relative addresses.

1. Click on a **cell**. The cell will be highlighted.

2. Click the **mouse pointer** on the input line. The insertion point will appear where you click.

3. Type + on the input line.

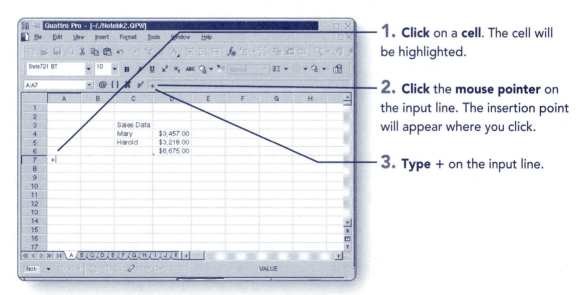

164 CHAPTER 12: WORKING WITH FUNCTIONS AND FORMULAS

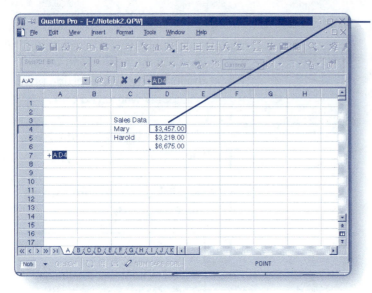

4. Click on **cell D4**. The cell will be highlighted and the cell reference will be inserted on the input line.

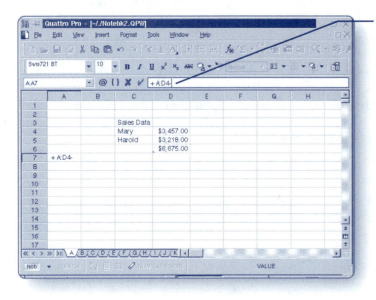

5. Type **−**. The operator will appear in the formula cell and on the input line.

USING ADDRESSES IN A FORMULA 165

6. Click on **cell D5**. The cell will be highlighted and the cell reference will be inserted on the input line.

7. Click on the **Accept button**. The value will be entered.

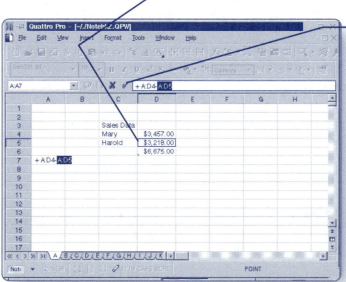

Using Absolute Addresses

Absolute addresses always reference the same cell, even if the cell and its values are moved. They should be used when your spreadsheet's layout is to remain static.

1. Click on a **cell**. The cell will be highlighted.

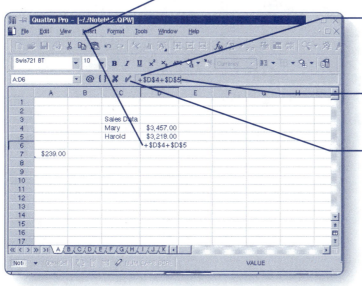

2. Click the **mouse pointer** on the input line. The insertion point will appear where you click.

3. Type **+$D$4+$D$5** on the input line.

4. Click on the **Accept button**. The value will be entered.

TIP

To change selected cell addresses on the input line from relative to absolute, press Shift+F4 with the insertion point on the actual cell address.

Using Functions

A *function* is just another kind of operator applied to values. Functions in Quattro Pro do not need operator symbols, although they often do the same work. For instance, +2*2*2 could be written as a @MULT(2,2,2) function. Don't worry about remembering all of Quattro Pro's 525 functions. A couple of tools do most of the work for you. The Function Composer is a great tool; it handles all of the function syntax for you.

1. Click on a **cell**. The cell will be highlighted.

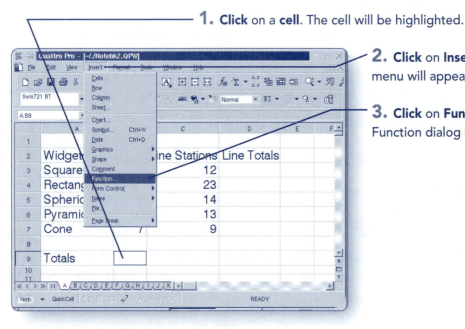

2. Click on **Insert**. The Insert menu will appear.

3. Click on **Function**. The Function dialog box will open.

USING FUNCTIONS   167

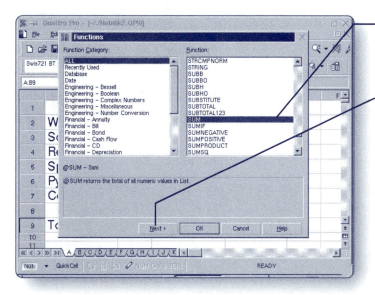

4. Click on **SUM** in the Function text box. The function will be selected.

5. Click on **Next**. The Function dialog box will change to the Formula Composer dialog box.

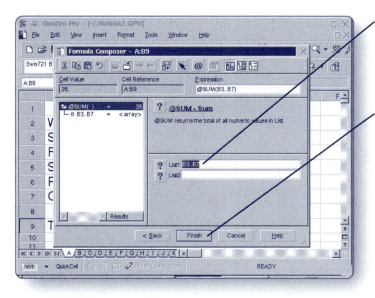

6. Type B3..B7 in the box next to List1. The cell range will be inserted into the SUM function in the box below Expression.

7. Click on **Finish**. The Function Composer dialog box will close and the new function will appear in the proper cell in the spreadsheet.

13

Formatting Notebooks

In our image-conscious world, what the data in a spreadsheet conveys depends on how that data *looks*. In this chapter, you'll learn how to:

- Format numerical data
- Change row heights and column widths
- Apply font changes to values
- Add borders to cells
- Customize your Quattro Pro workplace

Formatting Numbers

You can express numeric data in many different forms: dates, times, and currency, just to name a few. You can change the format of your data in just a few steps in Quattro Pro.

Changing the Decimal Point Places

When dealing with decimals in numeric data, you must be sure that you use the proper number of decimal places. After all, in the United States, a soda pop can cost $.55, not $.54678.

1. Click on a **cell** with a numeric value. The cell will be highlighted.

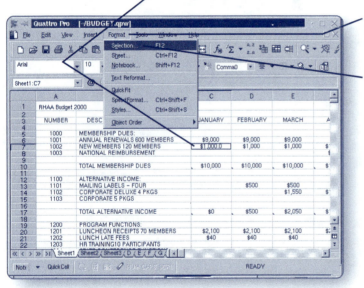

2. Click on **Format**. The Format menu will appear.

3. Click on **Selection**. The Active Cells dialog box will appear.

TIP
Press F12 to open the Active Cells dialog box.

FORMATTING NUMBERS 171

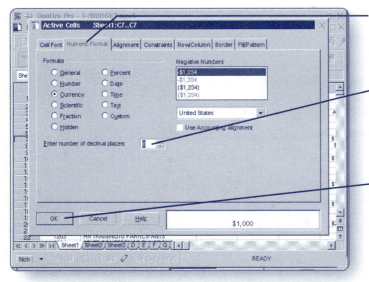

4. Click on the **Numeric Format tab**. The tab will come to the front.

5. Type a **number** in the **box** next to Enter number of decimal places. The value will be displayed.

6. Click on **OK**. The Active Cells dialog box will close and the cell will be reformatted as desired.

Applying New Data Formats

Many of your spreadsheets might use specialized data presentations. Here's how you get Quattro Pro to treat your numbers correctly.

1. Click on a **cell** with a numeric value. The cell will be highlighted.

2. Click on **Format**. The Format menu will appear.

3. Click on **Selection**. The Active Cells dialog box will open.

172 CHAPTER 13: FORMATTING NOTEBOOKS

4. Click on the **Numeric Format tab**. The tab will come to the front.

5. Click on **Number**. The option is selected.

6. Click on the **red −1234** option. A preview of the selected number will appear in the Preview.

7. Click on **OK**. The Active Cells dialog box will close and the numeric data will be formatted to the new style.

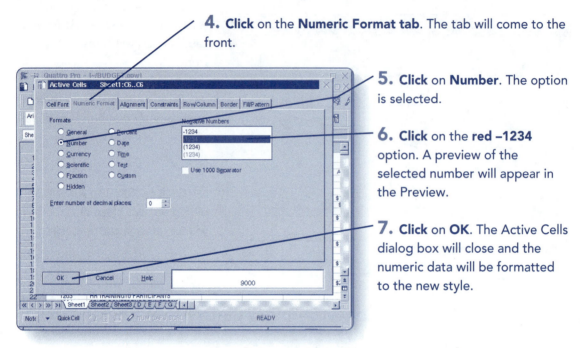

Applying New Formats with QuickFormat

QuickFormat enables you to copy the format of one cell onto another with just a click of the mouse.

1. Click on a **cell** with a format you want to copy. The cell will be highlighted.

2. Click the **QuickFormat** button. The pointer will change to the QuickFormat cursor.

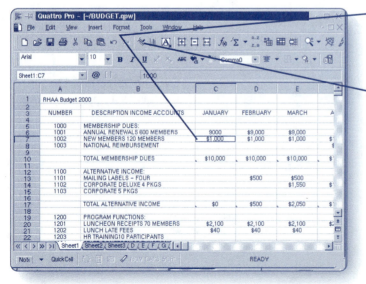

ADJUSTING COLUMN WIDTHS 173

3. Click on a **cell** to apply the new format. The cell format will be changed to reflect that of the original selected cell.

4. Click the **QuickFormat** button when finished. The cursor will change to the text cursor.

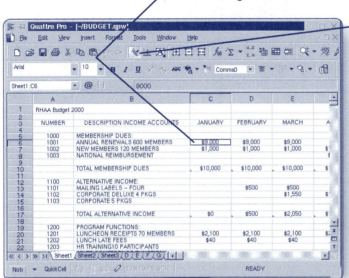

Adjusting Column Widths

If you have a lot of data to fit within a cell, you might have to change the size of the cell. You do this by adjusting the column width and row height.

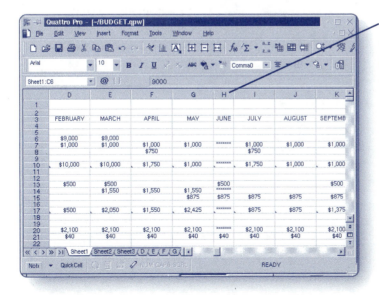

1. Click the **mouse pointer** on the line next to the column heading. The pointer will change to the resizing cursor.

174 CHAPTER 13: FORMATTING NOTEBOOKS

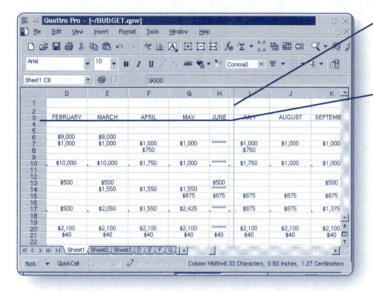

2. Drag the **column line**. The column width will increase or decrease.

3. Click the **mouse pointer** on the line next to the row heading. The pointer will change to the resizing cursor.

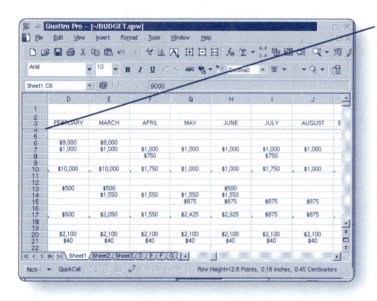

4. Drag the **row line**. The column height will increase or decrease.

TIP

To automatically size a column or row, double-click on the column or row line.

Setting Cell Alignment

Like paragraphs in WordPerfect, you can align values within their cells.

Adjusting Cell Alignment

Cell alignment in Quattro Pro takes one of four forms: left, right, centered, or general.

1. Click on a **cell**. The cell will be highlighted.

2. Click on the **Alignment button**. The Alignment menu will appear.

3. Click on **Left**. The cell's contents will be aligned to the left side of the cell.

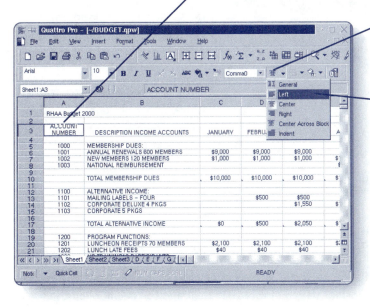

Aligning across Multiple Cells

To create a heading within a Quattro Pro document, you need to align the text across multiple cells.

1. Click on a **cell** with the heading. The cell will be highlighted.

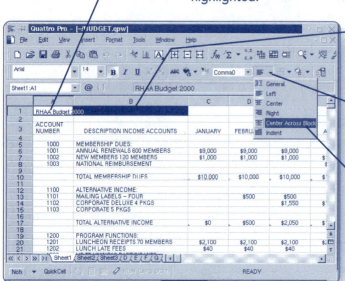

2. Select the **range** of cells you want the heading to appear in. The range is highlighted.

3. Click on the **Alignment button**. The Alignment menu will appear.

4. Click on **Center Across Block**. The cell's contents will be aligned in the center of the selected cell range.

Formatting with Fonts

When changing the fonts of cell values in Quattro Pro, it is important to remember that selecting the cell applies changes to all of the cell's values. Selecting a portion of the value in the cell's input line applies font changes to only those selected values.

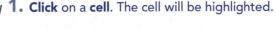

Changing a Font

Changing the font of a cell is a piece of cake.

1. Click on a **cell**. The cell will be highlighted.

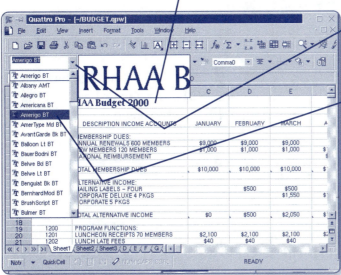

2. Click on the **down arrow (↓)** next to the Font box. The Font drop-down list will appear.

3. Click on **Amerigo BT**. The drop-down list will close and the new font will be applied to the cell.

Changing a Font Size

When you need to make data look bigger or smaller, you can change the size of its displayed font.

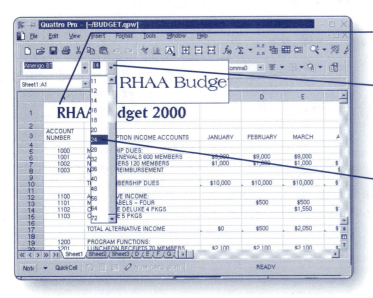

1. Click on a **cell**. The cell will be highlighted.

2. Click on the **down arrow (↓)** next to the Font Size box. The Font Size drop-down list will appear.

3. Click on **24**. The drop-down list will close and the new font size will be applied to the cell.

Applying a Font Attribute

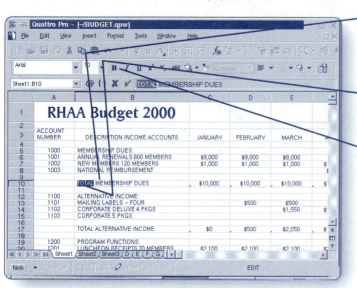

1. **Double-click** on a **cell**. The cell will be placed into edit mode.

2. **Select** a **portion** of the value. The text will be highlighted.

3. **Click** on the **Bold button**. The selected text will take the bold attribute.

Adding Borders

By default, the cell borders within a Quattro Pro spreadsheet are invisible when printed and difficult to see onscreen. You can make the borders visible for a sharper presentation.

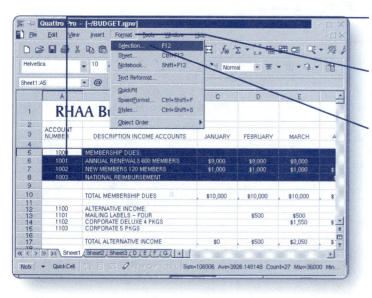

1. **Select** a **cell range**. The cell range will be highlighted.

2. **Click** on **Format**. The Format menu will appear.

3. **Click** on **Selection**. The Active Cells dialog box will open.

ADDING BORDERS 179

4. Click on the **Border tab**. The Border tab will come to the front.

5. Click on **Outline**. Solid lines will appear in the preview.

6. Click on the **down arrow (↓)** next to the Border Type button. The Border Type palette will be displayed.

7. Click on a **border type**. The palette will close and the change will be applied to the preview.

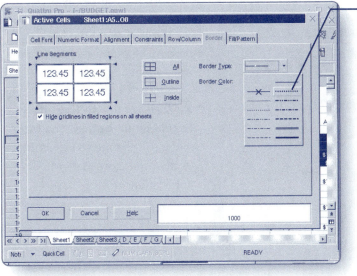

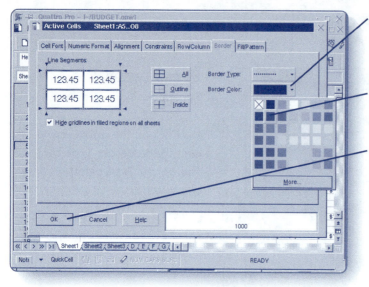

8. Click on the **down arrow (↓)** next to the Border Color button. The Color palette will appear.

9. Click on a **color** in the Color palette. The palette will close.

10. Click on **OK**. The Active Cells dialog box will close and the changes will be applied to the selected range of cells.

Customizing Your Workspace

In a tip of the hat to all the users out there who are used to using other spreadsheet applications, Quattro Pro lets you change your workspace to match that of other applications.

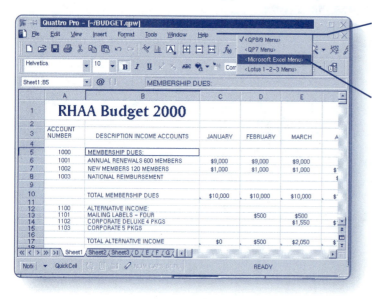

1. Right click on the **Main menu**. The menu selection menu will appear.

2. Click on the **<Microsoft Excel Menu> option**. The Main menu will change to reflect that of the *other* spreadsheet application.

14

Completing Your Spreadsheet

Although we are moving closer to pure electronic media, it is still readily apparent that people have a great love for paper. It is important to know how to prepare and print your Quattro Pro notebooks into hardcopy. In this chapter, you'll learn how to:

- Establish paper size and margins
- Preview a print job
- Print a spreadsheet

Preparing to Print

In WordPerfect, it is not too difficult to see how pages are set up. In a Quattro Pro spreadsheet, however, such settings as margins and page breaks are not always apparent.

Setting Up Margins

The margins of a spreadsheet page are typically hard to see. In fact, they only appear after you examine the document in Print Preview (discussed later in this chapter) or you initially change the page margins. This is a strange feature, to be sure, which emphasizes the need to always preview your document before printing.

1. Click on **File**. The File menu will appear.

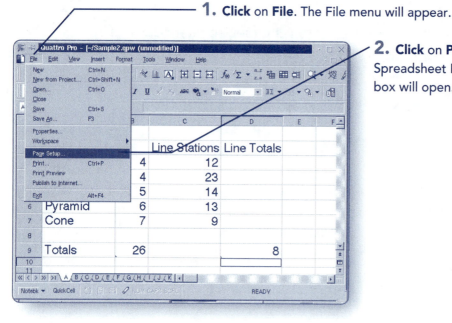

2. Click on **Page Setup**. The Spreadsheet Page Setup dialog box will open.

PREPARING TO PRINT 183

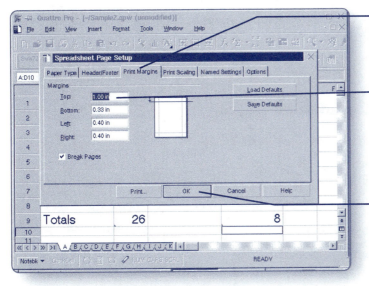

3. Click on the **Print Margins tab**. The Print Margins tab will come to the front.

4. Type new margin values in the boxes below Margins. Values will be displayed in the boxes next to Top, Bottom, Left, and Right.

5. Click on **OK**. The Spreadsheet Page Setup dialog box will close and the spreadsheet will reflect the changes.

Setting Page Orientation and Size

Spreadsheets usually do not appear in portrait orientation, but rather landscape. In this section, discover how to change the page orientation and paper size for your spreadsheet.

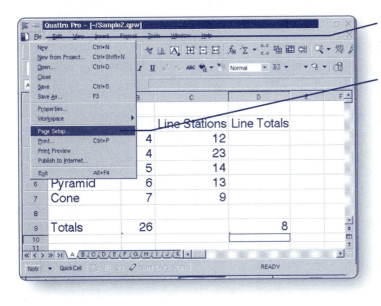

1. Click on **File**. The File menu will appear.

2. Click on **Page Setup**. The Spreadsheet Page Setup dialog box will open.

184 CHAPTER 14: COMPLETING YOUR SPREADSHEET

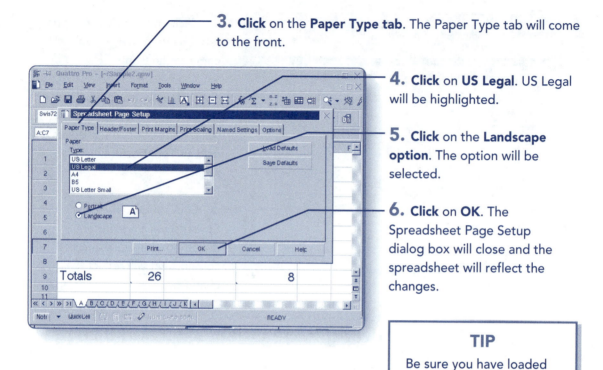

3. Click on the **Paper Type tab**. The Paper Type tab will come to the front.

4. Click on **US Legal**. US Legal will be highlighted.

5. Click on the **Landscape option**. The option will be selected.

6. Click on **OK**. The Spreadsheet Page Setup dialog box will close and the spreadsheet will reflect the changes.

TIP
Be sure you have loaded the right paper size in your printer before you change the paper size of the spreadsheet.

Getting It All on One Page

Many times your spreadsheet overflows off of the page onto another. When you print them out, you could get something akin to a jigsaw puzzle. You can fool around with the margins and paper size until it all fits onto one page, or you can use print scaling to make your life a lot easier.

PREPARING TO PRINT

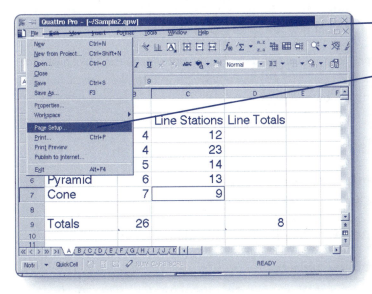

1. Click on **File**. The File menu will appear.

2. Click on **Page Setup**. The Spreadsheet Page Setup dialog box will open.

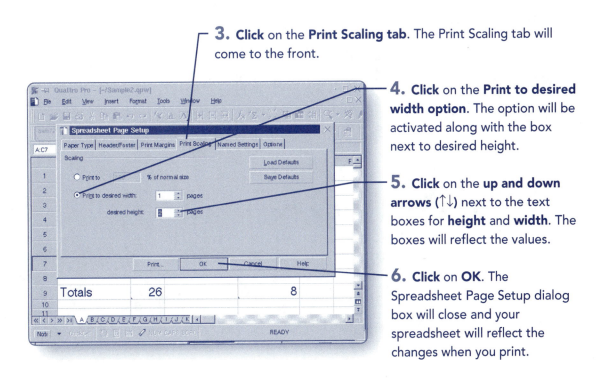

3. Click on the **Print Scaling tab**. The Print Scaling tab will come to the front.

4. Click on the **Print to desired width option**. The option will be activated along with the box next to desired height.

5. Click on the **up and down arrows** (↑↓) next to the text boxes for **height** and **width**. The boxes will reflect the values.

6. Click on **OK**. The Spreadsheet Page Setup dialog box will close and your spreadsheet will reflect the changes when you print.

Printing a Spreadsheet

Once you set up the page for the spreadsheet, you can print it. But first, you should preview the page to make sure all your data fits on one page.

Using Print Preview

Print Preview works with your printer to show you how your page will look on actual paper.

1. Click on **File**. The File menu will appear.

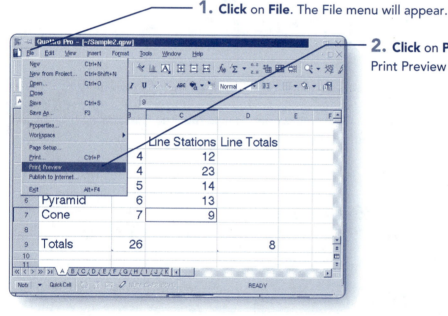

2. Click on **Print Preview**. The Print Preview window will open.

PRINTING A SPREADSHEET 187

3. Click on the **Zoom In** button to see more detail. The view of the spreadsheet will enlarge.

4. Click on the **Previous Page** or **Next Page** buttons to navigate through the entire document. The preview of each page to be printed will appear with each click.

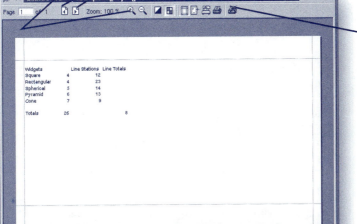

5. Click on the **Close button** (❌) to leave Print Preview. The Normal view will appear.

Printing Your Work

When creating a Quattro Pro spreadsheet, you should print your work toward the end of the creation process, after previewing the pages. You can print just the current sheet, the entire notebook, or a selected range of cells.

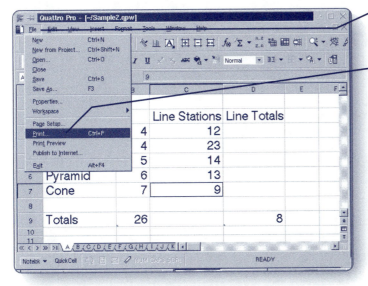

1. Click on **File**. The File menu will appear.

2. Click on **Print**. The Spreadsheet Print dialog box will open.

TIP

You also can open the Spreadsheet Print dialog box by pressing Ctrl+P.

CHAPTER 14: COMPLETING YOUR SPREADSHEET

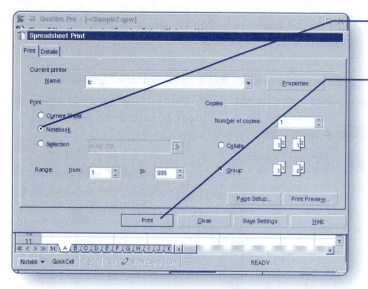

3. Click on the option you want. The option will be selected.

4. Click on **Print**. The spreadsheet will print and the Spreadsheet Print dialog box will close.

TIP

Click on the Print button in the Notebook toolbar to immediately print the spreadsheet on the default printer with the default settings for such items as the pages to print and the number of copies.

15

Manipulating Data

After you enter your data into a spreadsheet, you can do several more things with it than simply add and subtract numbers. Quattro Pro enables you to set up data-entry restrictions so no "wrong" data gets into your calculations and enables you to filter data so you can see only the figures you need to make a decision. Quattro Pro even accelerates data entry itself. In this chapter, you'll learn how to:

- Use QuickType to enter data more efficiently
- Filter your data to see only what you need
- Make data input rules
- Group and sort your data

Entering Data Faster

Data manipulation begins with a question you ask before you even start a Quattro Pro document: What data do you want to enter? After you answer this question, you start putting data into your spreadsheet. If you are fortunate enough to have software that directly imports data into Quattro Pro, then your work is minimal. The rest of us take the old finger-dance approach. Luckily, Quattro Pro has some neat features that accelerate the data-entry process.

Using QuickType

If you are like most people, endless typing of data can be a tedious process. QuickType remembers data you have entered previously so you can input data that much faster.

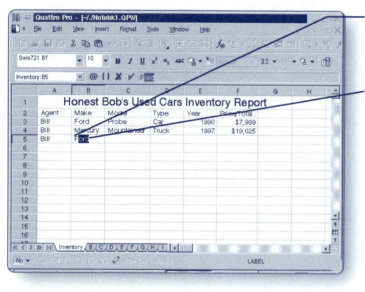

1. Click on a **cell** in the first empty row. The cell will be highlighted.

2. Type Ford. Values from the Make column will appear in the row. In fact, you need only type *F* before the entire Ford value will fill in the cell.

ENTERING DATA FASTER 191

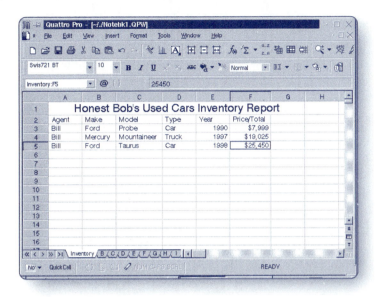

3. Press the **tab key** to skip to the next cell. The pointer will move to the next cell, where you can fill in additional values.

> **NOTE**
> The QuickType method only works for text values. You must completely enter any other value type.

Using QuickFill

QuickFill will let you enter sequential data in the blink of an eye.

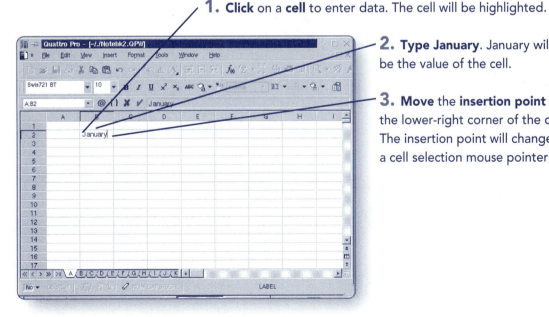

1. Click on a **cell** to enter data. The cell will be highlighted.

2. Type January. January will be the value of the cell.

3. Move the **insertion point** to the lower-right corner of the cell. The insertion point will change to a cell selection mouse pointer.

192 CHAPTER 15: MANIPULATING DATA

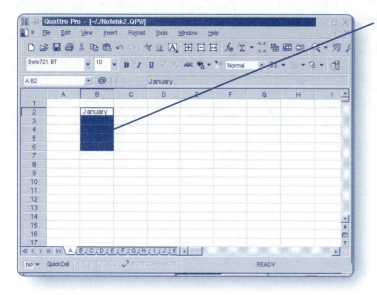

4. Click and **drag** the **selection mouse pointer** down the column. The empty cells will be selected.

5. Release the **mouse button**. The months of the year will be filled into the selected cells.

Filtering Data

Filtering enables you to visually strip out unnecessary data. This is a visual action only; the data does not go anywhere. Rather, Quattro Pro hides it away until you want to view the data in its entirety again.

Using the QuickFilter to Filter Data

The QuickFilter can use as many different criteria as there are columns in the sheet. Any data can become a filter.

1. Select the **cell range** to filter. The cell range will be highlighted.

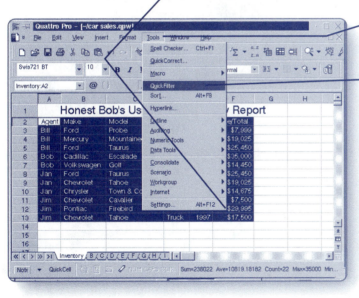

2. Click on **Tools**. The Tools menu will appear.

3. Click on **QuickFilter**. The QuickFilter down arrows will appear in the first row of the range.

4. Click on the **down arrow** (↓) next to the Agent cell. A filter selection drop-down list will appear, listing all available agents as well as five other filter types:

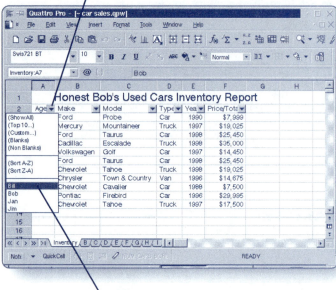

- **Show All**. Cancels any previously applied filter by allowing all values to be displayed.

- **Top 10**. In a larger spreadsheet, displays only rows with the top 10 values in this column.

- **Custom.** Enables the creation of customized filter criteria.

- **Blanks**. Will display only rows where data in the column is blank.

- **Non Blanks**. Will display only rows where data in the column is not blank.

5. Click on **Bill**. Only the rows with Bill will be displayed.

FILTERING DATA

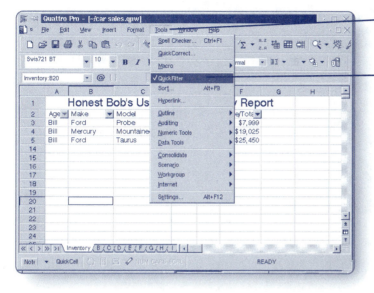

6. **Click** on **Tools**. The Tools menu will appear.

7. **Click** on **QuickFilter**. The QuickFilter controls will close.

Using the Custom Filter

You use the custom filter for more defined work. The custom filter enables you to select three criteria with which to filter data.

1. **Select** the **cell range** to filter. The cell range will be highlighted.

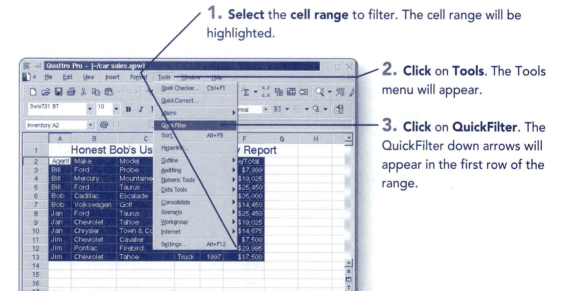

2. **Click** on **Tools**. The Tools menu will appear.

3. **Click** on **QuickFilter**. The QuickFilter down arrows will appear in the first row of the range.

196 CHAPTER 15: MANIPULATING DATA

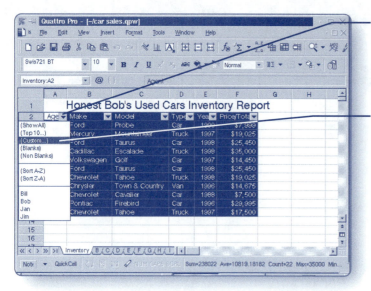

4. Click on the **down arrow (↓)** next to the Agent cell. A filter selection drop-down list will appear.

5. Click on **Custom**. The Custom QuickFilter dialog box will open.

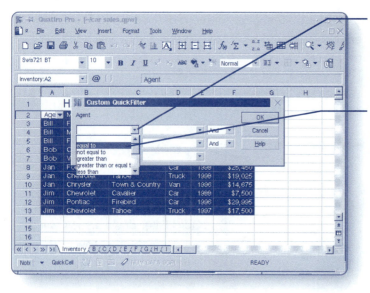

6. Click on the **down arrow (↓)** next to the first Condition box. The Condition drop-down list will appear.

7. Click on **equal to**. It will be selected and will appear in the Condition box.

FILTERING DATA 197

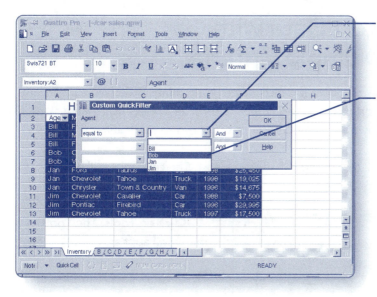

8. Click on the **down arrow** (↓) next to the first Value box. The Value drop-down list will appear.

9. Click on **Bob**. It will be selected and will appear in the Value box.

10. Click on the **down arrow** (↓) next to the Operator box. The Operator drop-down list will appear.

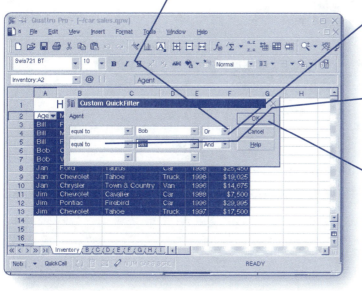

11. Click on **Or**. It will be selected and will appear in the Operator box.

12. Enter more **data** in the remainder of the fields as needed.

13. Click on **OK**. The Custom QuickFilter dialog box will close and the results of the filter will appear in the spreadsheet.

Sort Data with Multiple Criteria

Sorting data is a nice way to keep things orderly in a disorderly world. Data rarely comes to us in an alphabetical manner or any other orderly form. It's up to us to make sense of it.

1. **Select** the **cell range** to sort. The cell range will be highlighted.

2. **Click** on **Tools**. The Tools menu will appear.

3. **Click** on **Sort**. The Data Sort dialog box will open.

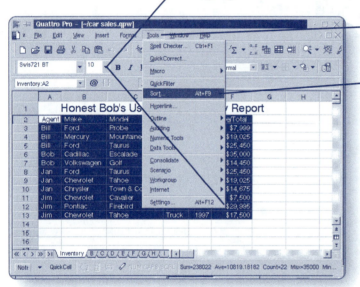

TIP
If you press Alt+F9, the Data Sort dialog box will open.

SORT DATA WITH MULTIPLE CRITERIA 199

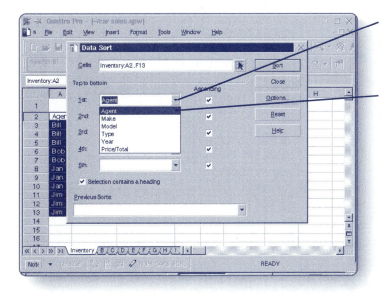

4. **Click** on the **down arrow** (↓) next to the 1st box. The Sort by drop-down list will appear.

5. **Click** on **Agent**. It will be selected and will appear in the 1st box.

6. **Click** on the **down arrow** (↓) next to the 2nd box. The Sort by drop-down list will appear.

7. **Click** on **Type**. It will be selected and will appear in the 2nd box.

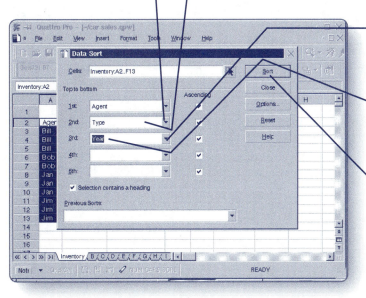

8. **Click** on the **down arrow** (↓) next to the 3rd box. The Sort by drop-down list will appear.

9. **Click** on **Year**. It will be selected and will appear in the 3rd box.

10. **Click** on **Sort**. The Data Sort dialog box will close and the data will be sorted according to your criteria.

Grouping Your Data

In WordPerfect, you can outline your work. In that component, you typically outline prior to creating the main document. In Quattro Pro, you find outlining useful after you've created the bulk of a document.

Quattro Pro refers to the outlining function as grouping. Use grouping when you want to drop large amounts of data from view while also being able to quickly expand it when more detail is desired.

1. Select the **rows** to group. The rows will be highlighted.

2. Click on **Tools**. The Tools menu will appear.

3. Move the **mouse pointer** to **Outline**. The Outline menu will appear.

4. Click on **Group**. The selected rows will be grouped.

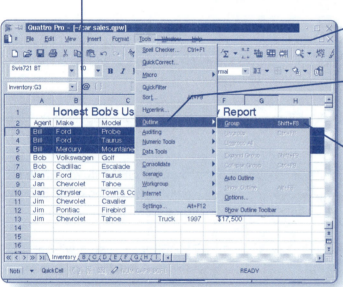

TIP

If you press Shift+F8, the rows are automatically grouped.

GROUPING YOUR DATA

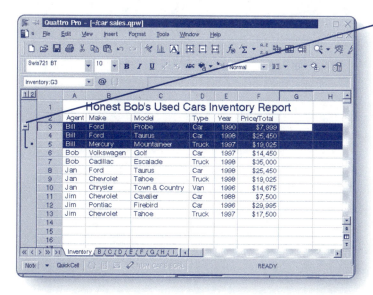

5. Click on the **group control**. That section of the outline will collapse.

6. Select the **grouped rows**. The rows will be highlighted.

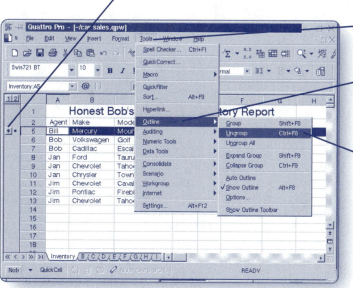

7. Click on **Tools**. The Tools menu will appear.

8. Move the **mouse pointer** to **Outline**. The Outline menu will appear.

9. Click on **Ungroup**. The selected rows will be ungrouped.

TIP
If you press Ctrl+F8, the rows are automatically ungrouped.

16
Charting Data

Let's face it: Charts are simply cool. There is nothing like that "Aha!" feeling you get when you look at incomprehensible raw data, and then see it again neatly organized in a chart.

Quattro Pro works well to create these cool charts. The data within Quattro Pro is more than ready to be charted and graphed. All it takes is a little planning and effort to yield a lot of result. In this chapter, you'll learn how to:

- Create pie, bar, line, and 3D charts
- Resize a chart
- Edit a chart
- Change a chart's style

Creating a Chart

In Quattro Pro, you can create several types of charts: pie, bar, line, and three-dimensional (3D) among them. There are dozens of variants to these four categories. They are all easy to create thanks to Quattro Pro's Chart Expert and QuickChart tools.

Making a Chart with Chart Expert

Pie charts provide an excellent vehicle for showing percentage values in a clear fashion. When we can see a given piece of the pie in relation to the other pieces, we get a pictorial representation in our minds that holds more meaning than mere numbers.

1. Select the **cell range** to chart. The cell range will be highlighted.

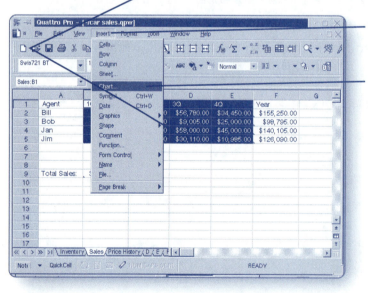

2. Click on **Insert**. The Insert menu will appear.

3. Click on **Chart**. The first Chart Expert dialog box will open.

CREATING A CHART 205

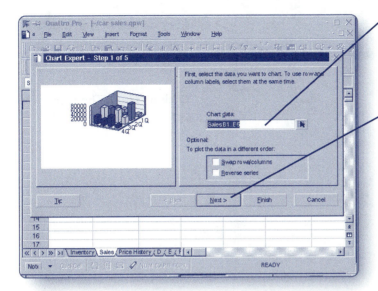

4. Confirm the **selected range** in the Chart data box. The references to the range should match what you selected.

5. Click on **Next**. The second Chart Expert dialog box will open.

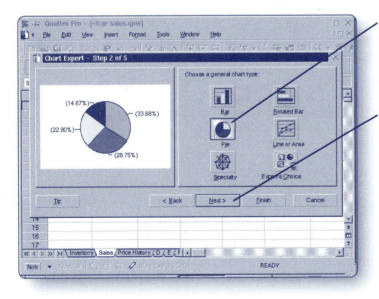

6. Click on the **Pie button**. The button will be selected and the Preview window will display the chart type.

7. Click on **Next**. The third Chart Expert dialog box will open.

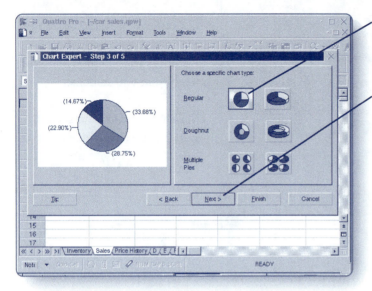

8. Click on **one** of the Regular buttons. The button will be selected.

9. Click on **Next**. The fourth Chart Expert dialog box will open.

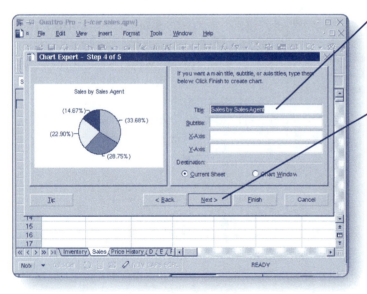

10. Type a new **title** for the chart in the Title box. The title will appear in the Preview window.

11. Click on **Next**. The fifth Chart Expert dialog box will open.

CREATING A CHART

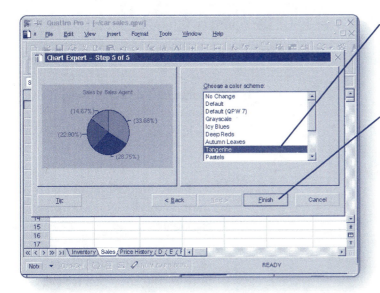

12. **Click** on the **color scheme** you want. The color scheme will be highlighted and displayed in the Preview window.

13. **Click** on **Finish**. The Chart Expert dialog box will close and the chart pointer will be visible in the spreadsheet.

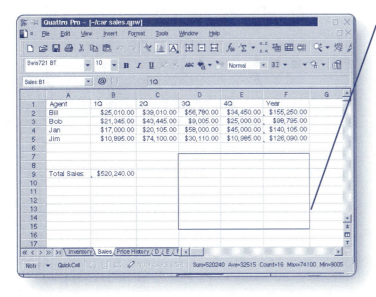

14. **Click** and **drag** the **chart pointer** over an area of your spreadsheet. The chart outline will appear over the selected area.

15. **Release** the **mouse button**. The chart will appear in the selected area with a new Property Bar for chart editing.

CHAPTER 16: CHARTING DATA

Making a Chart with QuickChart

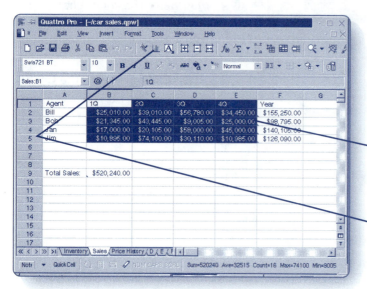

Making a chart with Chart Expert is an easy but rather lengthy process. If you simply want to see your data graphically, perhaps QuickChart is the way to go.

1. Select the **cell range** to chart. The cell range will be highlighted.

2. Click on the **QuickChart button**. The chart pointer will be visible in the spreadsheet.

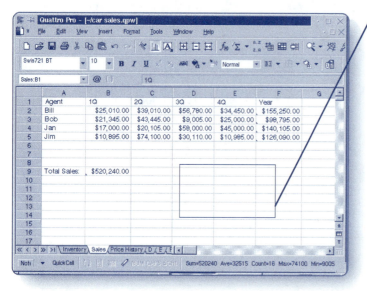

3. Click and drag the **chart pointer** over an area of your spreadsheet. The chart outline will appear over the selected area.

4. Release the **mouse button**. The chart will appear in the selected area with a new Property Bar for chart editing.

Modifying a Chart

After you have a chart in your document, you might need to make some changes to make it flow in your document better.

Resizing a Chart

When Quattro Pro first creates a chart within a document, the chart might not be the correct size. There is usually a discrepancy between the size of the chart and the size of the chart object, which is the big box surrounding the chart. Here's how to resize the chart and the chart object.

1. **Click** on the **chart object edge**. The chart object handles will appear.

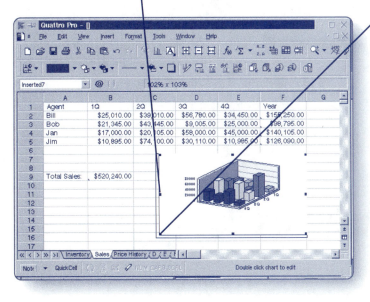

2. **Click and drag** any **edge** or **corner handle** on the border of the chart object. The border will move with the mouse pointer.

3. **Release** the **mouse button**. The chart object will be resized to the desired size.

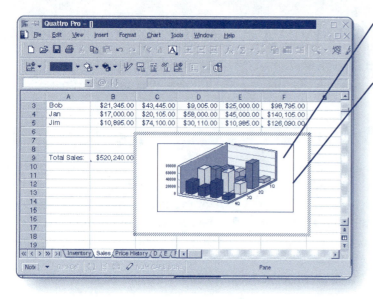

4. Click near the **chart**. The chart handles will appear.

5. Click and drag any **edge** or **corner handle** on the border of the chart. The border will move with the mouse pointer.

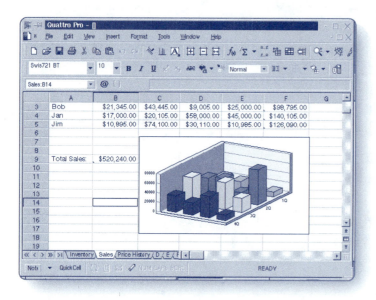

6. Release the **mouse button**. The chart will be resized to the desired size.

MODIFYING A CHART

Moving a Chart

Quattro Pro puts the chart where you want it, but what if you need to move it? Moving a chart is sometimes necessary to clean up your layout.

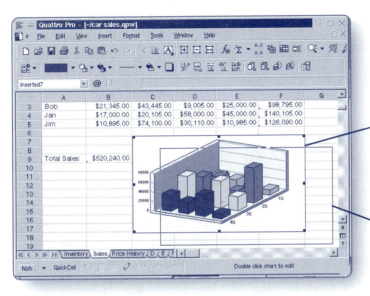

1. Click and hold the **mouse pointer** on the chart object edge. The move object pointer will appear.

2. Drag the **chart object** to the desired location. The chart object will move to match the action of your mouse pointer.

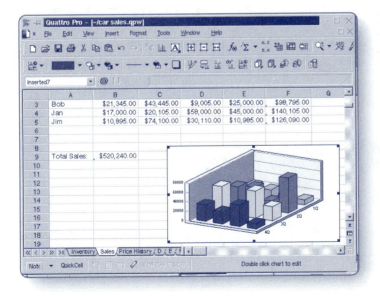

3. Release the **mouse button**. The chart object will be moved into the new location.

Changing a Chart Style

Sometimes, you might change your mind about the kind of chart to use. You don't need to start all over again, however. You can simply change the chart type on the fly.

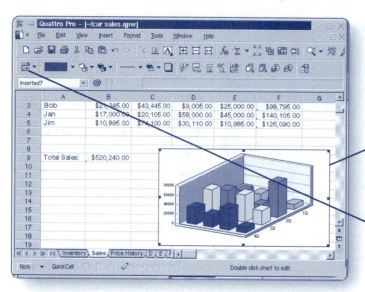

1. Click on the **chart object** to select it. The chart object handles will appear.

2. Click on the **Change the chart type button** on the Property Bar. The Chart Type palette will open.

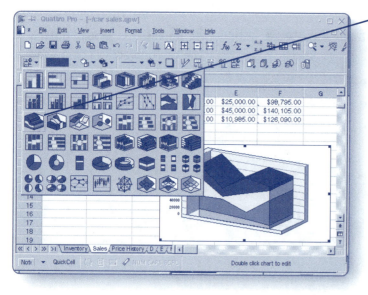

3. Click on a **desired chart type**. The chart type will be selected and the palette will close. The original chart will be changed to the new type.

Modifying Chart Data

Not only can you change the chart type on the fly, but you can also edit the chart's data without a lot of fuss.

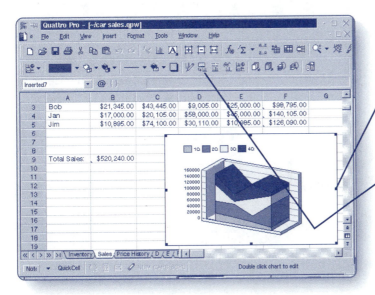

1. Click on the **chart object** to select it. The chart object handles will appear.

2. Click on the **Chart Data button**. The Chart Series dialog box will open.

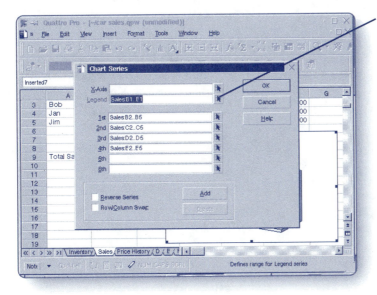

3. Click on the **Chart range button** next to the Legend box. The Chart Series dialog box will minimize.

214 CHAPTER 16: CHARTING DATA

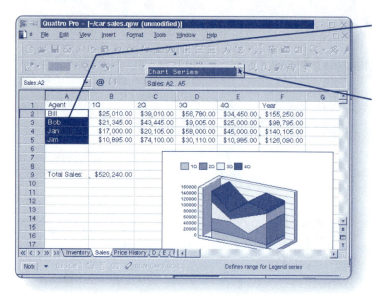

4. Select a new **range** for the chart legend. The new range will be highlighted.

5. Click on the **Chart range button** next to the minimized Chart Series dialog box. The Chart Series dialog box will maximize.

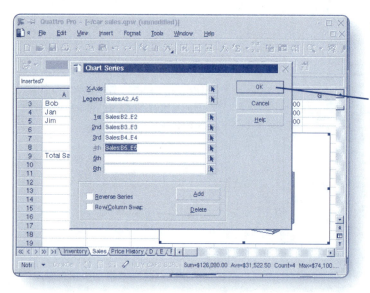

6. Repeat Steps 4 and 5 for the 1st, 2nd, 3rd, and 4th fields. Select the ranges across rows.

7. Click on **OK**. The Chart Series dialog box will close and the chart will change to reflect the new data ranges.

Deleting a Chart

If you must remove a chart, you can do so in just a few short steps.

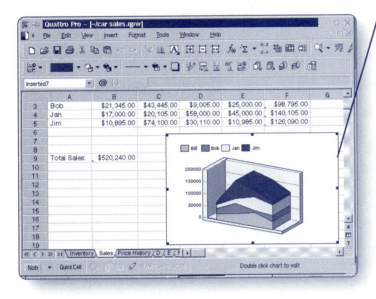

1. **Click** on the **chart object** to select it. The chart object handles will appear.

2. **Press** the **Delete key**. The chart will be removed.

Part III Review Questions

1. Where are formulas entered? See *"Exploring the Spreadsheet"* in Chapter 10.

2. How do you use multiple sheets in a notebook? See *"Using Multiple Sheets"* in Chapter 10.

3. How do you add rows and columns? See *"Inserting Rows and Columns"* in Chapter 11.

4. How do you shift data across a sheet? See *"Moving Data"* in Chapter 11.

5. What is an absolute address? See *"Using Absolute Addresses"* in Chapter 12.

6. How do you create a relative address? See *"Using Relative Addresses"* in Chapter 12.

7. How do you create large text labels? See *"Aligning across Multiple Cells"* in Chapter 13.

8. How can you preview your spreadsheet? See *"Using Print Preview"* in Chapter 14.

9. How many criteria can you use in the custom filter? See *"Using the Custom Filter"* in Chapter 15.

10. How do you change a chart style? See *"Changing a Chart Style"* in Chapter 16.

PART IV
Working with Advanced Data

Chapter 17
Learning Paradox Basics............219

Chapter 18
Working with Paradox...............243

17

Learning Paradox Basics

The average computer user increasingly deals with more data. A spreadsheet alone might not fulfill a user's data needs. This is where Paradox comes in. Paradox is recognized as one of the world's best relational databases, and it's now available on the Linux platform, just for you. In this chapter, you'll learn how to:

- Master database concepts
- Navigate the Paradox environment
- Build basic database components
- Create a unique StarBase database

Database Concepts

Four different types of objects compose databases. All of these objects working together make up the database. Any of them taken separately do not have much use. These objects are tables, forms, queries, and reports. Before examining the workings of an actual database, it helps to review the functionality of each object.

You're probably familiar with tables. They are essentially simplified spreadsheets. A database table is simpler because the purpose of the rows and columns is set, whereas a spreadsheet has more flexibility in how you can use rows and columns. Also, spreadsheets allow cells to interact with each other, whereas database tables don't. If you need to make mathematical comparisons, put your data in a spreadsheet.

In a database table, each row is a database record. A database record is a collection of related data. In a database of books, for example, one record might be:

Ivanhoe, Sir Walter Scott, New American Library, September 1987

This record has five fields: Book Title, Author, Publisher, Published Month, and Published Year. All other records in this database table use the same fields. If a record needs to contain more information, then the database table needs additional fields. In database programmer lingo, including more information is sometimes referred to as adding columns.

A form is the interface structure between the user and the table. Although you can directly enter data into a table (and some prefer this), a form gives the user visual cues to help enter data more quickly, rather than tediously tab across row after row of the database table.

DATABASE CONCEPTS

At the very least, a good database needs tables and forms. If the database had only a table, it would be rather dull. If the database had only a form, it would only be a shell surrounding nothingness.

Queries are little programming scripts that pull specific information out of a database. Don't panic if you don't think you can program anything. You can master queries after you understand the way they are structured.

After a query gathers information, it displays it. This is done in a report, the final piece of the database puzzle. Reports are similar to spreadsheets in that they typically present data in tabular form. Reports, however, are not interactive. They simply place the data requested by a query into a read-only file, which can be printed or displayed onscreen. If you need to change the data, you must change it in the table (through the form).

Databases can have multiple versions of all of these objects. In a climatology database, you could have a table of known temperature highs and lows for a region and another table of rainfall amounts, each accessed by separate forms. The possibilities are limitless.

Examining the Paradox Environment

Before you can begin to use Paradox, you need to first learn the tools it has for you to use.

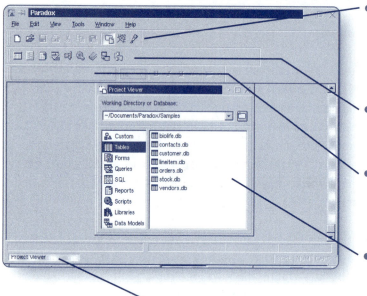

- **Standard Bar**. Contains the normal set of file and text commands found in all WordPerfect Office 2000 applications.

- **Property Bar**. Contains specific tools for handling Paradox elements.

- **Text Formatting Bar**. Contains design tools for formatting text within Paradox.

- **Project Viewer**. Manages the Paradox elements within a directory.

- **Status Bar**. Indicates status of tasks being performed.

Creating a Database

There is no magic wand to wave to build a database from scratch in Paradox, though there are projects that you can use as templates. But for a unique database, you need to build it one step at a time.

Creating a Table with Table Expert

The logical place to start in creating a database is to build the container to hold the data: the table. Fortunately, Paradox gives you a great tool to use called (appropriately enough) the Table Expert. Even if the tables provided do not completely match your desired goal, you can modify the template fields easily.

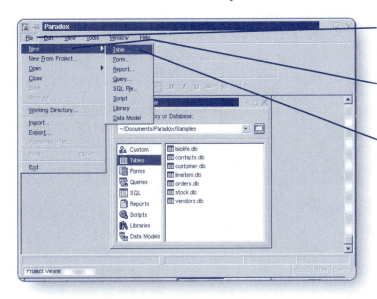

1. Click on **File**. The File menu will appear.

2. Move the **mouse pointer** to New. The New menu will appear.

3. Click on **Table**. The New Table dialog box will open.

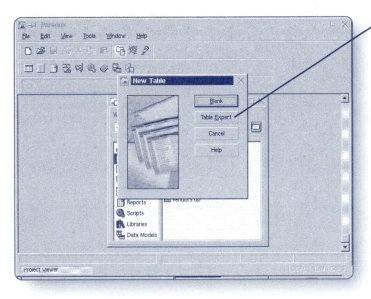

4. Click on **Table Expert**. The Table Expert dialog box will open.

224 CHAPTER 17: LEARNING PARADOX BASICS

5. Click on the **Personal option**. The Table templates list will change to personal-oriented templates.

6. Click on **Albums**. Albums will be highlighted and the Available Fields list will change to reflect the appropriate fields from the Albums table.

7. Click on the **Add All button**. All of the fields in the Available Fields list will be added to the Fields in my table list.

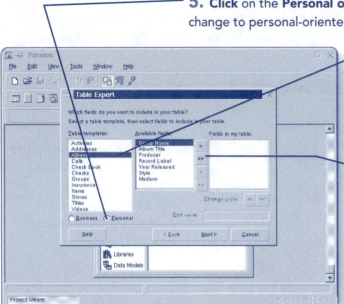

8. Click on **Group Name**. The option will be highlighted and will appear in the Edit name box.

9. Change Group Name to **Publisher**. The change will be reflected in the Edit name box.

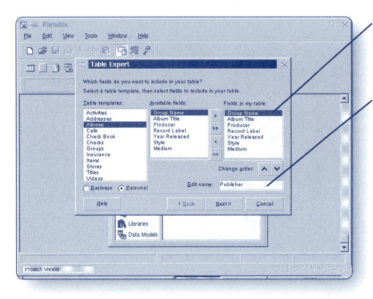

CREATING A DATABASE 225

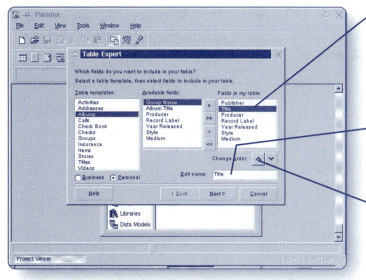

10. **Click** on **Album Title**. The option will be highlighted and will appear in the Edit name box. Publisher will now appear in the Fields in my table list.

11. **Change Album Title** to **Title**. The change will be reflected in the Edit name box.

12. **Click** on the **up arrow** (↑) next to Change order. The Title field will be moved up one line on the list.

13. **Repeat steps 10-12** as needed until the fields in the Fields in my table list are the same as those reflected in Table 17-1.

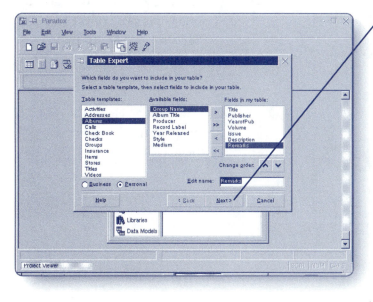

14. **Click** on **Next**. The next Table Expert dialog box will open.

Table 17.1. Fields for the New Table

Title
Publisher
YearofPub
Volume
Issue
Description
Remarks

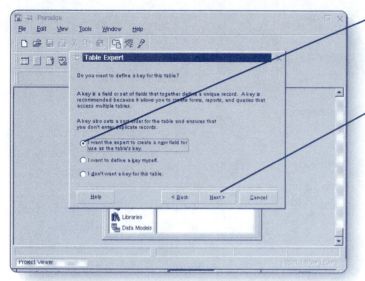

15. Confirm the **selection** of the first option. The I want the expert... option should be selected.

16. Click on **Next**. The next Table Expert dialog box will open.

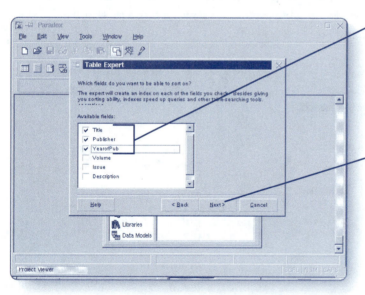

17. Click in the **check box** of the fields you want to be able to sort; in this case, **select Title**, **Publisher**, and **YearofPub**. A check (√) will be placed in each check box.

18. Click on **Next**. The next Table Expert dialog box will open.

CREATING A DATABASE 227

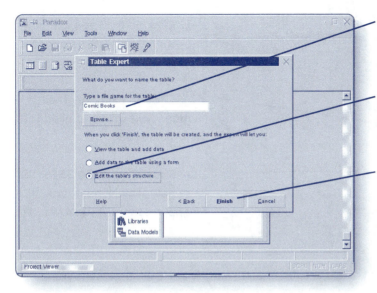

19. **Type** a **name** for the table. The name will appear in the Type a file name for the table box.

20. **Click** the **Edit the table's structure option**. The option will be selected.

21. **Click** on **Finish**. The Table Expert dialog box will close and the Restructure Paradox 7,8,9 Table dialog box will open.

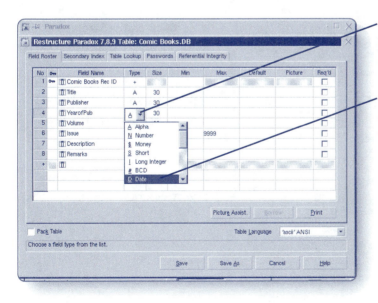

22. **Click** on the **Type cell** of the YearofPub row. The field type drop-down list will appear.

23. **Click** on **Date**. The Date type will be applied to the YearofPub row.

228 CHAPTER 17: LEARNING PARADOX BASICS

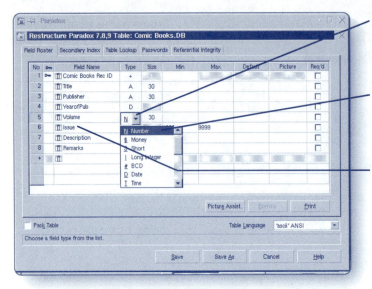

24. **Click** on the **Type cell** of the Volume row. The field type drop-down list will appear.

25. **Click** on **Number**. The Number type will be applied to the Volume row.

26. **Repeat steps 24-25** for the Issue field. The Number type will be applied to the Issue row.

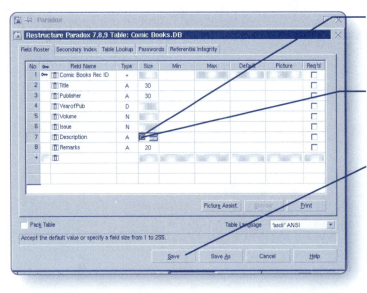

27. **Click** on the **Size cell** of the Remarks row. The size cell will be selected.

28. **Type 70**. The new field length will be applied to the Remarks row.

29. **Click** on **Save**. The table's new structure will be saved.

Creating a Form with Form Expert

You can, if you want, enter data directly into a database's table. But this would be tedious and time-consuming. Instead, use a form to make data entry more efficient. And use the Form Expert tool to make form creation that much easier.

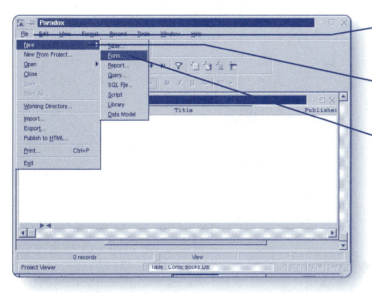

1. Click on **File**. The File menu will appear.

2. Move the **mouse pointer** to New. The New menu will appear.

3. Click on **Form**. The New Form dialog box will open.

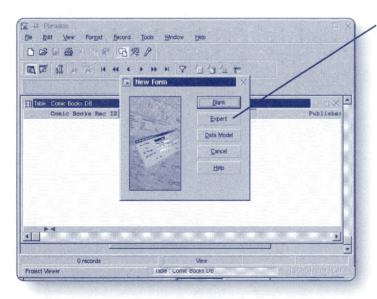

4. Click on **Expert**. The Form Expert dialog box will open.

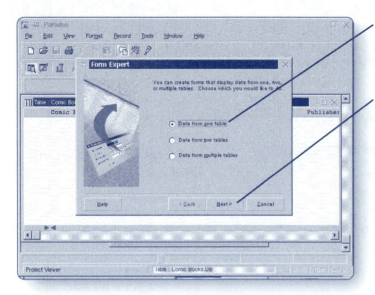

5. Click on the **Data from one table option**. The option will be selected.

6. Click on **Next**. The next Form Expert dialog box will open.

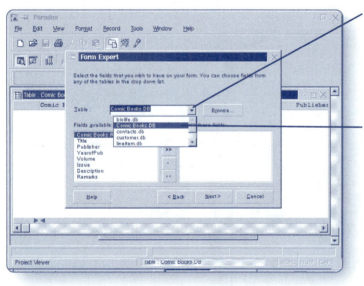

7. Click on the **down arrow (↓)** next to the Table box. A drop-down list of all of the tables in the current directory will be displayed.

8. Click on **Comic Books.DB**. The fields from the table will be listed in the Fields available box.

CREATING A DATABASE 231

9. Click the **Add All button**. All of the fields will be moved to the Display these fields box.

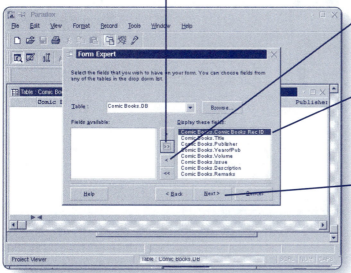

10. Click on **Comic Books.Comic Books Rec ID**. It will be selected.

11. Click on the **Remove button**. The ID field will be moved to the Available fields box.

12. Click on **Next**. The next Form Expert dialog box will open.

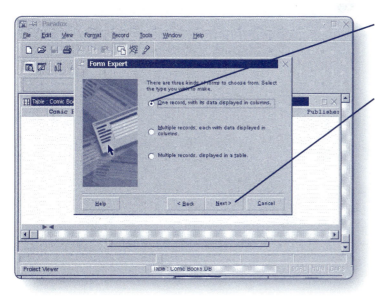

13. Click on the **One record option**. The option will be selected.

14. Click on **Next**. The next Form Expert dialog box will open.

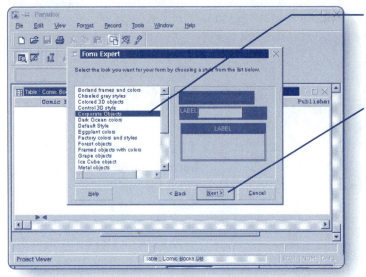

15. **Click** on **Corporate Objects**. The line will be selected and a preview of the style will appear in the Preview box.

16. **Click** on **Next**. The next Form Expert dialog box will open.

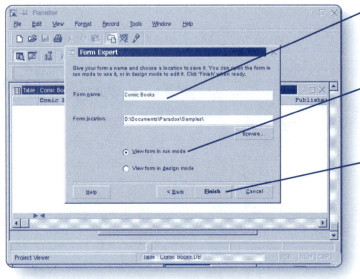

17. **Type** a **name** for the form. The name will appear in the Form name box.

18. **Click** the **View form in run mode option**. The option will be selected.

19. **Click** on **Finish**. The Form Expert dialog box will close and the form will be displayed.

Creating a Query with Query Expert

A query is a set of instructions that tells the database to pull out certain pieces of information and store them in a query table, which is like a subtable. You can even edit records from the query table and have those changes reflected in the main database table.

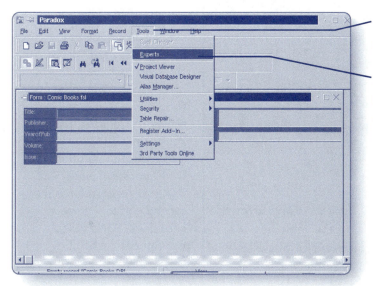

1. Click on **Tools**. The Tools menu will appear.

2. Click on **Experts**. The Paradox Experts dialog box will open.

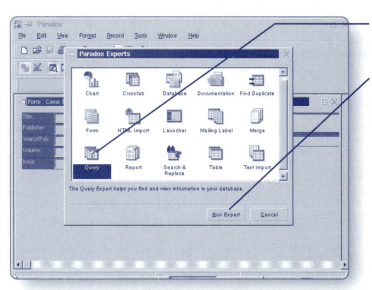

3. Click on **Query**. The Query will be selected.

4. Click on **Run Expert**. The Query Expert dialog box will open.

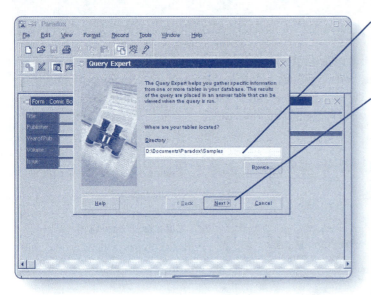

5. Type or **confirm** the **directory** where your tables reside. Use Browse if necessary.

6. Click on **Next**. The next Query Expert dialog box will open.

> **NOTE**
>
> Don't worry if you see notations such as "C:\" or "D:\" on your Linux machine. The Windows Emulator (WINE) that allows WordPerfect Office 2000 to run on Linux interprets disk partitions in the Windows manner. So, if your Linux partition is the second partition on your hard drive, WINE calls it D:\, rather than hda2.

7. Click the **down arrow** (↓) next to the Table box. A drop-down list of available tables in the directory will appear.

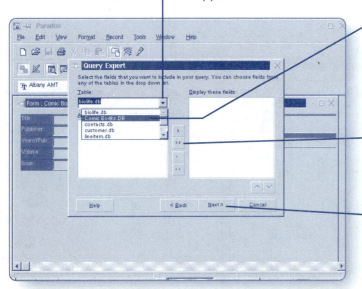

8. Click on **Comic Books.DB**. The Comic Books.DB table will be selected and the fields in that table will be displayed in the Available fields box.

9. Click the **Add All button**. All of the fields will be moved to the Display these fields box.

10. Click on **Next**. The next Query Expert dialog box will open.

CREATING A DATABASE 235

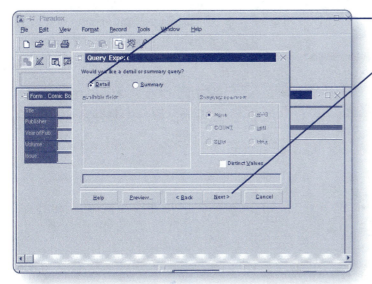

11. **Click** on the **Detail option**. The option will be selected.

12. **Click** on **Next**. The next Query Expert dialog box will open.

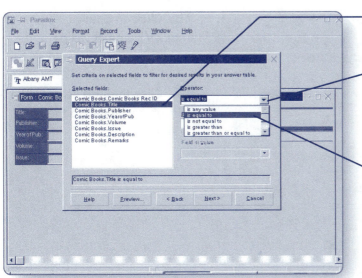

13. **Click** on **Comic Books.Title**. It will be selected.

14. **Click** the **down arrow** (↓) next to the Operator box. A drop-down list of available operators will appear.

15. **Click** on **is equal to**. It will be selected and the Field or value box will be activated.

236 CHAPTER 17: LEARNING PARADOX BASICS

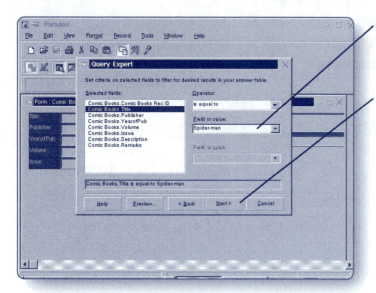

16. Type Spider-man in the Field or value box. The data will appear in the field.

17. Click on **Next**. The next Query Expert dialog box will open.

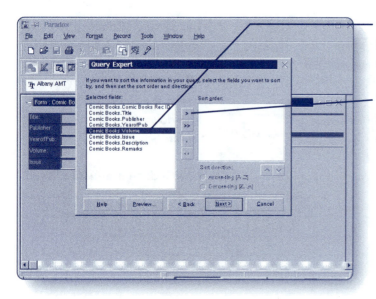

18. Click on **Comic Books.Volume**. It will be selected.

19. Click the **Add button**. The field will be moved to the Sort order box.

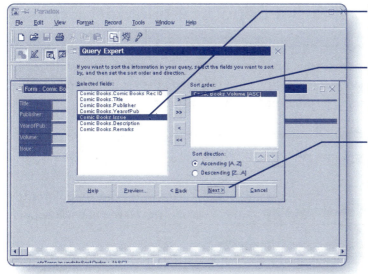

20. Click on **Comic Books.Issue**. It will be selected.

21. Click the **Add button**. The field will be moved to the Sort order box.

22. Click on **Next**. The next Query Expert dialog box will open.

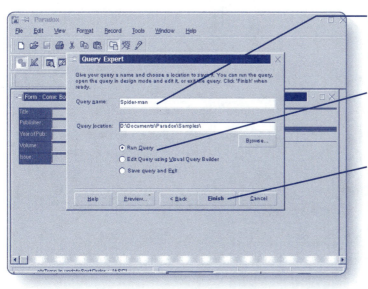

23. Type a **name** for the query. The name will appear in the Query name box.

24. Click on the **Run Query option**. The option will be selected.

25. Click on **Finish**. The Query Expert dialog box will close and the results of the query will be displayed.

Creating a Report with Report Expert

A report differs from a query only in its type of output. Reports are read-only. After information is in a report, you cannot change it there. You have to change data in the database table and rerun the report to make changes in the report.

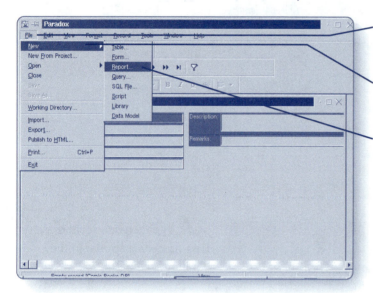

1. Click on **File**. The File menu will appear.

2. Move the **mouse pointer** to New. The New menu will appear.

3. Click on **Report**. The New Report dialog box will open.

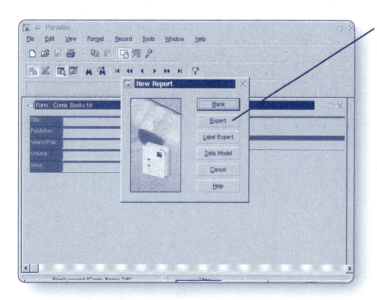

4. Click on **Expert**. The Report Expert dialog box will open.

CREATING A DATABASE

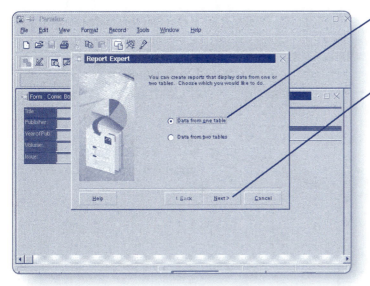

5. Click on the **Data from one table option**. The option will be selected.

6. Click on **Next**. The next Report Expert dialog box will open.

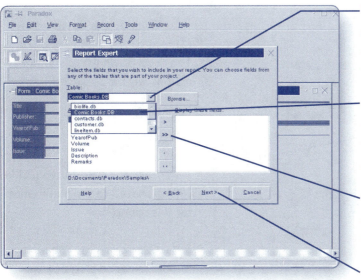

7. Click the **down arrow (↓)** next to the Table box. A drop-down list of available tables in the directory will appear.

8. Click on **Comic Books.DB**. It will be selected and the fields in that table will be displayed in the Available fields box.

9. Click the **Add All button**. All of the fields will be moved to the Display these fields box.

10. Click on **Next**. The next Report Expert dialog box will open.

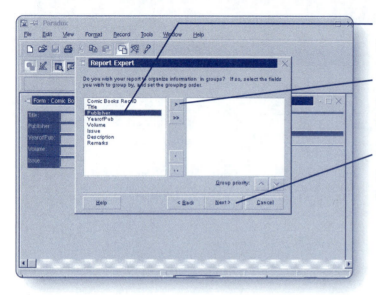

11. Click on **Publisher**. It will be selected.

12. Click the **Add button**. The field will be shifted to the Group box.

13. Click on **Next**. The next Report Expert dialog box will open.

14. Click on **Title**. It will be selected.

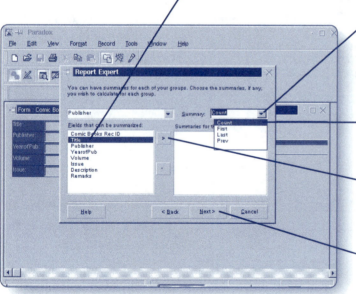

15. Click on the **down arrow** (↓) next to the Summary box. The drop-down list of summary actions will be displayed.

16. Click on **Count**. It will be selected.

17. Click the **Add button**. Title will be shifted to the Summaries for this group box.

18. Click on **Next**. The next Report Expert dialog box will open.

CREATING A DATABASE 241

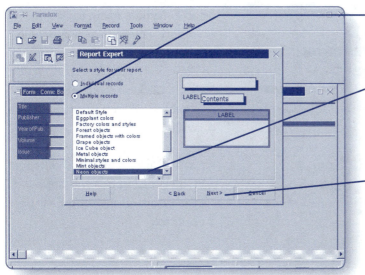

19. **Click** on the **Multiple records option**. The option will be selected.

20. Click on **Neon Objects**. It will be selected and the new style will appear in the Preview box.

21. Click on **Next**. The next Report Expert dialog box will open.

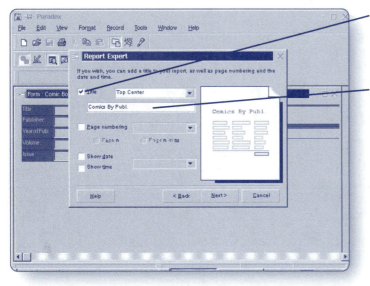

22. Click on the **check box** next to Title. A check (√) will be placed in the check box.

23. Type a **title** for the report. The title will appear in the Preview.

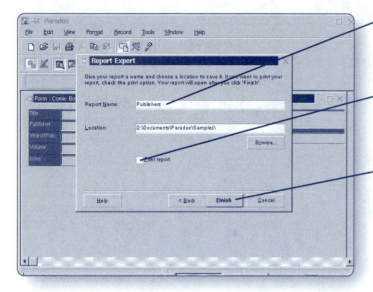

24. **Type** a **name** for the report. The name will appear in the Report Name box.

25. **Click** on the **check box** next to Print report. A check (√) will be placed in the check box.

26. **Click** on **Finish**. The Report Expert dialog box will close and the results of the report will be printed.

18

Working with Paradox

If you are a collector like me, then using a database is not such a far-fetched idea. After all, what collector would not want his prized collection of Burmese bottle caps indexed and cross-referenced for condition, weight, and angle of bend? Non-collectors, take heart—Paradox has plenty of uses for you, as you will soon read. In this chapter, you'll learn how to:

- Make mailing labels using information in a Paradox database
- Send data directly to a Web page
- Use data directly in a Quattro Pro spreadsheet
- Import and export data to and from a variety of formats

Creating Mailing Labels

Every holiday season it happens: You need to send cards to the people you know. Or you want to send the latest marketing brochures to a database full of customers. If the information is in Paradox, here's how you can get it onto mailing labels.

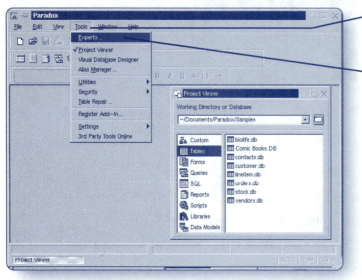

1. Click on **Tools**. The Tools menu will appear.

2. Click on **Experts**. The Paradox Experts dialog box will open.

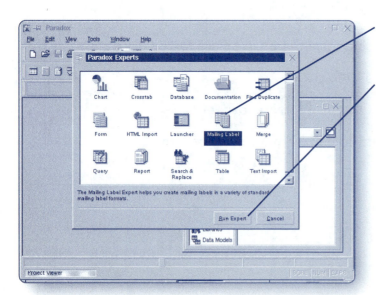

3. Click on **Mailing Label**. The option will be selected.

4. Click on **Run Expert**. The Mailing Label Expert dialog box will open.

CREATING MAILING LABELS   245

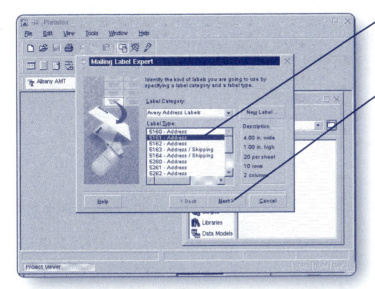

5. Click on **5161 – Address**. That Avery mailing label type will be selected.

6. Click on **Next**. The next Mailing Label Expert dialog box will open.

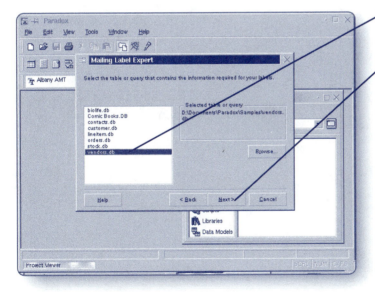

7. Click on **vendors.db**. The database table will be selected.

8. Click on **Next**. The next Mailing Label Expert dialog box will open.

CHAPTER 18: WORKING WITH PARADOX

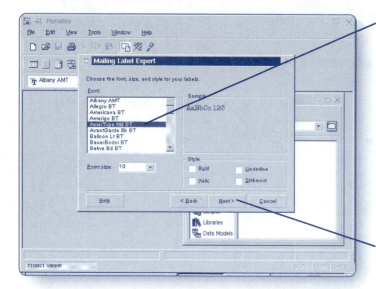

9. Click on **AmerType Md BT**. The font will be selected.

TIP
It's a good idea to leave the text size for mailing labels fairly small, so all of the address can actually fit on the label.

10. Click on **Next**. The next Mailing Label Expert dialog box will open.

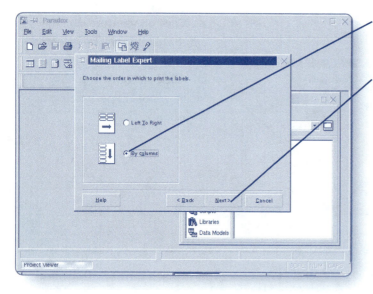

11. Click on **By columns**. The option will be selected.

12. Click on **Next**. The next Mailing Label Expert dialog box will open.

CREATING MAILING LABELS

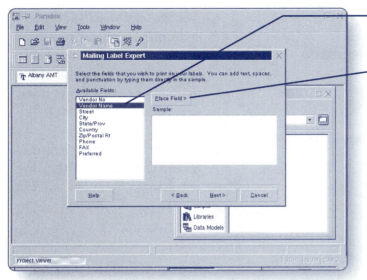

13. **Click** on **Vendor Name**. The field will be selected.

14. **Click** on **Place Field**. The Vendor Name field will be moved to the Sample window.

15. **Click** on the **line** below {Vendor Name} in the Sample window. The line will be selected.

16. **Click** on **Street**. The field will be selected.

17. **Click** on **Place Field**. The Street field will be moved to the Sample window at the insertion point.

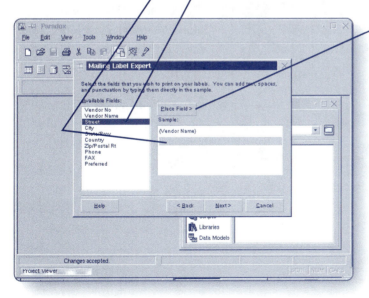

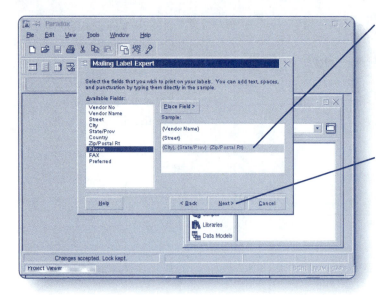

18. Repeat Steps 15–17 to insert the City, State/Prov, and Zip/Postal Rt fields in the Sample window. Use punctuation and spacing between the field names as needed.

19. Click on **Next**. The next Mailing Label Expert dialog box will open.

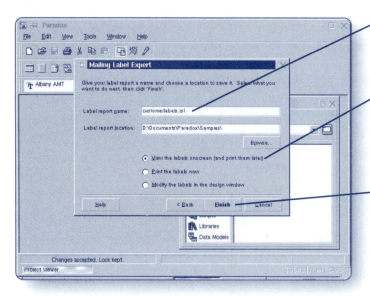

20. Type a **name** for the labels. The name will appear in the Label report name text box.

21. Click on the **View the labels onscreen (and print them later) option**. The option will be selected.

22. Click on **Finish**. The Mailing Label Expert dialog box will close and the labels will be displayed.

Publishing Data to a Web Page

The pervasiveness of the Internet in the business world today means that we need new ways of sharing information. Paradox steps up to this challenge by enabling you to create a report completely ready for the World Wide Web.

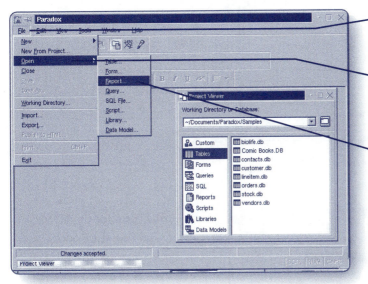

1. Click on **File**. The File menu will appear.

2. Move the **mouse pointer** to Open. The Open submenu menu will appear.

3. Click on **Report**. The Open Report dialog box will open.

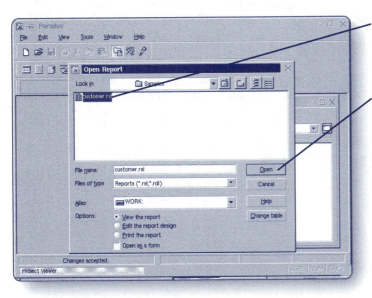

4. Click on the **report** you want to open. The file name will be selected.

5. Click on **Open**. The report will open.

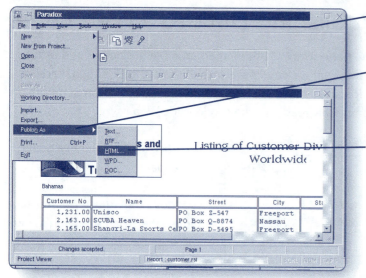

6. Click on **File**. The File menu will appear.

7. Move the **mouse pointer** to Publish As. The Publish As submenu will appear.

8. Click on **HTML**. The HTML Report Expert dialog box will open.

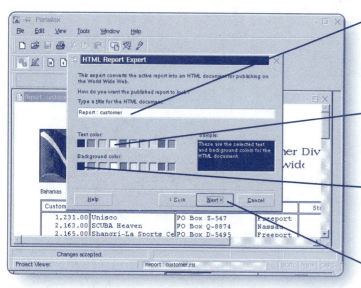

9. Type a **title** for the HTML report. The title will appear in the Type a title for the HTML document text box.

10. Click on a **text color**. The Sample will change to match the selection.

11. Click on a **background color**. The Sample will change to match the selection.

12. Click on **Next**. The next HTML Report Expert dialog box will open.

PUBLISHING DATA TO A WEB PAGE 251

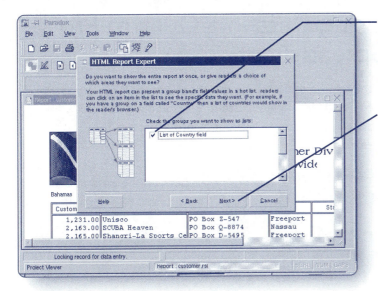

13. **Click** on the **List of Country field check box**. A check (√) will be placed in the check box.

14. **Click** on **Next**. The next HTML Report Expert dialog box will open.

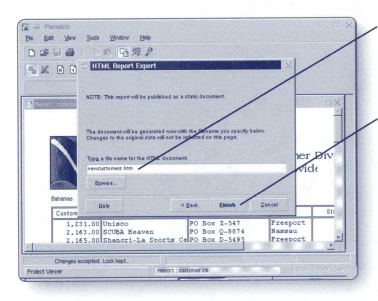

15. **Type** a **name** for the HTML report. The name will appear in the Type a file name for the HTML document text box.

16. **Click** on **Finish**. The HTML Report Expert dialog box will close and the Web page will be generated.

Using Data in a Quattro Pro Spreadsheet

Although database tables and spreadsheets look very similar, in reality they're very different. But you easily can still grab data from a database and put in into a Quattro Pro spreadsheet.

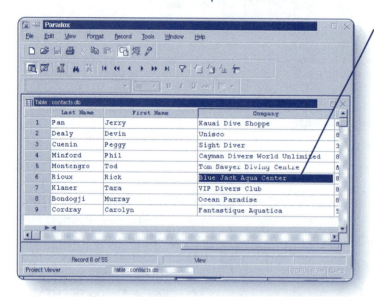

1. Click on the **data** to copy. The data will be selected.

2. Press Ctrl+C. The data will be copied.

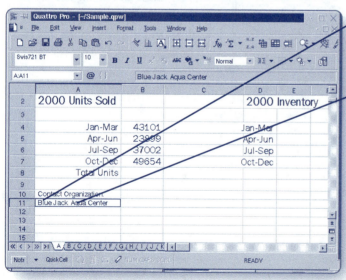

3. Click on the **cell** in Quattro Pro where you want to copy the data. The cell will be selected.

4. Press Ctrl+V. The data will be pasted into the cell.

Importing and Exporting Data

Beyond the simple cutting and pasting of data, you can import whole files of data—and export databases to new types of data files as well.

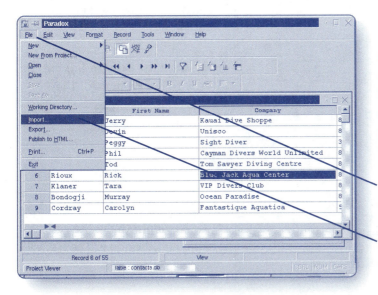

Importing Data

Paradox lets you import an amazing array of data files, including text files and spreadsheets. You can even pull in data from alternate formats, such as Excel.

1. Click on **File**. The File menu will appear.

2. Click on **Import**. The Import dialog box will open.

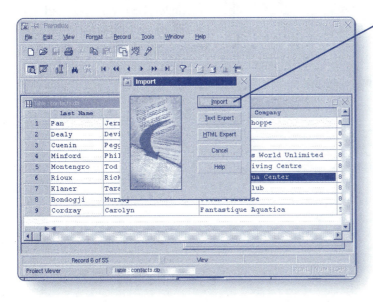

3. Click on **Import**. The Import Data dialog box will open.

CHAPTER 18: WORKING WITH PARADOX

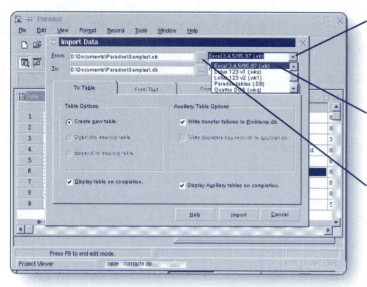

4. Click on the **down arrow (↓)** next to the From field. The data type drop-down menu will appear.

5. Click on **Excel 3,4,5/95,97 (.xls)**. The option will be selected.

6. Click the **Browse (...) button** next to the From field. The Select File dialog box will open.

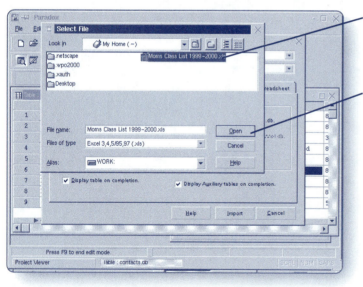

7. Navigate to the **file** you want and **click** on it. The file will be selected.

8. Click on **Open**. The Select File dialog box will close and the full file name of the file to be imported will appear in the From text box.

IMPORTING AND EXPORTING DATA 255

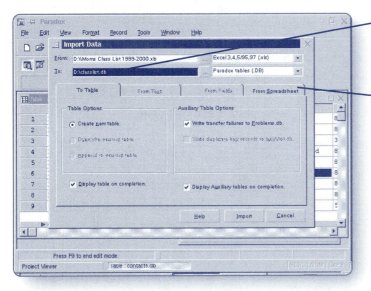

9. Type a **name** for the new database. The name will appear in the To text box.

10. Click on the **From Spreadsheet tab**. The From Spreadsheet tab will come to the front.

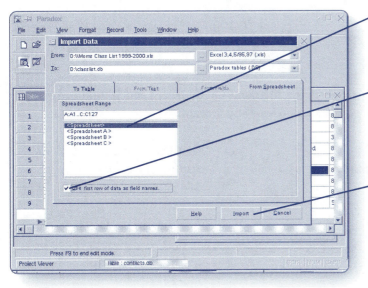

11. Click on the **sheet name** where the data resides. The name will be selected.

12. Click on the **Use first row of data as field names check box**. A check (√) will be placed in the check box.

13. Click on **Import**. The new database table will be created from the spreadsheet.

Exporting Data

If you need to share your data with others, you might need to export it to a common file format they can work with or import into their own database. The most common file format is a text file, with the data separated and delimited.

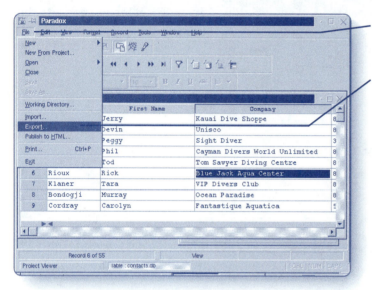

1. Click on **File**. The File menu will appear.

2. Click on **Export**. The Export Data dialog box will open.

3. Confirm the **file names** in the From and To text boxes. They should match what you want.

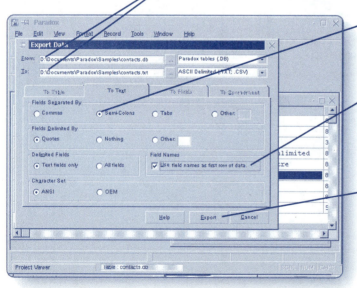

4. Click on the **Semi-Colons option**. The option will be selected.

5. Click on the **Use field names as first row of data check box**. A check (√) will be placed in the check box.

6. Click on **Export**. The new text file will be created from the database.

Part IV Review Questions

1. What are the elements of a database? See *"Creating a Database"* in Chapter 17.

2. How is a table made in Paradox? See *"Creating a Table with Table Expert"* in Chapter 17.

3. Why is a form helpful to use? See *"Creating a Form with Form Expert"* in Chapter 17.

4. What do queries and tables have in common? See *"Creating a Query with Query Expert"* in Chapter 17.

5. How are reports made? See *"Creating a Report with Report Expert"* in Chapter 17.

6. How can Paradox help you contact others? See *"Creating Mailing Labels"* in Chapter 18.

7. How do you create a Web-page ready report? See *"Publishing Data to a Web Page"* in Chapter 18.

8. How can you share data with a Quattro Pro spreadsheet? See *"Using Data in a Quattro Pro Spreadsheet"* in Chapter 18.

9. How do you pull in data from alternate sources? See *"Importing Data"* in Chapter 18.

10. How can you share data with someone who does not have Paradox? See *"Exporting Data"* in Chapter 18.

PART V
Working with Ideas

Chapter 19
Learning Presentations Basics **261**

Chapter 20
Editing a Slide Show **271**

Chapter 21
Working with Presentations
Special Effects **285**

Chapter 22
Drawing with Presentations **297**

19
Learning Presentations Basics

Because many people fear public speaking second only to death, most would rather not become fiery orators to get their points across. That leaves the second option: Use another way to communicate, such as visual stimuli. We simply remember things better if we see them with our eyes. As a result, the corporate slide show was born.

It started with placards at first, showing charts created by people whose job was to do nothing but. Overheads appeared next, lending presenters the ability to support their points on-the-fly. Then came slides, which added color and speed to presentations. Finally, slides were created directly on a computer and projected from there, as well.

Presentations is the component in WordPerfect Office 2000 that gets this job done for you. In this chapter, you'll learn how to:

- Start Presentations
- Create a Presentations slide show
- Use the different views to modify your slide show

Starting Presentations

Unlike the other components of WordPerfect Office 2000, Presentations does not start right after you call it up. Instead, PerfectExpert steps in to help guide the beginning of your work in Presentations.

1. Click on the **Application Starter**. The main menu will appear.

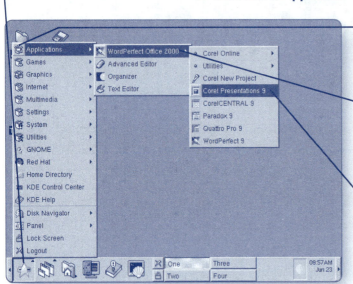

2. Move the **mouse pointer** to Applications. The Applications menu will appear.

3. Move the **mouse pointer** to WordPerfect Office 2000. The WordPerfect Office 2000 menu will appear.

4. Click on **Corel Presentations 9**. The PerfectExpert dialog box will open.

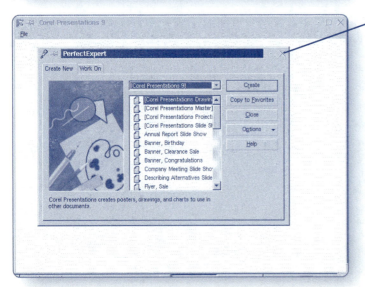

5a. Click on the **Close button** (☒) to circumnavigate PerfectExpert. The Startup Master Gallery dialog box will appear.

STARTING PRESENTATIONS 263

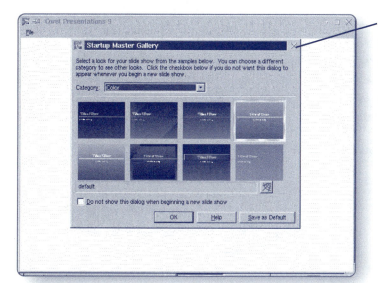

6a. Click on the **Close button** (**X**). The Presentations window will appear.

OR

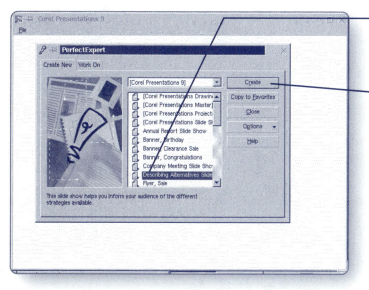

5b. Click on the desired **project** to start. The project will be highlighted.

6b. Click on **Create**. The Presentations window will appear, opened to the desired project.

Creating a Basic Slide Show

Creating a Presentations slide show is fairly routine when you use PerfectExpert. It is important to outline your presentation at least roughly before you begin so you have some idea what slides to create.

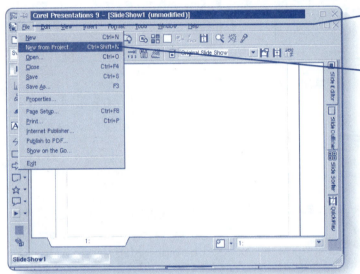

1. Click on **File**. The File menu will appear.

2. Click on **New from Project**. The PerfectExpert dialog box will open.

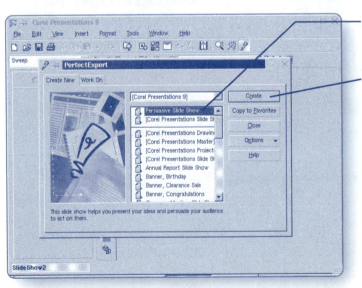

3. Click on **Persuasive Slide Show**. It will be selected.

4. Click on **Create**. The Presentations window will appear with the PerfectExpert in one pane and the slide show in the other pane.

Switching Views

Before you start learning how to modify the slide show templates Presentations provides, or create a slide show from scratch, it's important to understand the Presentations interface. More than any of the other WordPerfect Office 2000 applications, Presentations has the ability to view a single document in many different ways.

Viewing with the Slide Editor

The most prevalent view within Presentations is the Slide Editor, where slides get the most hands-on treatment. This is where you can edit text and graphics.

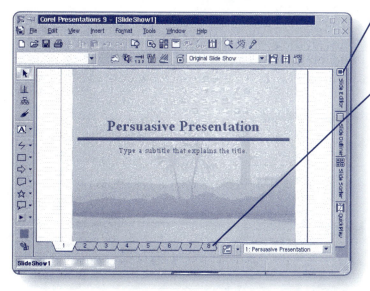

1. **Click** on the **Slide Editor tab**. The Slide Editor will come to the front.

2. **Click** on a **slide tab** to navigate to a new slide. The slide will come to the front.

266 CHAPTER 19: LEARNING PRESENTATIONS BASICS

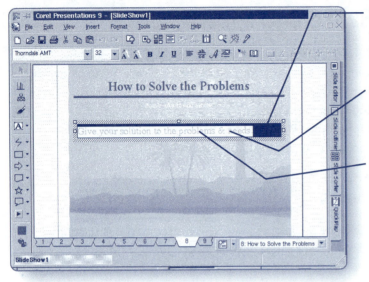

3. **Double-click** on some **text** to edit it. The text box will be highlighted.

4. **Select** the **text** within the text box. The text will be highlighted.

5. **Type** new **text**.

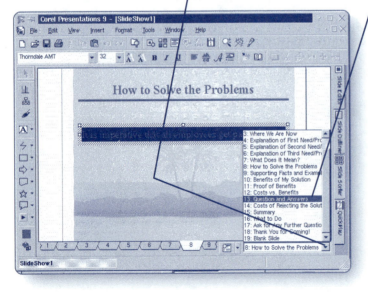

6. **Click on** the **down arrow** (↓) next to the Slide Navigator box. A drop-down list of all slides in the slide show will appear.

7. **Click** on a different **slide**. The Slide Editor will open to that slide.

Using Slide Outliner

After you create the slide show, you often need to edit the outline. After all, Presentations slide shows are essentially one big outline chopped into different slides.

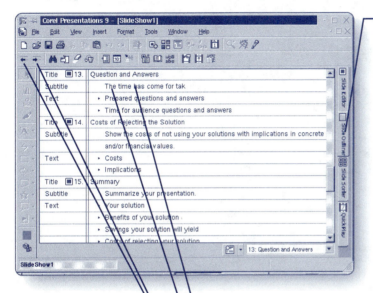

1. Click on the **Slide Outliner tab**. The Slide Outliner window will come to the front.

2. Select some text to edit. The text will be highlighted.

3. Type new **text**.

4. Click on the **Demote** or **Promote buttons** to change the outline level of a selected line of text. The text will be indented or outdented as selected.

TIP
Double-clicking on any slide icon in the Slide Outliner opens that slide in the Slide Editor.

Using Slide Sorter

With the Slide Sorter, you can quickly arrange slides into the order you want.

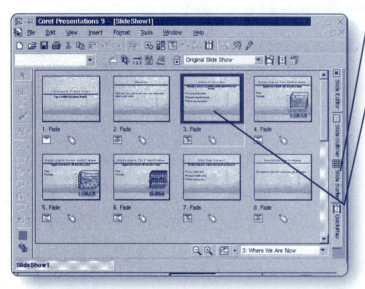

1. Click on the **Slide Sorter tab**. The Slide Sorter window will come to the front.

2. Click on a **slide**. The slide will be highlighted.

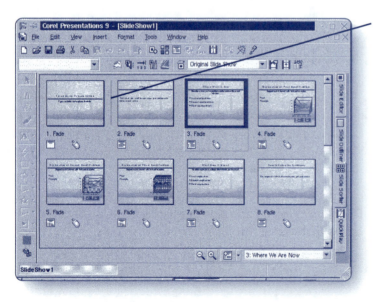

3. Drag the **slide** to a new location in the presentation. The slide placeholder will move with the mouse pointer.

SWITCHING VIEWS 269

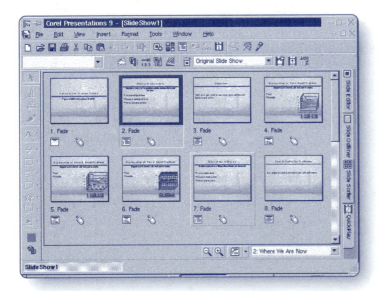

4. **Release** the **mouse button**. The slide will be placed in its new location.

TIP
Double-clicking on any slide in the Slide Sorter opens that slide in the Slide Editor.

QuickPlay a Slide Show

After all is said and done, you need to view the slide presentation in its entirety. That's what QuickPlay is for.

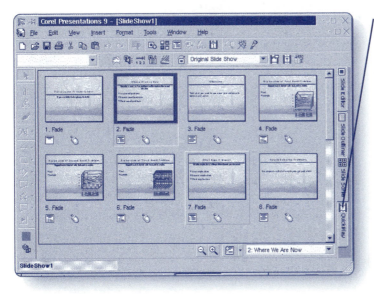

1. **Click** the **QuickPlay tab**. The slide show will appear full-screen.

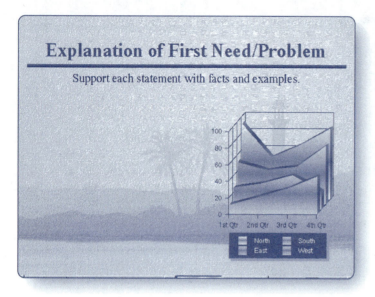

2. Press the **Spacebar**. The presentation will progress through each slide and each slide effect.

3. Press the **Esc key**. The QuickPlay view will close before the presentation is complete.

20

Editing a Slide Show

You can enhance Presentations slide shows in a multitude of ways beyond the good-looking, but basic, templates generated by the PerfectExpert. A word of caution before beginning the examination of these enhancements: Don't get carried away. Keep the look of your slides simple and uncluttered. Don't go crazy with five different kinds of transitions for a six-slide presentation. A lot of flashy tricks in your presentation serve only to distract. Simplicity and consistency are the watchwords for a good presentation. In this chapter, you'll learn how to:

- Add, delete, and rearrange slides as needed
- Edit text in a slide
- Place graphics in your presentation
- Alter presentation and slide designs
- Create speaker notes
- Print a presentation

Working with Slides

In Chapter 19, "Learning Presentations Basics," you see how the Slide Sorter lets you view all the slides in the presentation at once. The Slide Sorter is an important tool when working with slides, but it's not the only one at your disposal.

Adding Slides

Nothing in the world is static. Ideas change, as do ways of presenting those ideas. You can have Presentations add slides to your slide show with just one button.

1. Click on a **slide tab**. Be sure it is the slide you want the new slide to appear after. The slide will come to the front.

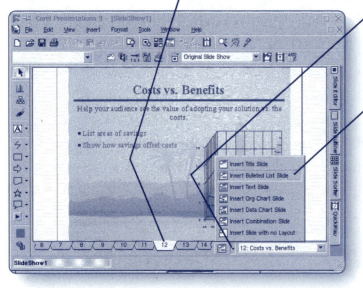

2. Click on the **down arrow (↓)** next to the Insert Slide button. A list of slide templates to add will appear.

3. Click on **Insert Bulleted List Slide**. A new bulleted list slide will appear after the slide you initially selected.

Deleting Slides

It is much easier to remove something than build it. Such is the way of the world and Presentations when you remove a slide.

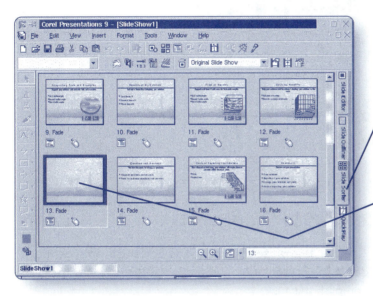

1. Click on the **Slide Sorter tab**. The Slide Sorter window will come to the front.

2. Click on the **slide** to be deleted. The slide is selected.

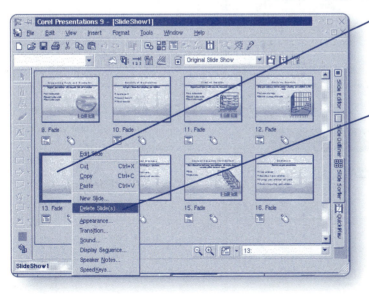

3. Press the **right mouse button** (*right-click*) on the slide. The slide's context menu will appear.

4. Click on **Delete Slide(s)**. A Delete Slide dialog box will appear to confirm the action.

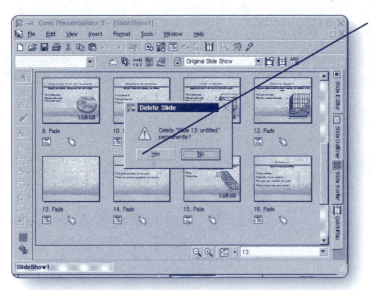

5. Click on **Yes**. The Delete Slide dialog box will close and the slide will be removed from the presentation.

Rearrange Slides

In Chapter 19, you see how the Slide Sorter can arrange the slides in the presentation. But that's not the only way to accomplish this task.

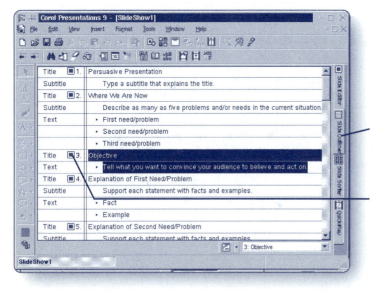

1. Click on the **Slide Outliner tab**. The Slide Outliner window will come to the front.

2. Click on a **slide icon**. The text of the slide will be selected.

WORKING WITH SLIDES 275

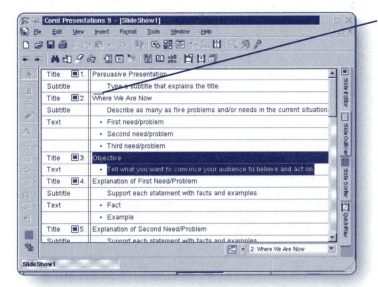

3. Drag the **slide icon** up or down the outline. The slide text placeholder will move with the mouse pointer.

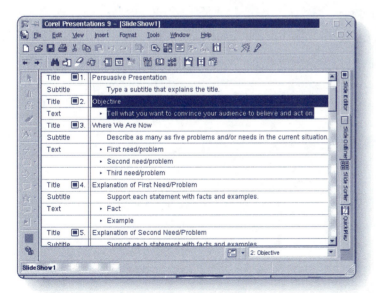

4. Release the **mouse button**. The slide will be placed in its new location.

Manipulating Text

You do not have to be a rocket scientist to work with text in a Presentation slide show. All you need to do is think about what you want to say.

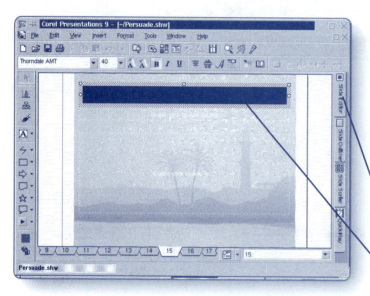

Adding Text to a New Slide

When you create a new slide, you have to visualize what you want to say and how you want it to look on the slide itself.

1. **Click** on the **Slide Editor tab**. The Slide Editor window will come to the front.

2. **Double-click** an **empty text box** in a new slide. The text insertion point will appear and the text box will be highlighted.

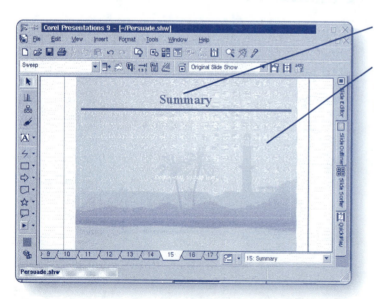

3. **Type** the **new text**.

4. **Click anywhere** outside of the text area. The changes will be made.

Editing Text

You typically edit text on a slide in the Slide Editor, but there are other ways to skin a cat, especially when you need to see a lot of the text in the presentation at once.

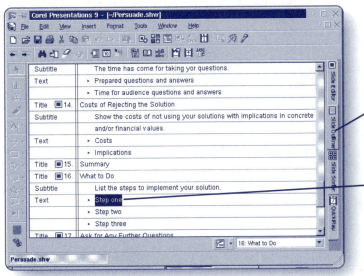

1. Click on the **Slide Outliner tab**. The Slide Outliner window will come to the front.

2. Select some text in the outline. The text will be highlighted.

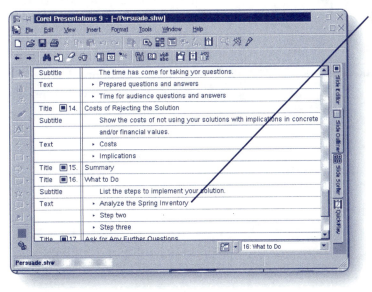

3. Type the **new text**.

Changing the Font

Changing the font of a slide's text is a simple process.

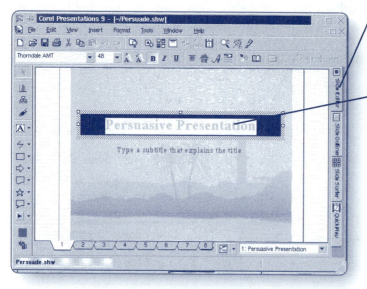

1. **Click** on the **Slide Editor tab**. The Slide Editor window will come to the front.

2. **Select some text** in a slide. The text will be highlighted.

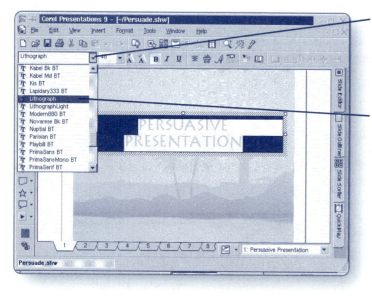

3. **Click** on the **down arrow (↓)** next to the Font Selection box. The Font drop-down list will appear.

4. **Click** on **Lithograph**. The selected text's font will change to the Lithograph font.

Deleting a Text Object

Text on Presentations slides is contained within text box objects. You can remove the text objects to make room for other objects when needed.

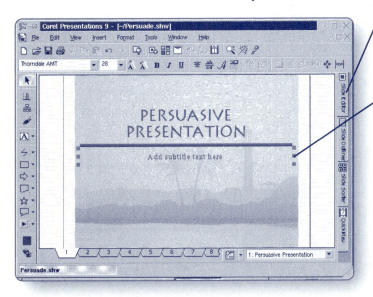

1. Click on the **Slide Editor tab**. The Slide Editor window will come to the front.

2. Click on **some text** in a slide. The text box borders will appear.

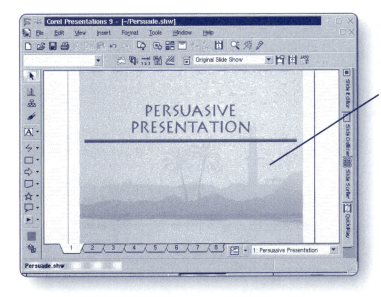

3. Press the **Delete key**. The contents of text box will be removed.

4. Press the **Delete key** again. The text box will be removed.

Changing Slide Designs

Changing an individual slide's basic design is pretty easy, leaving you plenty of time to think of what you want to say.

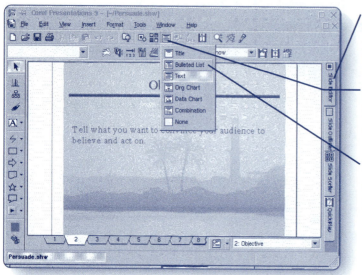

1. Click on the **Slide Editor tab**. The Slide Editor window will come to the front.

2. Click the **Select Format button**. The Select Format menu will appear.

3. Click on **Bulleted List**. The slide will change to the new layout style.

Changing Slide Show Designs

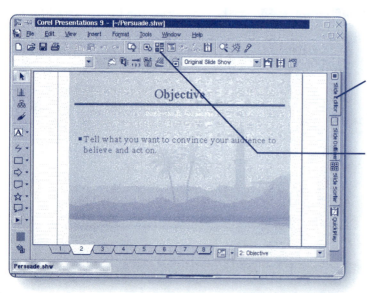

Presentations lets you quickly modify the look and feel of the entire slide show.

1. Click on the **Slide Editor tab**. The Slide Editor window will come to the front.

2. Click the **Master Gallery button**. The Master Gallery dialog box will appear.

CHANGING SLIDE SHOW DESIGNS 281

3. Click on the **down arrow** (↓) next to the Category box. The Category drop-down list will appear.

4. Click on **Theme**. The styles of the Theme category will be displayed.

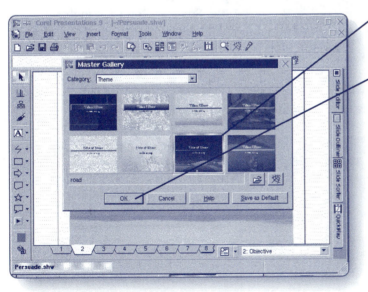

5. Click on **Road**. The theme will be selected.

6. Click on **OK**. The Master Gallery dialog box will close and the new theme will be applied to all of the slides in the presentation.

Making Speaker Notes

When you're up there in front of the audience, no matter how many times you've practiced, you likely need some speaker notes to help guide you through your speech. Presentations lets you create speaker notes that are associated with any slide you desire, so you can get through the rough spots.

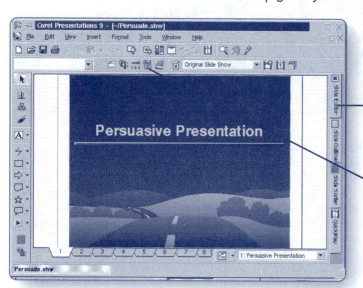

1. Click on the **Slide Editor tab**. The Slide Editor window will come to the front.

2. Click on the **Speaker Notes button**. The Slide Properties dialog box will open, with the Speaker Notes tab in the foreground.

3. Click the **down arrow** (↓) next to the Slide Navigator box. The list of slides in the presentation will appear.

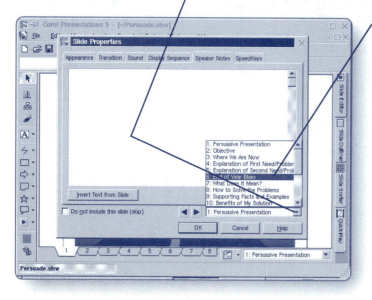

4. Click on the **slide** you want to add notes to. The slide will be selected.

PRINTING IN PRESENTATIONS

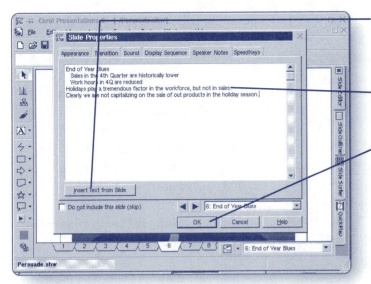

5. Click the **Insert Text from Slide**. The text from the slide will appear in the notes.

6. Type additional **notes**. The text will appear in the notes.

7. Click on **OK**. The speaker notes for the slide will be set.

Printing in Presentations

Most of the time, you use Presentations to project slide show presentations onscreen. At times, you might need to print a hard copy of the presentation, if only for posterity.

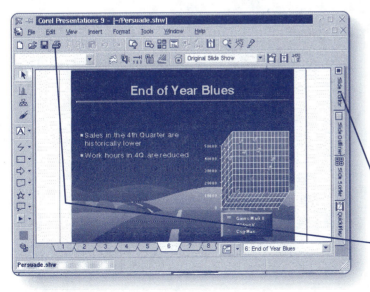

Printing a Slide Show

Printing a presentation in Presentations is just like printing a document anywhere else in WordPerfect Office 2000.

1. Click on the **Slide Editor tab**. The Slide Editor window will come to the front.

2. Click on the **Print button**. The presentation will be printed.

Printing Speaker and Audience Notes

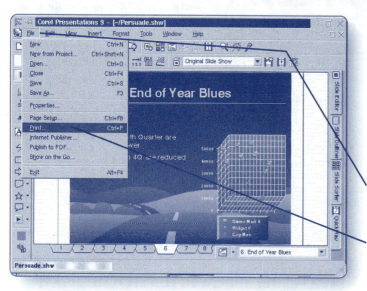

Another common printing task in Presentations is printing speaker notes and audience notes. Audience notes are a miniature printout of the slides in your presentation that viewers can use to make their own notes on what you have to say.

1. Click on **File**. The File menu will appear.

2. Click on **Print**. The Print to lp, WINEPS dialog box will open.

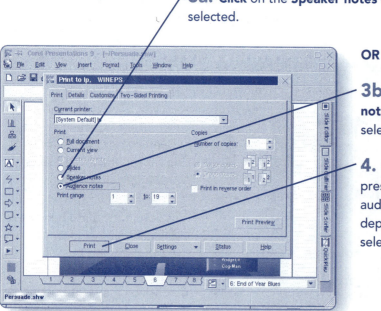

3a. Click on the **Speaker notes option**. The option will be selected.

OR

3b. Click on the **Audience notes option**. The option will be selected.

4. Click on **Print**. The presentation's speaker or audience notes will be printed, depending on the option selected.

21

Working with Presentations Special Effects

You've seen them before: those fabulous presentations that have all the bells and whistles. Presentations lets you include these features in your slide shows as well. Remember, however, that it is more important what you say than how you say it. In this chapter, you'll learn how to:

- Add tables to your presentation
- Insert charts into a slide
- Add stunning transitions between slides
- Place sound effects in your slide show

Adding Tables

Unlike WordPerfect, Presentations has no inherent table tools of its own. To create a table effect, you need to insert a specialized table chart.

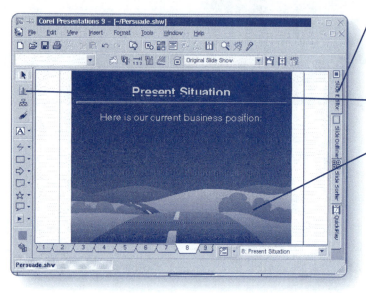

1. Click on the **Slide Editor tab**. The Slide Editor window will come to the front.

2. Click the **Chart button**. The Chart mouse pointer will appear.

3. Click and **drag** the **Chart mouse pointer** across the slide. The position of the chart will appear as an outlined box.

4. Release the **mouse button**. The Data Chart Gallery dialog box will open.

ADDING TABLES 287

5. Click on **Table** in the Chart type box. Table will be highlighted and examples of table charts will appear on the right side of the dialog box.

6. Click on a **table example**. The example will be selected.

7. Click in the **Use sample data check box**. A check (√) will be placed in the check box and the example will be cleared.

8. Click on **OK**. The Data Chart Gallery dialog box will close and the chart will appear in the slide with the Datasheet dialog box open in the foreground.

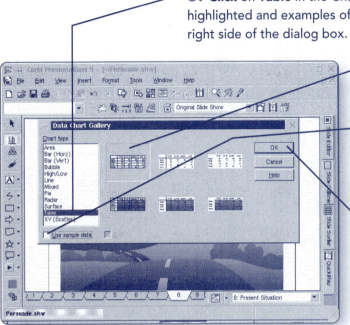

9. Type some **data** into the spreadsheet.

10. Click the **Close button** (**X**). The Datasheet dialog box will close.

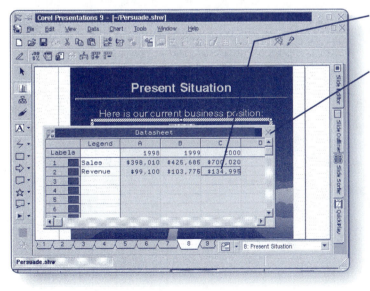

288 CHAPTER 21: WORKING WITH PRESENTATIONS SPECIAL EFFECTS

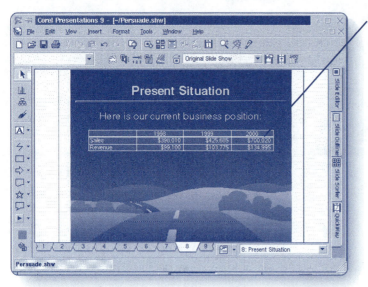

11. Double-click the **table**. The Table Properties dialog box will be opened.

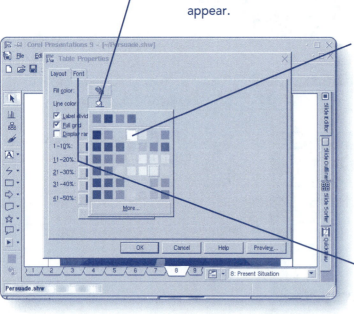

12. Click the **Line Color button**. The Line Color palette will appear.

13. Click on a **new color**. The color will be selected and the palette will close.

14. Click on the **Font tab**. The Font tab will come to the front.

INSERTING CHARTS 289

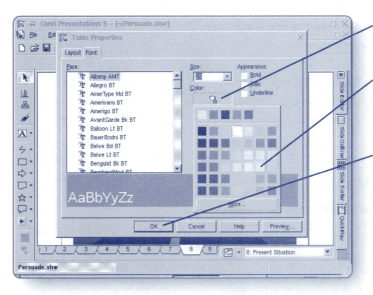

15. Click the **Color button**. The Color palette will appear.

16. Click on a **new color**. The color will be selected and the palette will close.

17. Click on **OK**. The Table Properties dialog box will close and the table will have a new appearance.

Inserting Charts

You can't have a business presentation without a chart, it seems. Making a graphic chart is much like making a table, as you can see.

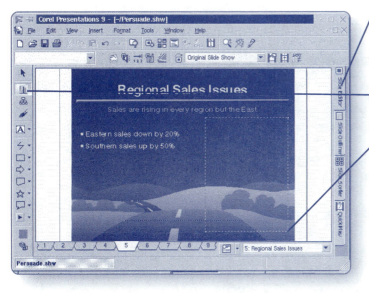

1. Click on the **Slide Editor tab**. The Slide Editor window will come to the front.

2. Click the **Chart button**. The Chart mouse pointer will appear.

3. Click and **drag** the **Chart mouse pointer** across the slide. The position of the chart will appear as an outlined box.

4. Release the **mouse button**. The Data Chart Gallery dialog box will open.

5. Click on **Mixed** in the Chart type box. Mixed will be highlighted and examples of table charts will appear on the right side of the dialog box.

6. Click on a **table example**. The example will be selected.

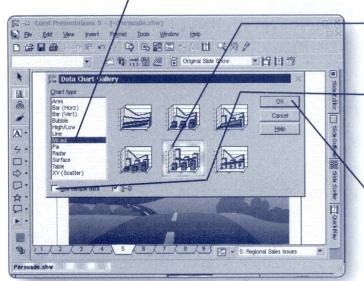

7. Click in the **Use sample data check box**. A check (√) will be placed in the check box and the example will be cleared.

8. Click on **OK**. The Data Chart Gallery dialog box will close and the chart will appear in the slide with the Datasheet dialog box open in the foreground.

9. Type some **data** into the spreadsheet.

10. Click the **Series button**. The Series Properties dialog box will open.

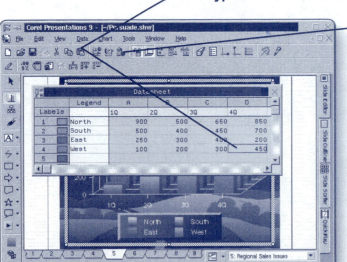

INSERTING CHARTS 291

11. Click on the **Area option**. The option will be selected for Series 1: North.

12. Click on the **Fill tab**. The Fill tab will come to the front.

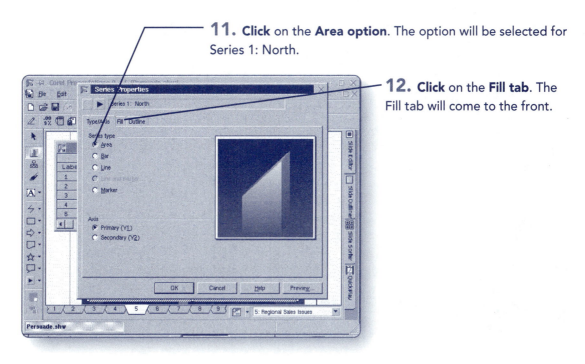

13. Click the **Foreground button**. The Foreground palette will appear.

14. Click on a **new color**. The color will be selected and the palette will close.

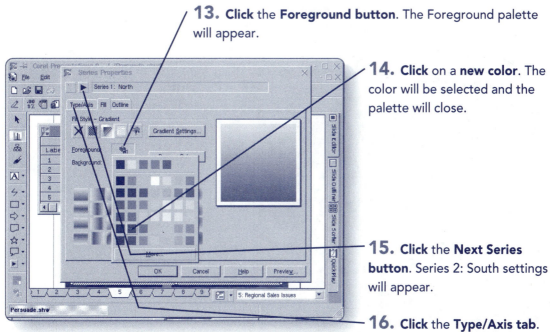

15. Click the **Next Series button**. Series 2: South settings will appear.

16. Click the **Type/Axis tab**. The Type/Axis tab will come to the front.

292 CHAPTER 21: WORKING WITH PRESENTATIONS SPECIAL EFFECTS

17. Click on the **Bar option**. The option will be selected for Series 2: South.

18. Click the **Next Series button**. Series 3: East settings will appear.

19. Click on the **Line option**. The option will be selected for Series 3: East.

20. Click the **Next Series button**. Series 4: West settings will appear.

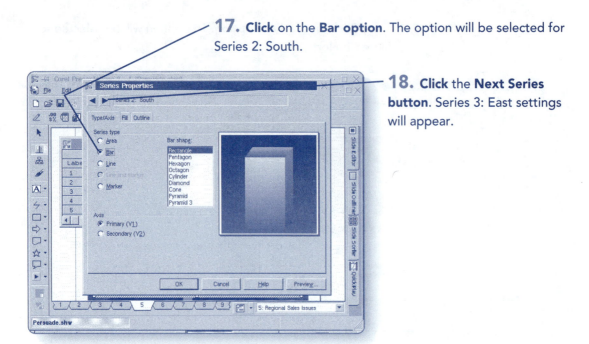

ADDING TRANSITIONS 293

21. Click on the **Marker option**. The option will be selected for Series 4: West.

22. Click the **Star button**. The star will be selected.

23. Click on **OK**. The Series Properties dialog box will close and the chart will have a new appearance.

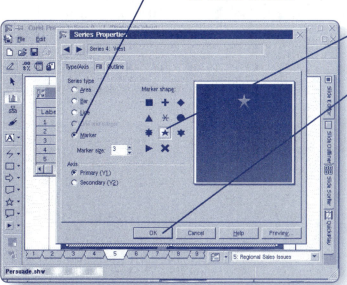

Adding Transitions

When you move from one slide to another in a presentation, the screen often shows more than an instant switch. These effects are called transitions, and they are easy to add to any slide.

1. Click on the **Slide Sorter tab**. The Slide Sorter window will come to the front.

2. Press and **hold** the **Shift key**.

3. Click on **all slides**. The slides will be highlighted.

4. Release the **Shift key**.

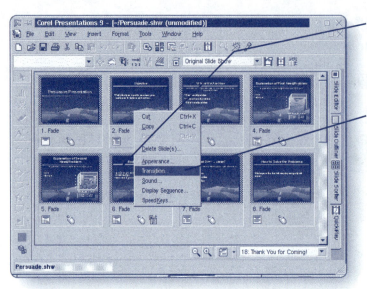

5. Press the **right mouse button** (*right-click*) on any slide. The slide context menu will appear.

6. Click on **Transition**. The Slide Properties dialog box will appear.

7. Click on **Clock** in the Effect box. The effect will be selected and a demonstration of the transition will be shown in the Preview window.

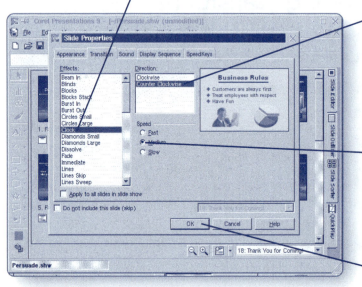

8. Click on **Counter clockwise** in the Direction box. The direction will be selected and a demonstration of the transition will be shown in the Preview window.

9. Click on the **Medium option** in the Speed box. The option will be selected and a demonstration of the transition will be shown in the Preview window.

10. Click on **OK**. The Slide Properties dialog box will close and the slides' transitions will be changed.

Applying Sound Effects

Slide transitions are not the only cool events you can put in a presentation. Neat effects such as sound can be applied to text and any other object in Presentations.

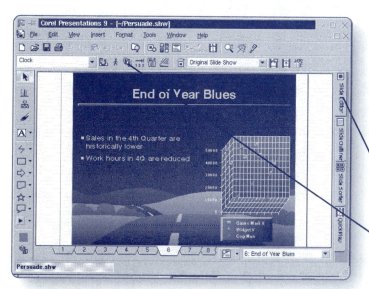

You might be tempted to load your file with a lot of bells and whistles. For the sake of simplicity and not drowning your own message in hype, avoid using a lot of gimmickry.

1. Click on the **Slide Editor tab**. The Slide Editor window will come to the front.

2. Click on the **Sound button**. The Slide Properties dialog box will appear.

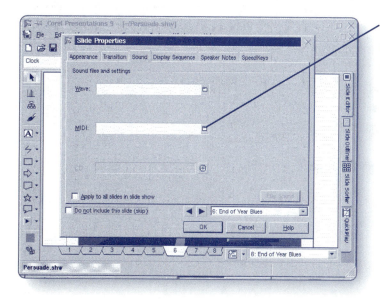

3. Click the **Open file button** next to the MIDI box. The Open dialog box will open.

296 CHAPTER 21: WORKING WITH PRESENTATIONS SPECIAL EFFECTS

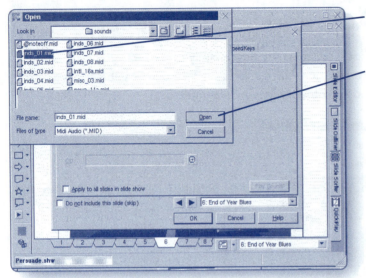

4. Click on a **MIDI file**. The file will be selected.

5. Click on **Open**. The Open dialog box will close and the MIDI file will be attached to this slide.

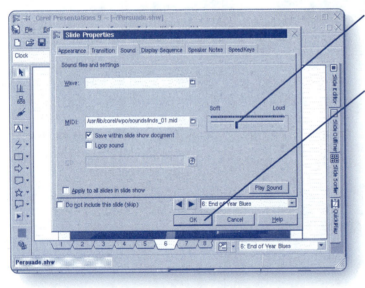

6. Click and **drag** the **volume control**. The volume of the MIDI sound clip will be adjusted.

7. Click on **OK**. The Slide Properties dialog box will close.

22

Drawing with Presentations

The ability to create stunning art becomes more accessible to the layperson every day. With its strong set of drawing tools, Presentations clearly steps in the right direction toward this accessibility, giving you endless opportunities to customize your slide shows. Because of this object-oriented treatment of items in a drawing, you can more easily manipulate and interact with the objects—especially given the tools Presentations includes. In this chapter, you'll learn how to:

- Maneuver around the drawing tools and the Bitmap Editor
- Create various shapes
- Draw lines and curves
- Create tool buttons for your Web pages

Exploring the Drawing Tools

If you thought that Presentations was only good for making slides, you might be pleasantly surprised to find it can help you make all sorts of drawn items—posters, banners, placards; you name it!

There are two sets of drawing tools used within Presentations: the main Tool Palette and the Bitmap Editor. The Tool Palette contains tools you use for creating basic shapes.

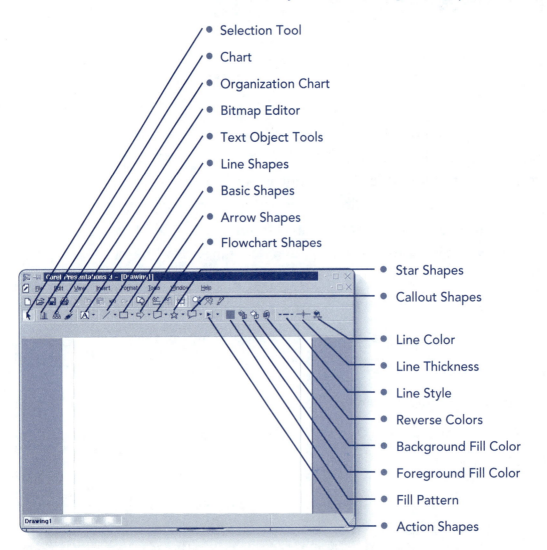

- Selection Tool
- Chart
- Organization Chart
- Bitmap Editor
- Text Object Tools
- Line Shapes
- Basic Shapes
- Arrow Shapes
- Flowchart Shapes
- Star Shapes
- Callout Shapes
- Line Color
- Line Thickness
- Line Style
- Reverse Colors
- Background Fill Color
- Foreground Fill Color
- Fill Pattern
- Action Shapes

EXPLORING THE DRAWING TOOLS   299

Clicking on the Bitmap Editor calls up this set of tools. You use the Bitmap Editor to create more detailed works that can be inserted into the greater picture. The different and additional tools of the Bitmap Editor give you a lot more flexibility.

- Cancel Bitmap
- Close
- Clear
- Paint Brush
- Flood Fill
- Air Brush
- Pickup Color
- Text Box
- Text Line
- Selective Replace
- Erase
- Select Area
- Air Brush Density
- Bitmap Brush Size
- Bitmap Brush Shape

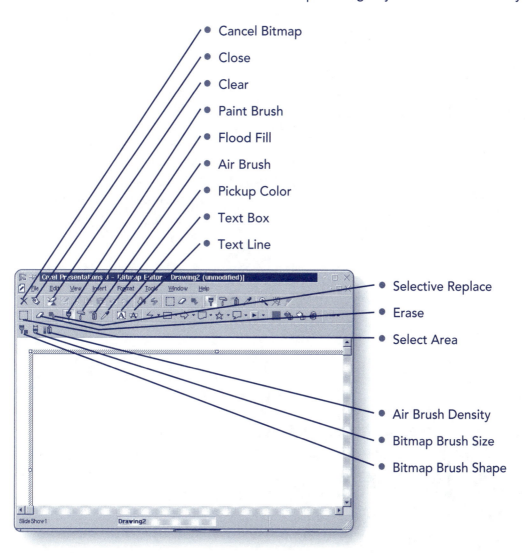

Creating Shapes

Don't be intimidated by your artistic abilities or lack thereof. In Presentations, you repeat a basic operation time and again: Select an object type, place the object, and configure the object.

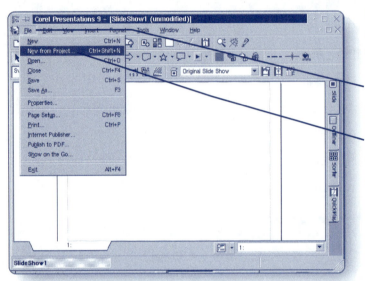

Remember, if you make a mistake, you can always click on the Undo button!

1. Click on **File**. The File menu will appear.

2. Click on **New from Project**. The PerfectExpert dialog box will appear.

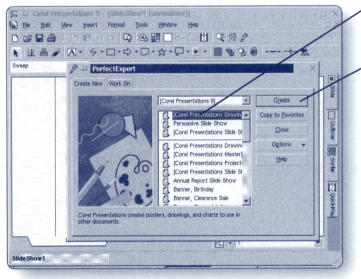

3. Click on **Corel Presentations Drawing**. It will be selected.

4. Click on **Create**. The PerfectExpert dialog box will close and a blank drawing will open.

CREATING SHAPES **301**

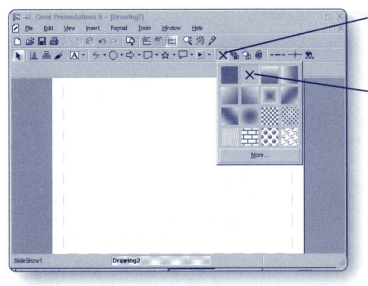

5. Click the **Fill Pattern button** on the Tool Palette. The Fill Pattern palette will appear.

6. Click on **No Pattern (X)**. The no fill pattern will be indicated by a big X.

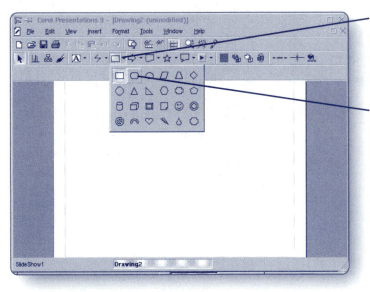

7. Click on the **down arrow (↓)** next to the Basic Shapes button on the Tool Palette. The Basic Shapes palette will appear.

8. Click on **Rounded Rectangle**. The Rectangle mouse pointer will appear.

302 CHAPTER 22: DRAWING WITH PRESENTATIONS

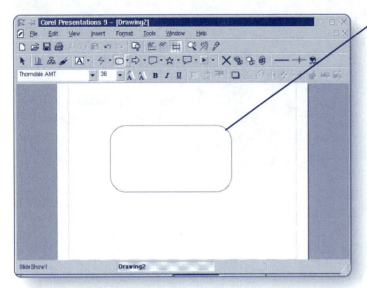

9. Click and **drag** the **mouse pointer** across the drawing canvas. The outline of the rectangle object will move with the mouse pointer.

TIP
To create a square using any of the rectangle tools, hold the Shift key while dragging the rectangle mouse pointer across the screen.

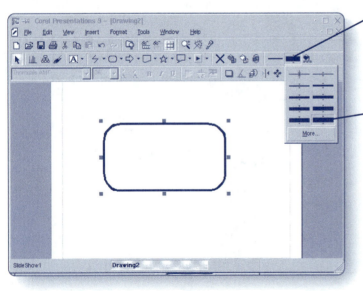

10. Click the **Line Width button** with the object still selected. The Line Width palette will appear.

11. Click on the **line width** you want. The width of the shape's line will increase to the specified amount.

CREATING SHAPES 303

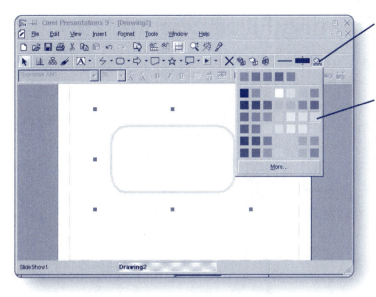

12. Click on the **Line Color button**. The Line Color palette will appear.

13. Click on **Turquoise**. The color will be selected and the shape's line will appear in that color.

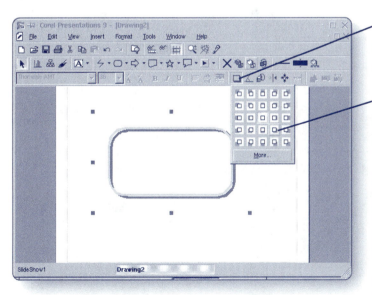

14. Click on the **Shadow button**. The Shadow palette will appear.

15. Click on a **shadow** you want. The shadow will appear next to the shape.

TIP

You can place a basic shape on the screen for later editing by just selecting a shape and then clicking anywhere on the drawing canvas.

Creating Filled Shapes

Creating an unfilled shape is pretty simple. A filled shape is just as easy and a lot more colorful.

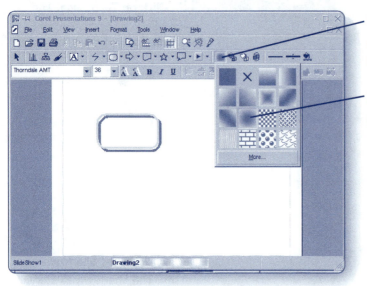

1. Click the **Fill Pattern button** on the Tool Palette. The Fill Pattern palette will appear.

2. Click on a **fill pattern**. The fill pattern will be selected.

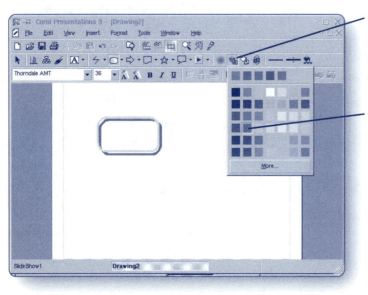

3. Click the **Foreground Fill Color button** on the Tool Palette. The Foreground Fill Color palette will appear.

4. Click on a **color**. The color will be selected.

CREATING FILLED SHAPES 305

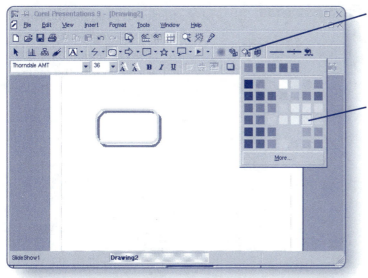

5. **Click** the **Background Fill Color button** on the Tool Palette. The Background Fill Color palette will appear.

6. **Click** on a **color**. The color will be selected.

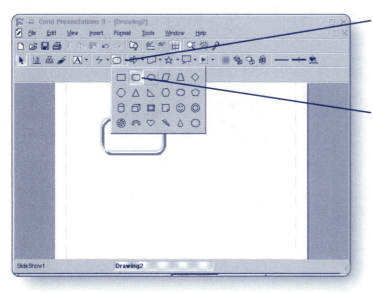

7. **Click** on the **down arrow (↓)** next to the Basic Shapes button on the Tool Palette. The Basic Shapes palette will appear.

8. **Click** on **Ellipse**. The Ellipse mouse pointer will appear.

306 CHAPTER 22: DRAWING WITH PRESENTATIONS

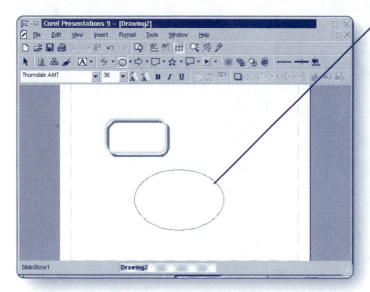

9. Click and **drag** the **mouse pointer** across the drawing canvas. The outline of the ellipse object will move with the mouse pointer.

TIP
To create a circle using any of the ellipse tools, hold the Shift key while dragging the ellipse mouse pointer across the screen.

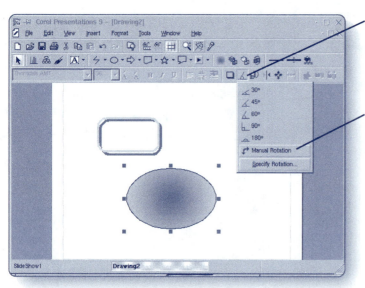

10. Click on the **Rotation button** with the ellipse still selected. The Rotation menu will appear.

11. Click on **Manual Rotation**. The rotation object handles will appear around the shape.

CREATING LINES AND CURVES 307

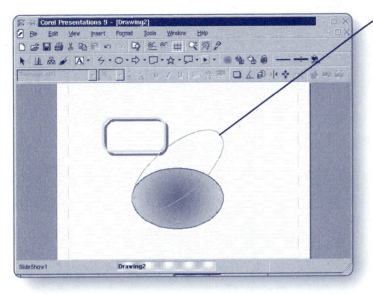

12. **Click** and **drag** a **rotation handle**. The shape will be "spun" to the new rotation angle.

13. **Release** the **mouse button**. The ellipse will be set at the new angle.

Creating Lines and Curves

More basic than shapes in a drawing are lines. Lines give shapes their form and help carry the eye from one part of a drawing to another.

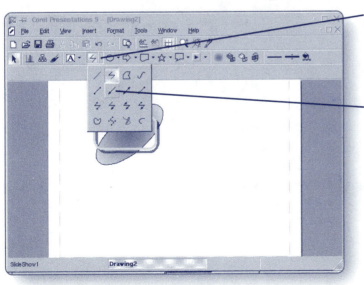

1. **Click** on the **down arrow** (↓) next to the Line Shapes button on the Tool Palette. The Line Shapes palette will appear.

2. **Click** on a **line**. The Line mouse pointer will appear.

CHAPTER 22: DRAWING WITH PRESENTATIONS

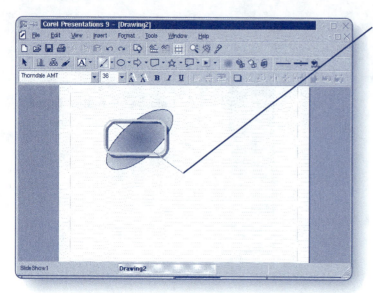

3. Click and **drag** the **mouse pointer** across the drawing canvas. The outline of the line object will move with the mouse pointer.

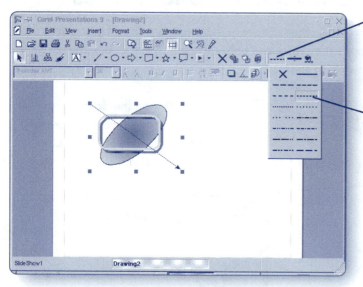

4. Click on the **Line Style button** with the line still selected. The Line Style palette will appear.

5. Click on the **Fine Dashed line**. The style will be selected and the line will change to the Fine Dashed style.

CREATING LINES AND CURVES 309

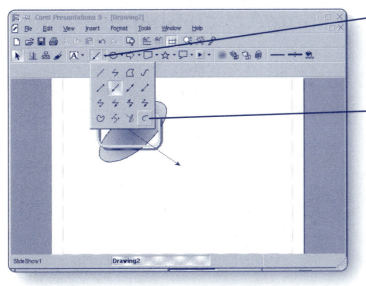

6. **Click** on the **down arrow** (↓) next to the Line Shapes button on the Tool Palette. The Line Shapes palette will appear.

7. **Click** on **Freeform Curve**. The curve mouse pointer will appear.

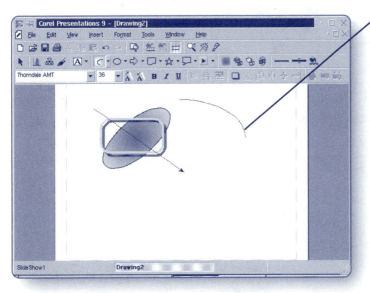

8. **Click** and **drag** the **curve pointer** across the screen. The curve object will move with the mouse pointer.

Creating Action Shapes

Action shapes are not some new kid's toy. Rather, they are specialized shapes that you can place on your drawing to use as navigation tools should you decide to use your drawing within a Web page.

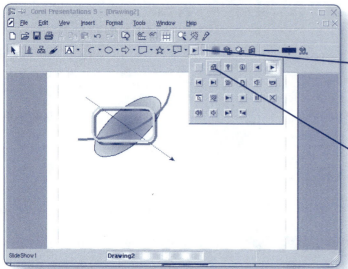

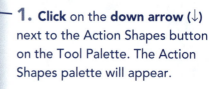

1. Click on the **down arrow (↓)** next to the Action Shapes button on the Tool Palette. The Action Shapes palette will appear.

2. Click on **Home Page**. The home page mouse pointer will appear.

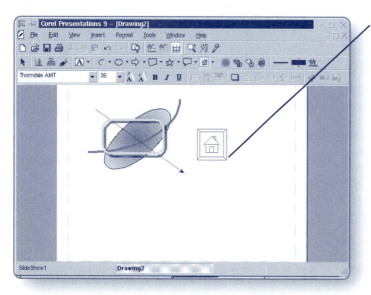

3. Click and **drag** the **mouse pointer** across the drawing canvas. The outline of the action shape will move with the mouse pointer.

Integrating the Bitmap Editor

When you want to create some artwork that is a little more detailed or a little more freeform, then you need to use the Bitmap Editor.

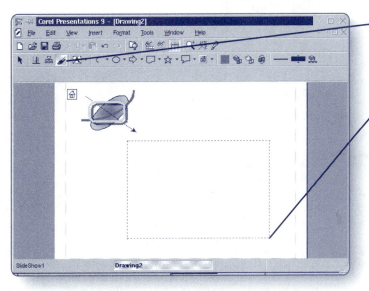

1. Click the **Bitmap Editor button** on the Tool Palette. The bitmap selector mouse pointer will appear.

2. Click and **drag** the **mouse pointer** across the drawing canvas. The outline of the bitmap canvas will move with the mouse pointer.

3. Release the **mouse button**. The bitmap canvas will be in place and the toolset will alter to that of the Bitmap Editor.

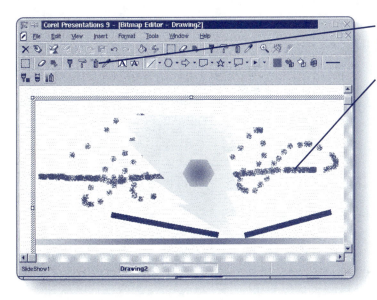

4. Click the **Air Brush button**. The button will be selected.

5. Click and **drag** the mouse pointer across the canvas. A speckled paint effect will appear.

6. Repeat Steps 4 and **5** with other tools. A drawing of your own will soon form.

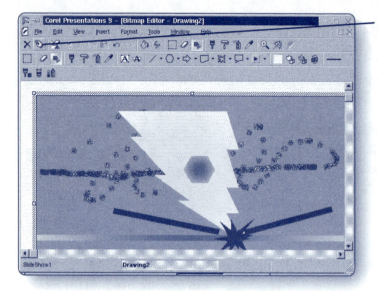

7. Click the **Close button**. The bitmap will be inserted into your initial drawing.

Part V Review Questions

1. How do you start all new slide shows? See *"Starting Presentations"* in Chapter 19.

2. What windows can you use in Presentations? See *"Switching Views"* in Chapter 19.

3. How do you view a slideshow in its entirety? See *"QuickPlay a Slide Show"* in Chapter 19.

4. What if your slides' order is wrong? See *"Rearrange Slides"* in Chapter 20.

5. How do you add more text? See *"Adding Text to a New Slide"* in Chapter 20.

6. How do you change the look of the slide show? See *"Changing Slide Show Designs"* in Chapter 20.

7. How does Presentations create a table? See *"Adding Tables"* in Chapter 21.

8. How do you add a chart to a slide? See *"Inserting Charts"* in Chapter 21.

9. What is a transition? See *"Adding Transitions"* in Chapter 21.

10. How can you add sounds to the slide show? See *"Applying Sound Effects"* in Chapter 21.

PART VI
Working with Time and People

Chapter 23
Learning the CorelCENTRAL Calendar . . **317**

Chapter 24
Using CorelCENTRAL Calendar to
Keep Organized **331**

Chapter 25
Using CorelCENTRAL Memo to
Keep Informed **339**

Chapter 26
Using CorelCENTRAL Address Book
to Keep in Touch **343**

23

Learning the CorelCENTRAL Calendar

It's all about time. You have a finite number of years to romp about this mortal coil. I say this not to panic anyone, but rather to raise another point. If you have only a set number of minutes to hang around, shouldn't you get the work done as efficiently as possible so you can go out and enjoy the rest of life? Thought so.

That brings us to CorelCENTRAL, WordPerfect Office 2000's Personal Information Manager. PIMs, as they are known in the computer biz, are software applications designed to help manage our busy days. CorelCENTRAL is actually three applications closely tied together: Calendar, Memo, and Address Book. The Calendar is the focus of this chapter, to help you start directly managing your time. In this chapter, you'll learn how to:

- Use the CorelCENTRAL Calendar interface
- Navigate the many different views in CorelCENTRAL Calendar
- Create an event on the calendar
- Create recurring events
- Edit existing events
- Delete events

Viewing CorelCENTRAL Calendar

Before learning to use the CorelCENTRAL Calendar component, first examine its interface because it has yet to appear in any of the other WordPerfect Office 2000 components.

- **Navigation calendar.** This pane helps with navigating to specific dates, tells you the currently selected day, and gives you the bigger picture on how busy your month is shaping up to be.

- **Event calendar.** This pane lists all of the events on a given day in block format. You can enter events directly into this pane and change times with the mouse, as you see later in this chapter.

- **New task input line.** You can quickly enter tasks in this field.

- **Task list.** View a list of the currently active tasks here.

> **NOTE**
>
> Tasks are the main topic of discussion in Chapter 24, "Using CorelCENTRAL Calendar to Keep Organized."

Changing the Calendar's View

The default view of CorelCENTRAL Calendar's Event calendar is the Day view. There are two other additional views as well. No one view is correct; which you use depends on your personal preferences.

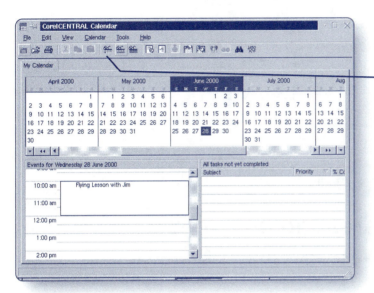

1. Click on the **Day button**. The Day view of the Event calendar will appear.

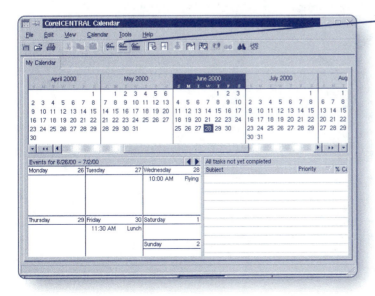

2. Click on the **Week button**. The Week view of the Event calendar will appear.

320 CHAPTER 23: LEARNING THE CORELCENTRAL CALENDAR

3. Click on the **Month button**. The Month view of the Event calendar will appear.

Creating an Event

CorelCENTRAL Calendar offers a pretty efficient way to create events, as you learn in this section.

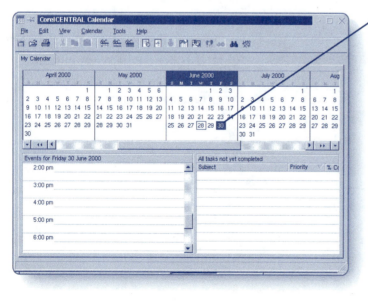

1. Click on a date. The day's schedule will appear in the Event calendar.

CREATING AN EVENT 321

2. Click on a **start time**. A half-hour block will be selected.

3. Click on the **Create a New Event button**. The Edit - New Event dialog box will appear.

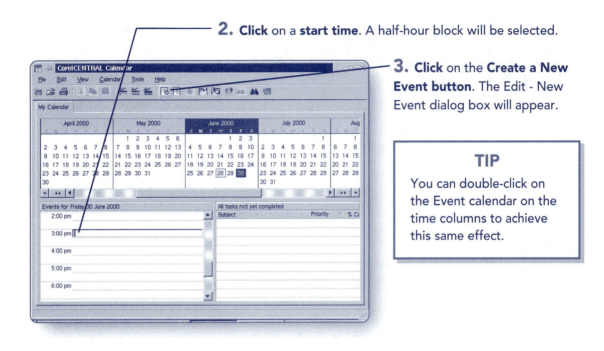

TIP
You can double-click on the Event calendar on the time columns to achieve this same effect.

4. Type the **subject** of your event. The information will appear in the Subject field.

5. Click the **down arrow (↓)** next to the Duration box. A drop-down list of durations for an event will appear.

6. Click on **2 Hours**. The duration will be selected.

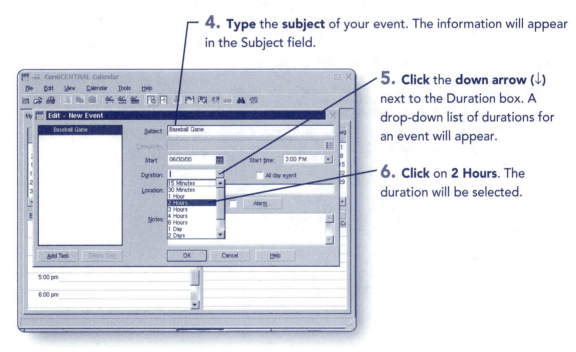

322 CHAPTER 23: LEARNING THE CORELCENTRAL CALENDAR

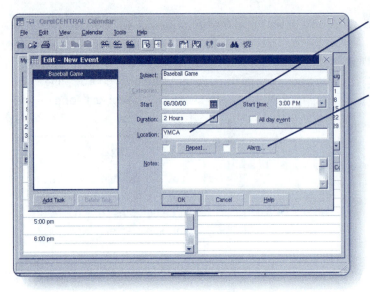

7. Type the **location** of the event. The information will appear in the Location box.

8. Click on **Alarm**. The Set Alarm dialog box will appear.

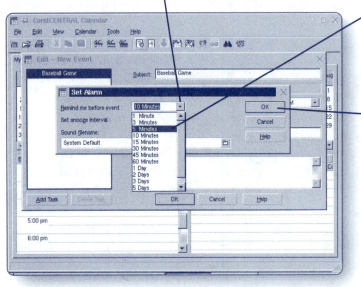

9. Click on the **down arrow** (↓) next to the Remind me before event box. A drop-down list will appear.

10. Click on **5 minutes**. The time will be selected and will appear in the Remind me before event box.

11. Click on **OK**. The Set Alarm dialog box will close.

CREATING RECURRING EVENTS 323

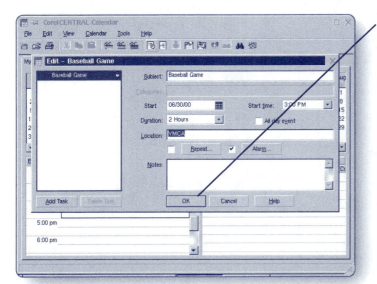

12. Click on **OK**. The Edit - New Event dialog box will close and the creation process will be completed.

TIP

You can change the start and end times of an event by clicking and dragging the bars above and below the event to the new times.

Creating Recurring Events

A recurring event repeats with some regularity, regularity being the key word. You can have repeated events, such as your child's Little League games or an important weekly event, but unless they occur at regular intervals, you have to treat them as single events in CorelCENTRAL Calendar.

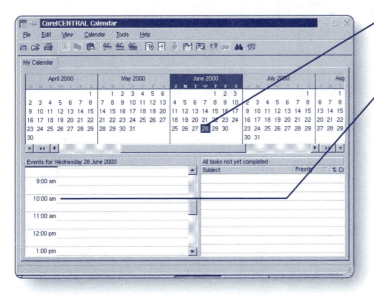

1. Click on a **date**. The day's schedule will appear in the Event calendar.

2. Double-click on a **start time**. A half-hour block will be selected and the Edit - New Event dialog box will appear.

324 CHAPTER 23: LEARNING THE CORELCENTRAL CALENDAR

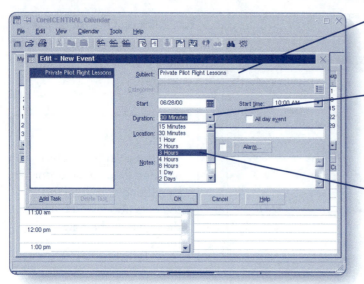

3. Type the **subject** of your event. The information will appear in the Subject field.

4. Click on the **down arrow** (↓) next to the Duration box. A drop-down list of durations for an event will appear.

5. Click on **3 Hours**. The duration will be selected.

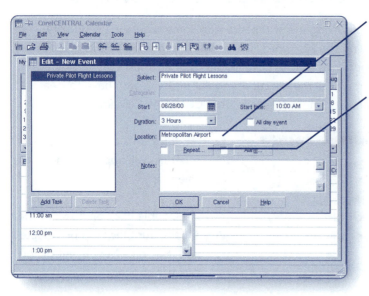

6. Type the **location** of the event. The information will appear in the Location box.

7. Click on **Repeat**. The Repeat Event dialog box will appear.

CREATING RECURRING EVENTS 325

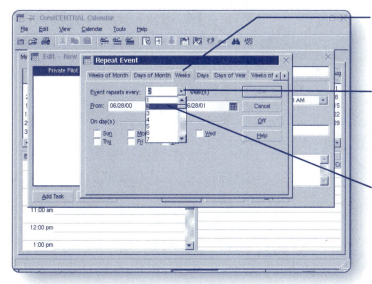

8. Click on the **Weeks tab**. The Weeks tab will come to the front.

9. Click on the **down arrow (↓)** next to the Event repeats every box. A list of numbers of weeks will appear.

10. Click on **2**. The number will be selected.

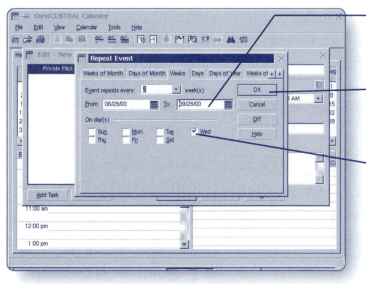

11. Type a new **end date**. The information will appear in the To box.

12. Click in the **Wed check box**. A check (√) will be placed in the check box.

13. Click on **OK**. The Repeat Event dialog box will close.

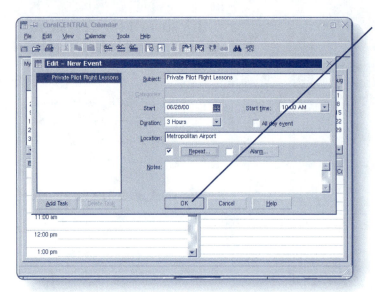

14. Click on **OK**. The Edit - New Event dialog box will close and the recurring event will be created.

Editing an Event

Nothing in the world is static. Events are postponed often. Changing your events in the Event calendar takes only a few seconds.

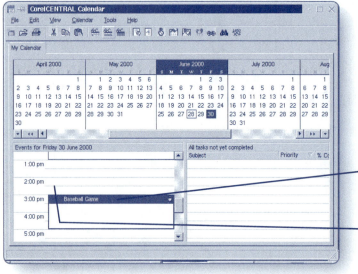

Moving to a Different Time

When moving an event to a different time, you can shift the entire event to the new time or extend the duration of the event to the new time.

1. Click and **hold** on an **event**. The event will be selected.

2. Drag the **event** to the new time. The event outline will move with the mouse pointer.

EDITING AN EVENT

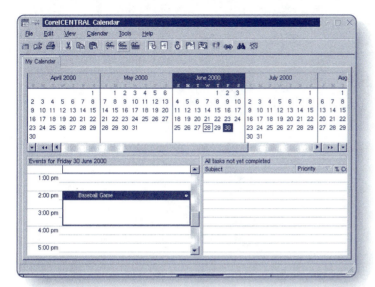

3. Release the **mouse button**. The event will be located at the new time.

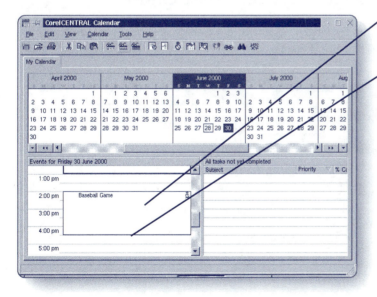

4. Click and **hold** on a **start** or **end time line** of an event.

5. Drag the **time line** to the new time. The time line outline will move with the mouse pointer.

CHAPTER 23: LEARNING THE CORELCENTRAL CALENDAR

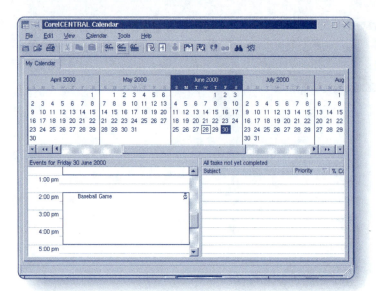

6. Release the **mouse button**. The event's duration will extend to the new time.

Moving to a Different Date

When moving an event to a different day, you can edit the event's properties with ease.

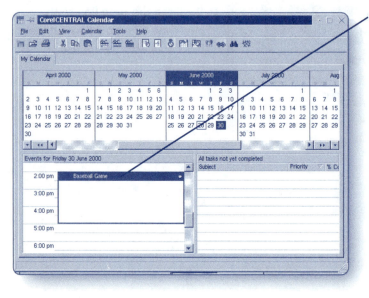

1. Double-click on an **event**. The Edit - New Event dialog box will appear.

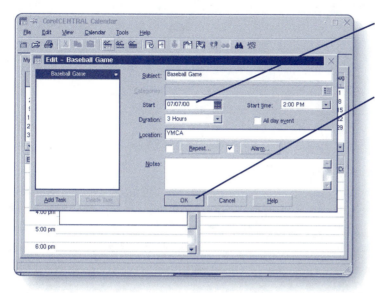

2. Type a new **start date**. The information will appear in the Start box.

3. Click on **OK**. The Edit - New Event dialog box will close and the event will be moved to the new date.

Deleting an Event

Tax audit appointment cancelled? While you're cheering, follow these steps to delete the event from CorelCENTRAL Calendar.

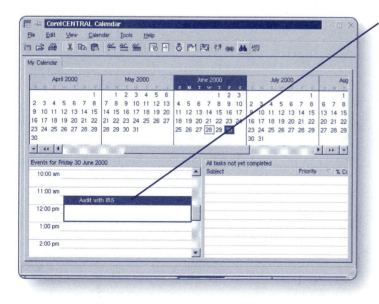

1. Click on an **event**. The event will be selected.

2. Press the **Delete key**. The event will be removed.

24

Using CorelCENTRAL Calendar to Keep Organized

Technology was supposed to make things easier for us. Remember that one? In case you had any doubts, try this statistic on for size: 50,000 years ago, it took the average man about 20 hours a week to feed, clothe, and house his entire family. The rest of the time, he could lollygag. Today, a person must work an average of 50 hours a week to achieve the same goal. Technology hasn't made things easier; it's just given us more stuff to do before we can relax with nuts and berries. In this chapter, you'll learn how to:

- Create tasks in CorelCENTRAL Calendar
- Link tasks to specific events
- Mark tasks as fully or partially complete
- Delete tasks from the task list

332 CHAPTER 24: USING CORELCENTRAL CALENDAR

Creating a Task

Using CorelCENTRAL Calendar is a pretty good way of tracking all of the tasks in your life. The interface to do so is deliberately simple. After all, why make the task list one more technological complication?

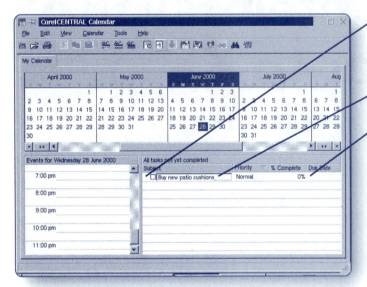

1. **Click** on the **line** at the top of the task list. The insertion point will appear on the line.

2. **Type** a **task** on the line.

3. **Double-click** the **task** anywhere on the line except in the Subject column. The Edit - Task dialog box will open.

> **TIP**
> Clicking on the Create a new task button on the main toolbar also starts the Edit - Task dialog box.

CREATING A TASK   333

4. Type a **category** for the task. The information will appear in the Category box.

5. Click the **mini-calendar button** next to the Start box if the task is to be started later. The mini-calendar will appear.

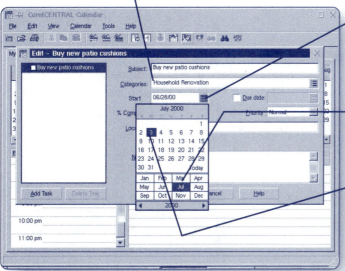

6. Click on the **month** of the date. The month shown on the mini-calendar will change.

7. Click on the **day** of the date. The mini-calendar will close and the new date will be displayed in the Start box.

8. Click on the **Due Date check box** if the task has a deadline. A check (√) will be placed in the check box and the Due Date box will be activated.

9. Click the **mini-calendar button** next to the Due Date box. The mini-calendar will appear.

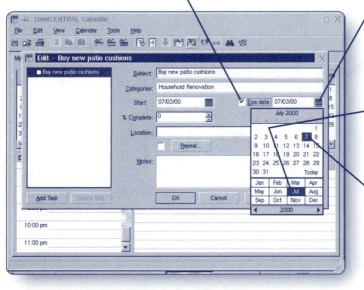

10. Click on the **month** of the date. The month shown on the mini-calendar will change.

11. Click on the **day** of the date. The mini-calendar will close and the new date will be displayed in the Due Date box.

12. **Click** on the **down arrow** (↓) next to the Priority box. The list of priority classifications will be displayed.

13. **Click** on **High**. The option will be selected.

14. **Click** on **OK**. The Edit - Task dialog box will close and the new task will appear in the task list.

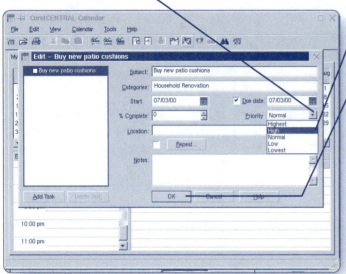

TIP

You can add additional tasks to the task list without leaving the Edit - Task dialog box. Simply click on the Add Task button to clear the boxes and start over again with a new task.

Completing a Task

When you finish a task, you need to mark it complete so it's off of your list of things to do.

1. **Click** on the **Complete check box** next to the completed task. A check (√) will be placed in the check box and the task will be marked as 100% complete.

2. **Double-click** on another **task**. The Edit - Task dialog box will appear.

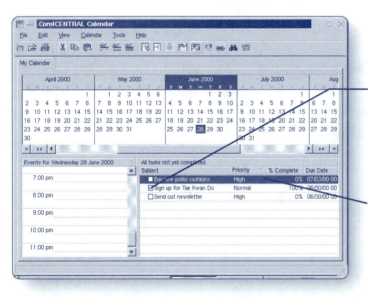

ASSIGNING A TASK TO AN EVENT 335

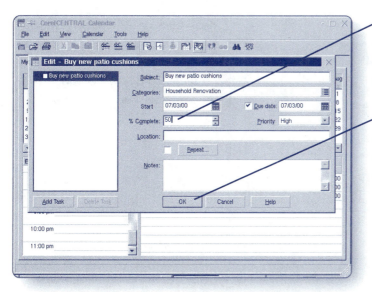

3. Type a **percentage of the task completed**. The information will appear in the % Complete box.

4. Click on **OK**. The Edit - Task dialog box will close and the updated task will appear in the task list.

Assigning a Task to an Event

Many times you have tasks that need to be done before, during, or after a specific event. CorelCENTRAL Calendar lets you create such tasks tied to individual events.

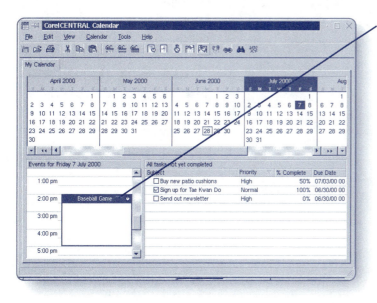

1. Double-click on an **event**. The Edit - Event dialog box will appear.

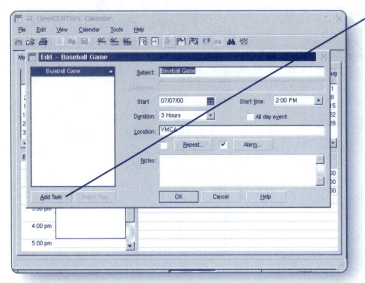

2. Click on **Add Task**. A new task will appear in the Event box, tied directly to the event, and the dialog box will change to an Edit - New Task dialog box.

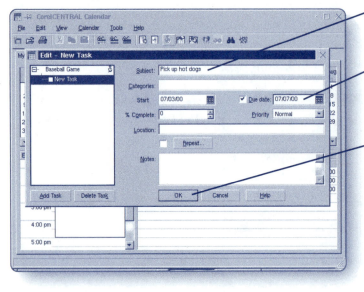

3. Type a **new subject** in the Subject box.

4. Type any **needed information** in the appropriate boxes.

5. Click on **OK**. The Edit - New Task dialog box will close and a task attachment icon will appear in the event.

DELETING A TASK 337

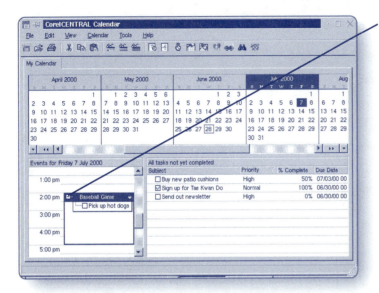

6. Click on the **task attachment icon** to view all of the tasks associated with an event. All of the tasks associated with the event will appear.

Deleting a Task

Even after a task is marked complete, it does not disappear from your task list. You need to follow active housekeeping procedures.

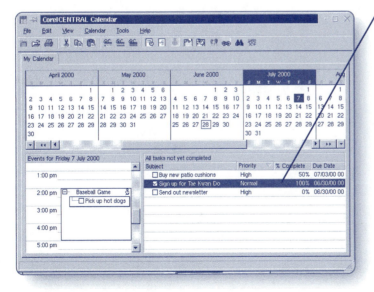

1. Click on the **task** you want to delete. The task will be selected.

2. Press the **Delete key**. The task will be removed.

25

Using CorelCENTRAL Memo to Keep Informed

There is an endangered species in the office place today, a form of communication that is quickly dying out. It is the memorandum, or memo, for short. This once-proud method of getting ideas across to other people has slowly, insidiously been replaced by the advent of the e-mail message and the sticky note.

Sadly, CorelCENTRAL Memo does not so much emulate the traditional memorandum as the sticky note, so don't look for any sudden revivals here. Still, sticky notes do have their uses, even when they are on your computer screen. In this chapter, you'll learn how to:

- Create memos in CorelCENTRAL Memo
- Organize memos

Creating a Memo

Making a memo is a simple process by anyone's standards. This makes a lot of sense, because a complicated process would detract from the whole point of the memo: something on which to jot down a thought or reminder quickly.

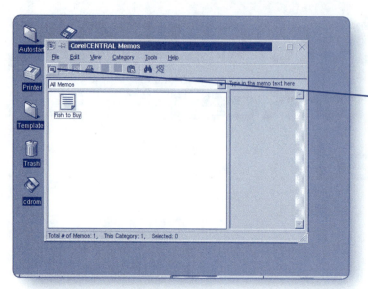

1. Click the **Create a memo button**. A new memo icon will appear in the memo window.

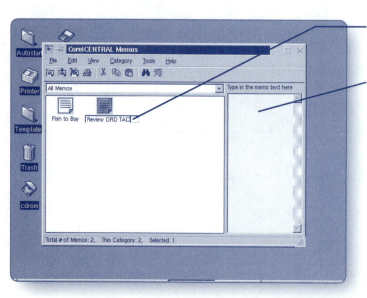

2. Type a **memo subject** at the subject placeholder.

3. Click in the **memo content** text box. The mouse pointer will appear in the text box.

ORGANIZING MEMOS 341

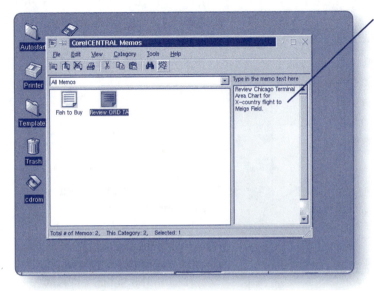

4. Type the **memo content** in the memo content text box. The memo will be completed.

Organizing Memos

As you can see, creating a memo is not a big deal. The nice thing about memos is that unlike real sticky notes that clutter up your appliances, doors, and computer screens, you can actually organize your memos into categories.

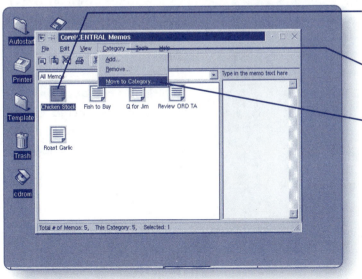

1. Click on a **memo**. The memo will be selected.

2. Click on **Category**. The Category menu will appear.

3. Click on **Move to category**. The Move to Category dialog box will appear.

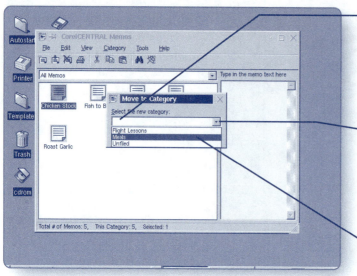

4a. **Type** a new **category**. The information will appear in the Select the new category box.

OR

4b. **Click** the **down arrow** (↓) next to the Select the new category box if a category exists for your memo. A drop-down list will appear.

5. Click on a **category**. The category will be selected and will appear in the Select the new category box.

6. Click on **OK**. The Move to Category dialog box will close and the memo text box will display all of the memos in the assigned category.

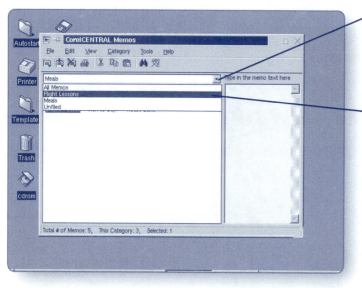

7. Click on the **down arrow** (↓) next to the category view box. A list of all assigned categories will appear.

8. Click on a **category**. The category will be selected and the memo window will display all of the memos in the assigned category.

26

Using CorelCENTRAL Address Book to Keep in Touch

The third component of the CorelCENTRAL application is the Address Book. It is here that you can compile and organize the contact information of all of your friends, colleagues, and associates into one easy-to-use interface. In this chapter, you'll learn how to:

- Add addresses to the Address Book
- Keep addresses updated
- Find addresses in your Address Book
- Create and manage multiple Address Books

Creating an Address

Made a new friend today? Picked up a new client off the corporate Web site? Then, you need to add her address information into the Address Book.

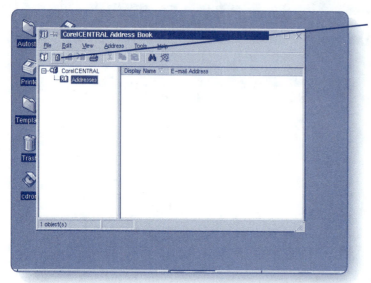

1. **Click** the **Create a new address entry button**. The New dialog box will appear.

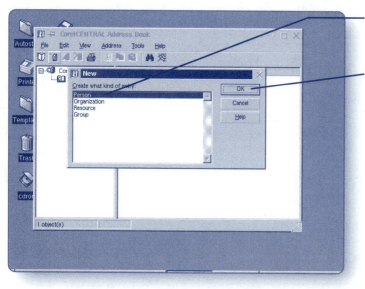

2. **Click** on **Person**. Person will be selected.

3. **Click** on **OK**. The New dialog box will close and the Person Properties dialog box will open.

CREATING AN ADDRESS 345

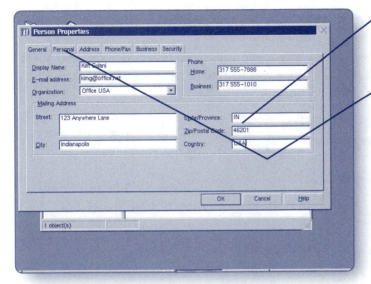

4. Type all **available information** in the appropriate boxes.

5. Click on the **Personal tab**. The Personal tab will come to the front.

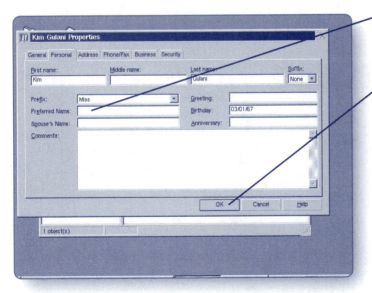

6. Type all **available information** in the appropriate boxes.

7. Click on **OK**. The Personal Properties dialog box will close and the entry will be added to the Address Book.

Editing Addresses

The average American moves three times in his life. And guess what? That means you need to edit the Address Book entries from time to time.

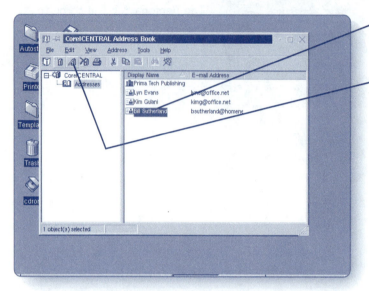

1. Click on an **address entry**. The entry will be selected.

2. Click the **Edit an address entry button**. The entry's Properties dialog box will appear.

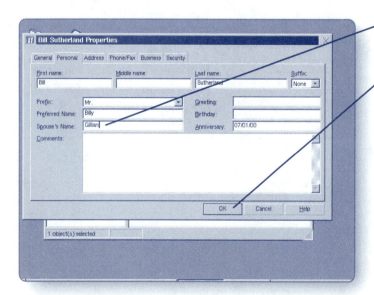

3. Type any **new or additional information** in the entry boxes.

4. Click on **OK**. The entry's Properties dialog box will close and the entry will be updated in the Address Book.

Importing Addresses

If you have just purchased WordPerfect Office 2000, you might not be very sanguine about retyping all of your old application's contact addresses into CorelCENTRAL Address Book. Here's a way to eliminate a lot of extra work on your part. All you need to do beforehand is export your legacy addresses into a text file, which many PIM applications can do with ease.

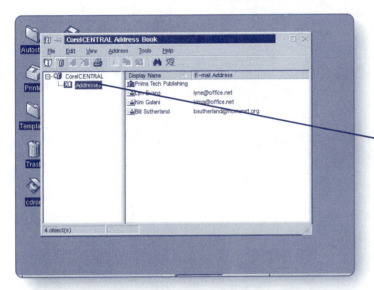

1. Click on an **Address Book**. The book will be selected.

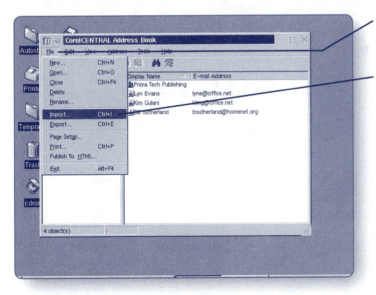

2. Click on **File**. The File menu will appear.

3. Click on **Import**. The Import dialog box will appear.

TIP
Pressing Ctrl+I will open the Import dialog box.

4. **Navigate** to the **appropriate file**. The file will be selected.

5. Click on **Open**. The Import dialog box will close and the ASCII Delimiter Setup dialog box will open.

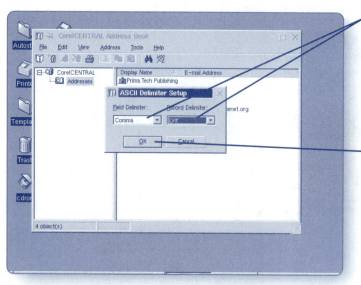

6. Confirm the **settings** for the field and record delimiters. Most ASCII versions of contact information use commas for field delimiters and line breaks for record delimiters.

7. Click on **OK**. The ASCII Delimiter Setup dialog box will close and the Field Mapping dialog box will open.

IMPORTING ADDRESSES 349

8. Click on a **line** in the Imported column. The line name will be selected.

9. Click on a **matching line** in the Address Book column. The matching line name will be selected.

10. Click on the **To Mapped button**. The relationship will appear in the Mapped column.

11. Repeat steps 8-10 until all necessary mappings are completed.

12. Click on **OK**. The addresses will be imported into the Address Book when the Imported Successfully! message appears.

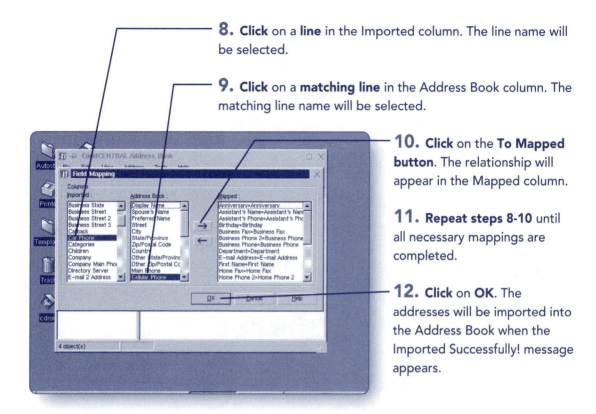

13. Click on **OK**. The process will be completed.

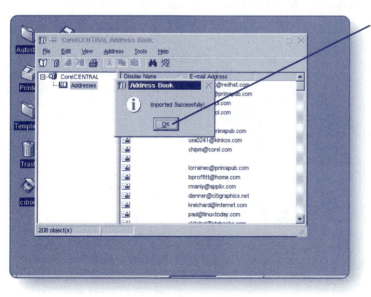

Searching for Addresses

When you have a lot of addresses in your Address Book, you need a way to quickly find them. Running a search in the Address Book is a piece of cake.

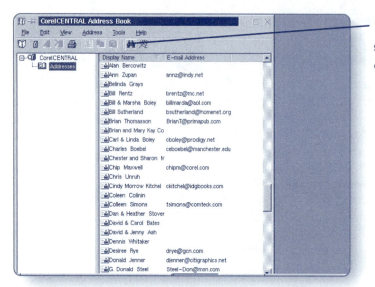

1. Click the **Search for specified text button**. The Find dialog box will appear.

2. Type in a **name** to find.

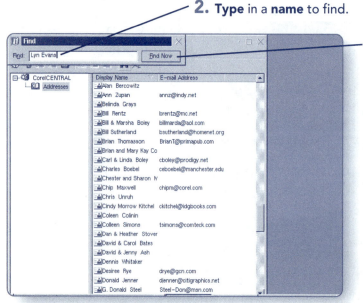

3. Click on **Find Now**. The Find dialog box will expand to list the address entry.

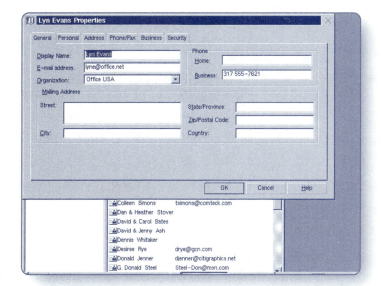

4. Double-click on the **entry**. The entry's Properties dialog box will appear for you to read or edit.

Creating New Address Books

After you have a number of entries in your Address Book, you might want to organize the entries by placing them in separate Address Books. To do this, you need to first create a new Address Book.

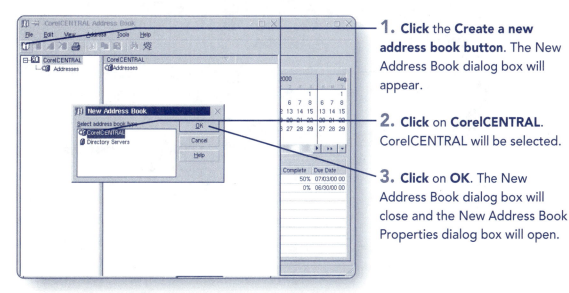

1. Click the **Create a new address book button**. The New Address Book dialog box will appear.

2. Click on **CorelCENTRAL**. CorelCENTRAL will be selected.

3. Click on **OK**. The New Address Book dialog box will close and the New Address Book Properties dialog box will open.

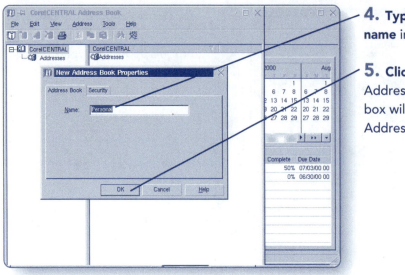

4. Type an **Address book name** into the Name box.

5. Click on **OK**. The New Address Book Properties dialog box will close and the new Address Book will appear.

Managing Address Books

After you have created a new Address Book, you can easily move entries into it for better organization.

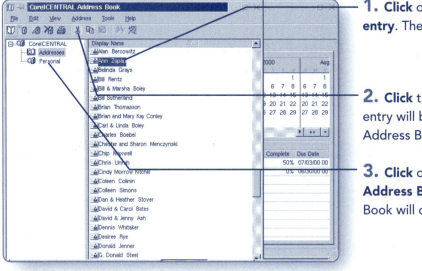

1. Click on an **Address Book entry**. The entry will be selected.

2. Click the **Cut button**. The entry will be cut from the Address Book.

3. Click on the **destination Address Book**. The Address Book will open.

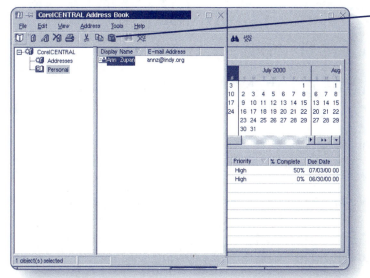

4. Click the **Paste button**. The entry will be placed into the Address Book.

Part VI Review Questions

1. What are the views in CorelCENTRAL Calendar? See *"Changing the Calendar's View"* in Chapter 23.

2. How do you set up an event? See *"Creating an Event"* in Chapter 23.

3. How do you create an all-day event? See *"Creating an Event"* in Chapter 23.

4. What is a recurring event? See *"Creating Recurring Events"* in Chapter 23.

5. How do you change an event's duration? See *"Moving to a Different Time"* in Chapter 23.

6. How do you change the date of an event? See *"Moving to a Different Date"* in Chapter 23.

7. Where can you create tasks? See *"Creating a Task"* in Chapter 24.

8. How do you indicate a partially completed task? See *"Completing a Task"* in Chapter 24.

9. How do you make a memo? See *"Creating a Memo"* in Chapter 25.

10. How do you find an address? See *"Searching for Addresses"* in Chapter 26.

PART VII

Appendixes

Appendix A
WordPerfect Office 2000 for
Linux Installation................357

Appendix B
Using Shortcut Keys................367

A

WordPerfect Office 2000 for Linux Installation

Before you can do any of the tasks outlined in this book, you will need to install the WordPerfect Office 2000 suite, among other things. In this appendix, you'll learn how to:

- Install WordPerfect Office 2000 for Linux
- Register the application
- Set up a printer to work with WordPerfect Office 2000

Installing the Software

After you buy a copy of WordPerfect Office 2000, it's time to start installing. As the root superuser, just insert Disc 1 into your mounted CD-ROM drive and follow the steps below.

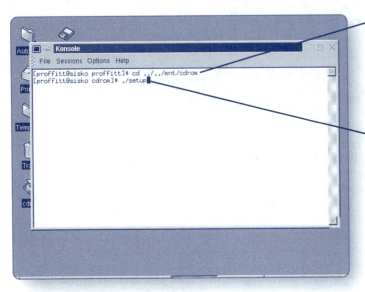

1. Type the **cd command** in a console window to navigate to the CD-ROM directories. The directory should be \mnt\cdrom on most Linux machines.

2. Type **./setup**. The WordPerfect Office 2000 setup wizard will start by opening the Corel WordPerfect Application Starter dialog box.

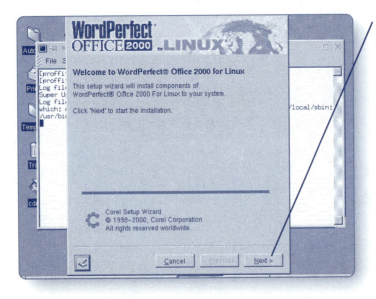

3. Click on **Next**. The License Agreement will appear.

INSTALLING THE SOFTWARE   359

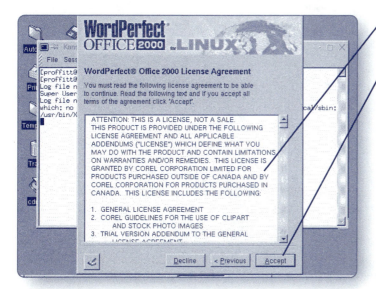

4. **Read** the **License Agreement**.

5. **Click** on **Accept**. The Setup Options will appear.

> **TIP**
>
> Unlike the Windows version, WordPerfect Office 2000 limits your choices for selecting installation options to either complete installation (with all of the applications) or minimal installation. It is recommended you install the complete option, to get the most value from the suite.

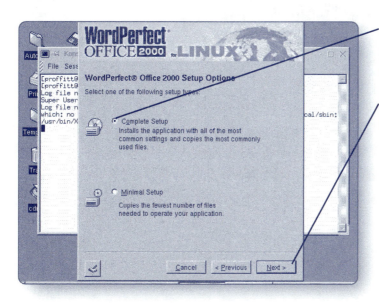

6. **Click** on the **Complete Setup option**. The option will be selected.

7. **Click** on **Next**. The Setup Review will appear.

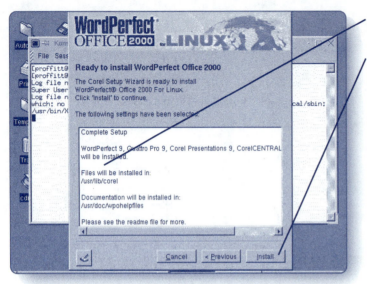

8. **Read** the **Setup Review**.

9. **Click** on **Install**. The installation will begin.

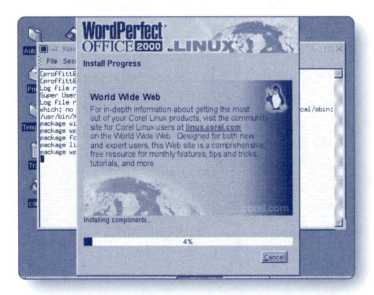

10. **Wait** for the **installation to complete**. The progress bar will mark the status of the installation. When finished, a message dialog box will appear.

REGISTERING THE SOFTWARE 361

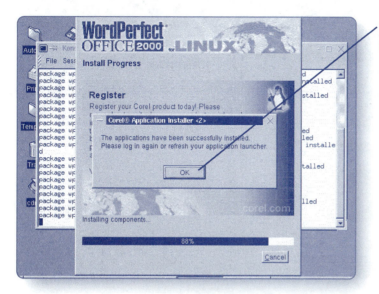

11. Click on **OK**. The installation will be complete.

Registering the Software

After the installation is complete, you should register the application. Follow these steps in any WordPerfect Office 2000 application to accomplish registration.

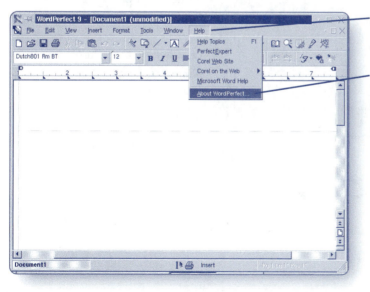

1. Click on **Help**. The Help menu will appear.

2. Click on **About WordPerfect**. The About WordPerfect 9 dialog box will appear.

APPENDIX A: WORDPERFECT OFFICE 2000 INSTALLATION

3. Click on **Edit Serial/PIN**. The Serial Number/PIN dialog box will appear.

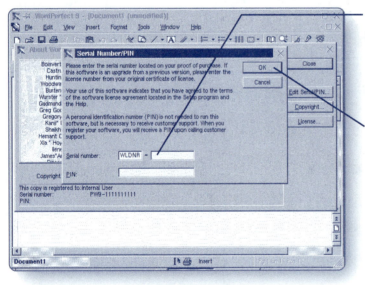

4. Type the **PIN Number** that came with your copy of WordPerfect Office 2000. The Serial Number will appear in the Serial Number box.

5. Click on **OK**. The Serial Number/PIN dialog box will close.

SETTING UP A PRINTER 363

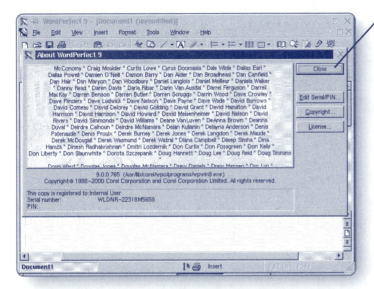

6. Click on **Close**. The About WordPerfect 9 dialog box will close.

Setting Up a Printer

After you have installed and registered WordPerfect Office 2000, the next thing you should do is get the printer talking to the office suite.

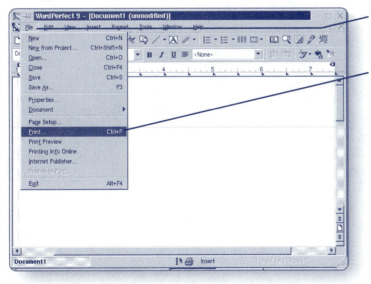

1. Click on **File**. The File menu will appear.

2. Click on **Print**. The Print to dialog box will appear.

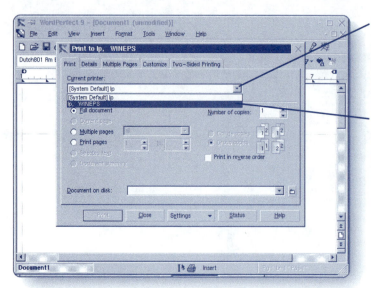

3. Click on the **down arrow (↓)** next to the Current Printer box. A drop-down list of available printers will appear.

4. Select a **printer**. The printer will be selected and will appear in the Current Printer box.

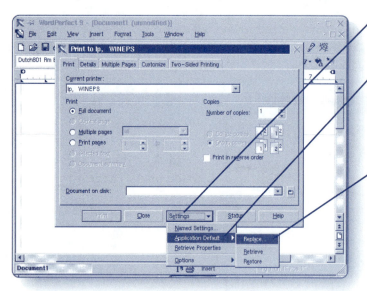

5. Click on **Settings**. The Settings menu will appear.

6. Move the **mouse pointer** to Application Default. The Application Default menu will appear.

7. Click on **Replace**. The Save as Default dialog box will appear.

SETTING UP A PRINTER   365

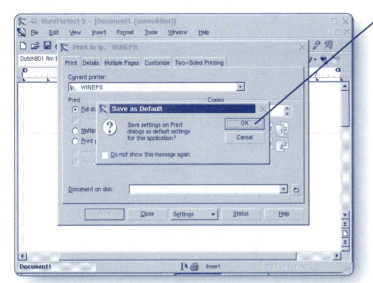

8. **Click** on **OK**. The Save as Default dialog box will close.

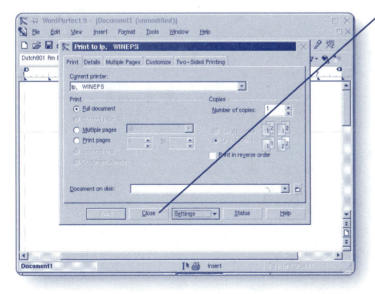

9. **Click** on **Close**. The Print to dialog box will close.

B
Using Shortcut Keys

In the WordPerfect Office 2000 suite, you can use many shortcut keys to start certain commands. I've mentioned quite a few of these combinations throughout this book, but they are also gathered here for your reference. In this appendix, you'll learn how to:

- Activate common WordPerfect Office 2000 tools with shortcut keys
- Activate specialized tools with shortcut keys

Using Common WordPerfect Office 2000 Shortcut Keys

Throughout WordPerfect Office 2000, some key combinations do the same thing in more than one application.

Applications	Shortcut Keys	Task
WP, QP, PR, CC, PX	F1	Help
WP, QP, PR	F3	Save file under new name
WP, PR	F7	Indent paragraph
WP, PR	F9	Format fonts
WP, PR	Alt+F1	Thesaurus
WP, PR	Alt+F3	Reveal codes
WP, QP, PR, CC	Alt+F4	Exit application
WP, PR	Alt+F7	Format line flush right
WP, QP	Alt+F9	Sort text
WP, PR	Alt+F10	Play macro
WP, QP	Alt+F12	Application settings
WP, PR	Alt+Shift+F1	Grammatik
WP, PR	Alt+Shift+F3	View ruler
WP, PR, CC	Ctrl+A	Select all text
WP, QP, PR, CC, PX	Ctrl+C	Copy selected text
WP, PR	Ctrl+E	Center paragraph
WP, QP, PR	Ctrl+F	Find and Replace
WP, QP, PR	Ctrl+G	Go To
WP, PR	Ctrl+L	Left align paragraph
WP, QP, PR, CC	Ctrl+N	Open new file
WP, QP, PR, CC	Ctrl+O	Open existing file
WP, QP, PR, CC, PX	Ctrl+P	Print open file
WP, PR	Ctrl+R	Right align paragraph
WP, QP, PR	Ctrl+S	Save open file
WP, QP, PR, CC, PX	Ctrl+V	Paste cut or copied text

USING COMMON SHORTCUT KEYS

Applications	Shortcut Keys	Task
WP, QP, PR	Ctrl+W	Insert symbol
WP, QP, PR, CC, PX	Ctrl+X	Cut selected text
WP, QP, PR	Ctrl+Z	Undo last action
WP, QP, PR	Ctrl+F1	Spell Checker
WP, QP, PR, CC	Ctrl+F4	Close file
WP, PR	Ctrl+F7	Hanging indent paragraph
WP, PR	Ctrl+F10	Record macro
WP, QP, PR	Ctrl+Shift+N	Open PerfectExpert
WP, QP	Ctrl+Shift+Z	Redo last action undone
WP, PR	Ctrl+Shift+F1	QuickCorrect
WP, PR	Ctrl+Shift+F7	Double indent paragraph
WP, PR	Ctrl+Shift+F10	Stop macro
WP, PR	Shift+F7	Format line center
WP, PR	Shift+F10	Pause macro
WP, QP, PR	Shift+Tab	Back tab

Using WordPerfect Shortcut Keys

WordPerfect contains several key combinations to make document creation faster and easier.

Shortcut Keys	Task
F12	Insert table
Alt+F5	Page view
Alt+F8	Format styles
Alt+Shift+F5	Hide bars
Ctrl+J	Justify paragraph
Ctrl+F5	Draft view
Ctrl+F8	Format margins
Ctrl+F11	Insert horizontal line
Ctrl+Enter	Insert new page
Ctrl+Shift+C	Drop cap paragraph
Ctrl+Shift+F3	Show nonprinting characters
Ctrl+Shift+F11	Insert vertical line
Shift+F9	Merge documents
Shift+F11	Edit graphic box

Using Quattro Pro Shortcut Keys

Quattro Pro contains many key combinations to make spreadsheet management faster and easier.

Shortcut Keys	Task
F12	Format selected cells
Alt+F2	Play macros
Alt+F8	Show outline
Ctrl+D	Insert date
Ctrl+F3	Insert named cells
Ctrl+F8	Ungroup cells
Ctrl+F9	Collapse grouped cells
Ctrl+F12	Format sheet
Ctrl+Shift+F	SpeedFormat
Ctrl+Shift+L	QuickFill
Ctrl+Shift+S	Format styles
Shift+F2	Macro debugger
Shift+F8	Group cells
Shift+F9	Expand grouped cells
Shift+F12	Format notebook

Using Presentations Shortcut Keys

With shortcut keys, you can create slide shows a lot more efficiently.

Shortcut Keys	Task
F6	Move object forward one layer
Alt+F8	Snap objects to grid
Alt+Shift+F8	Display gridlines
Ctrl+F8	Page setup
Ctrl+Shift+A	Apply object attributes
Ctrl+Shift+G	Get object attributes
Ctrl+Shift+R	Redo last action undone
Shift+F6	Move object back one layer

Using CorelCENTRAL Shortcut Keys

CorelCENTRAL does not have many unique shortcut keys, but the ones it does have are pretty useful.

Shortcut Keys	Task
Ctrl+E	Export addresses
Ctrl+F	Find item
Ctrl+I	Import addresses

Using Paradox Shortcut Keys

Paradox uses highly specialized shortcut keys to accomplish its functions.

Shortcut Keys	Task
F2	Field view
F5	Lock record
F7	QuickForm
F9	Edit data
F11	Go to previous record
F12	Go to next record
Ins	Insert record
Alt+Backspace	Undo last action
Ctrl+A	Locate next record
Ctrl+G	Format grid
Ctrl+H	Format heading
Ctrl+M	Format data
Ctrl+F2	Persistent field view
Ctrl+F5	Post record and keep locked
Ctrl+F7	QuickChart
Ctrl+F11	Go to first record
Ctrl+F12	Go to last record
Ctrl+Del	Delete record
Ctrl+Space	Lookup help
Ctrl+Shift+Space	Move help
Shift+F2	Memo view
Shift+F7	QuickReport
Shift+F11	Go to previous set
Shift+F12	Go to next set

Glossary

Absolute reference. A reference to a cell that does not change when copying or moving the referencing cell.

Active cell. The selected cell in a worksheet.

Address. An entry that appears in the CorelCENTRAL Address Book.

Alignment. The position of text in a document.

Application Starter. A KDE Windows tool that enables users to start applications and open files.

Attributes. The appearance of text such as bold, underlined, italic, or point size.

Bar chart. A type of chart that uses bars to represent values. Normally used to compare items.

Border. A line surrounding paragraphs, pages, table cells, or objects.

Browser. A feature application of most Linux platforms that allows users to view Web pages on the Internet and online Help files in WordPerfect Office 2000.

Button. A graphic representation used on toolbars and sometimes in dialog boxes to represent a function performed when the icon is clicked with a mouse.

Cell. The area defined by a rectangle at which a row and column intersect in a Quattro Pro worksheet.

Chart. A graphic representation of numerical data.

Click. Using the mouse to pick a menu item or option in a dialog box, as well as any other on-screen object, including document text.

Click and drag. A method of moving text or objects by clicking on an object with the mouse, dragging it to a new location, and releasing the mouse button to drop it into its new location.

Clipboard. An area of computer memory where you can temporarily store text or graphics.

Close button. Used to shut down or exit a dialog box, window, or application.

GLOSSARY

Column. A set of cells running vertically on a worksheet. Also, vertical divisions of text on a page.

Complex formula. A formula in a Quattro Pro spreadsheet that has multiple operators.

Coordinates. An alphanumeric reference to a cell.

Copy. To take a selection from the document and duplicate it on the Clipboard.

Cut. To take a selection from the document and move it to the Clipboard.

Data. Information that can be either numerical or textual.

Data area. The portion of a worksheet that is designated to print.

Data type. The category of numerical or textual data.

Database. A file composed of records, each containing fields together with a set of operations for searching or sorting.

Default. A setting or action predetermined by the program unless changed by the user.

Dialog box. A box that displays warnings or messages, or requests information from the user.

Document. Any file created in WordPerfect Office 2000.

E-mail. Messages sent electronically across a network, typically the Internet.

Endnote. Reference information that prints on the last page of a document.

Event. An entry in the CorelCENTRAL Calendar that spans less than one day to which no other individuals are invited.

Field. A piece of information used in a database. In a form letter, a field is a placeholder for corresponding data.

File. Information stored on a disk under a single name.

Filter. A setting to ensure that only cells meeting certain criteria are displayed in the worksheet.

Find. A feature used to locate characters in a WordPerfect Office 2000 document.

Font. A design set of letters, symbols, and numbers, also called a typeface.

Footer. Text repeated at the bottom of each page of a document or spreadsheet.

Footnote. Reference information that prints at the bottom of the page.

Form. A database window with spaces reserved for fields in which the user can enter data.

Format. To change the appearance of text or objects with features such as the font, style, color, borders, and size.

Formula. An equation that instructs Quattro Pro to perform certain calculations based on numerical data in designated cells.

Formula bar. The Quattro Pro toolbar control where all data and formulas are entered for a selected cell.

Function. A series of predefined formulas used in spreadsheets. Functions perform specialized calculations automatically.

Graph. A visual representation of numerical data. Also called a chart.

Gridlines. The lines dividing rows and columns in a table or worksheet.

Handles. Small squares that appear when you select an object and allow for its resizing or movement.

Header. Text entered in an area of the document for display at the top of each page of the document.

HTML. The language used to create documents for publication on the Web.

Hyperlink. A created element that consists of an address to a location, such as a folder on a computer or a Web page.

Indent. To place text inside the margin by a specific distance.

Justify. A type of alignment that spreads letters or words on a line or in a cell evenly between the left and right margin or across selected cells.

KDE. A graphical interface designed to be used in Linux systems.

Key combinations. A saved set of keystrokes that you can use to perform an action in lieu of a set of lengthier menu commands.

Landscape. A page orientation that prints a document with the long edge of the paper across the top.

Legend. In a chart, a box containing symbols and text that explains what each data series represents. Each symbol is a color pattern or marker that corresponds to one data series in the chart.

Line spacing. The amount of space between lines of text.

Line style. Effects using width, arrows, and dashes that can be applied to a line.

Linux. A UNIX-like operating system that gives users extensive control over all aspects of their work. Although it's a command-line-only operating system, several graphical interfaces can be used "over" the Linux operating system to make it more user-friendly.

Mail merge. A procedure that uses a form document, inserts placeholders for types of data, and merges that document with specific data to produce personalized letters, faxes, or e-mail messages.

Mathematical functions. Functions that produce mathematical results, such as SUM and PRODUCT.

Meeting. An entry in the CorelCENTRAL Calendar that spans less than one day to which others are invited.

Notebook. A single Quattro Pro file containing a collection of sheets.

Notes. Additional text displayed alongside a printed Presentations slide to prompt the presenter.

Object. A picture, chart, or other graphic element that you can place in a WordPerfect Office 2000 document.

Open. To start an application, to insert a document into a new document window, or to access a dialog box.

Operator. The parts of a formula that indicate an action to be performed, such as addition (+) or division (/).

Orientation. The way a document prints on a piece of paper; landscape prints with the longer side of a page on top, whereas portrait prints with the shorter edge at the top.

Outline. A hierarchy of lines of text that suggests major and minor ideas. Used extensively in Presentations.

Page break. A command that tells the application where to begin a new page.

Page setup. Settings that determine how the pages of the document are set up, including margins, orientation, and the size of paper on which each page prints.

Page View. A feature that lets you view a document onscreen as it will appear when printed.

Paste. To place text or an object previously placed on the Clipboard (through cutting or copying) into a WordPerfect Office 2000 document.

Portrait. A page orientation where a document prints with the short edge of the paper along the top.

Properties. The characteristics of text, objects, or devices. Text properties might include font or size.

Queries. Used in a Paradox database, a subset of data that meets certain criteria.

QuickCorrect. A feature of WordPerfect that automatically corrects common spelling mistakes.

QuickFill. A function that allows Quattro Pro to automatically complete a series of numbers or words by filling in cell data.

QuickFormat. AutoFormat enables the user to apply defined formatting settings to document.

QuickTips. A help feature that displays the name of a tool in a small box when you place the pointer over the tool.

Range. A collection of cells, ranging from the first-named cell to the last.

Redo. A feature that allows the restoration of an action that you reversed using the Undo feature.

Reference. In a formula, a name or range that refers the formula to a cell or set of cells.

Relative reference. A reference to a cell relative to the location of the cell where the reference is located.

Replace. A WordPerfect Office 2000 feature that locates text and replaces it with different text.

Row. A set of cells running from left to right across a worksheet.

Save. To take a document residing in the memory of the computer and create a file to be stored on a disk.

Scroll bars. The bars at the right side and bottom of a window that allow vertical and horizontal movements through a document.

Sheet. One of several pages in a Quattro Pro workbook.

Simple formula. A formula in a Quattro Pro spreadsheet that has only one operator.

Slide. An element in a Presentations document equivalent to a page.

Slide Sorter. A view in Presentations that lets you view all slides together in one screen.

Sort. To arrange data alphanumerically in either ascending (A-Z) or descending (Z-A) order.

Spell-As-You-Go. A feature that checks the spelling in a document against a dictionary and flags possible errors for correction.

Status bar. An area at the bottom of WordPerfect Office 2000 applications that shows information about the document.

Tab. A setting that you can place along the width of a line of text that enables the pointer to quickly jump to that setting.

Table. A collection of columns and rows, forming cells at their intersections, to organize sets of data.

Template. A collection of format settings that constitute a document type.

Text box. A floating object containing text that you can create with the drawing feature of WordPerfect Office 2000 programs to place text anywhere in a document.

Toolbars. Appear in the document window to access many of the commonly used features of the WordPerfect Office 2000 applications.

Transitions. In Presentations, elements added to a slide that determine the appearance of switching from slide to slide.

Undo. A feature that allows you to reverse the last action performed. You can undo multiple actions by repeatedly using this feature.

Web page. A document that appears on the World Wide Web. Also called a Web document.

World Wide Web. A series of HTML documents viewed on the Internet.

Zoom. To enlarge or reduce the way the text displays onscreen. It does not affect how the document prints.

Index

( ) (parenthesis), 161
+ (plus sign), 29
; (semicolon), 256

A

About WordPerfect 9 dialog box, 361–363
absolute addresses, 165
absolute reference, 375
Accept button, 143
Action Shapes tool, 310
Active Cells dialog box, 170–172, 179
Add Project Wizard, 15–17
Address Book. *See* CorelCENTRAL Address Book
addresses
   creating, 344–345
   defined, 375
   editing, 346
   importing, 347–349
   searching for, 350–351
alarms, calendar, 322
alignment
   cell contents, 175–176
   document text, 61–62
Alignment button, 175–176
application control icon, 7
Application Default menu, 364

Application Starter, 4, 375
applications. *See also* tools
   CorelCENTRAL, 315–354, 372
   exiting, 7–8
   Paradox, 217–257, 373
   Presentations, 259–313, 372
   Quattro Pro, 133–216, 371
   starting, 6
   WordPerfect, 37–131, 370
artwork. *See* graphics
ASCII Delimiter Setup dialog box, 348
attributes, 375
Audience Notes option, 284

B

Background Fill Color palette, 305
backgrounds
   fill color, 305
   Web pages, 250
Backspace key, 116
bar chart, 375
Basic Shapes palette, 301, 305
Bitmap Editor, 299, 311–312
Blanks filter, 194
bold text, 50–51
Border Type palette, 179
borders

cells, 178–180
   defined, 375
   graphics, 102
browsers, 28, 30, 375
bulleted lists
   documents, 59–60
   slides, 272
Bullets button, 59
buttons, 375. *See also specific buttons*

C

calendar. *See* CorelCENTRAL Calendar
capitalization, 52
ccaddressbook command, 6
cccalendar command, 6
ccmemo command, 6
cd command, 358
CD-ROM directories, 358
cells. *See also* spreadsheets
   addresses for, 140, 144–145
   aligning contents of, 175–176
   autofill features, 190–192
   borders for, 178–180
   changing size of, 173–174
   coordinates, 140
   copying, 155–156
   described, 136, 375
   editing contents of, 142–143
   entering data in, 138–140, 190–192
   fonts in, 176–178
   formatting, 172–173, 176–180
   moving, 157–158
   numeric data in, 139
   pasting, 155–156
   replacing contents, 141
   selecting, 138, 148–150
   sorting data in, 198–199
   text in, 138
Center button, 62

Chart Expert, 204–207
Chart Series dialog box, 213–215
Chart Type palette, 212
charts
   bar charts, 375
   defined, 375
   slide shows, 289–293
   spreadsheets, 203–215
circles, creating, 306
Clear All Tabs command, 66
click, 375
click and drag, 375
clipboard, 56, 375
Close button, 7–8, 375
Close command, 25
closing documents, 25
color
   charts, 207, 291
   fills, 305
   fonts, 288–289
   lines, 303
   tables, 288–289
   Web pages, 249
Color palette, 180
Column menu, 95–96
columns
   defined, 376
   documents, 95–97
   multi-column text boxes, 108–109
   spreadsheets, 136, 150, 152–154, 173–174
Columns button, 95, 96
Columns dialog box, 96–97, 108–109
command line, starting WordPerfect from, 5–6
commands. *See also specific commands*
   shortcuts for, 367–373
   for starting WordPerfect applications, 6
Console icon, 5
contents, table of, 124–127
Convert Case menu, 52
coordinates, 376

INDEX

copying
    cells, 155–156
    defined, 376
    text, 56–57
CorelCENTRAL Address Book, 6, 343–353
    adding addresses to, 344–345
    creating new address books, 351–352
    cutting/pasting addresses, 352–353
    editing addresses, 346
    importing addresses into, 347–349
    managing address books, 352–353
    searching for addresses, 350–351
CorelCENTRAL applications, 315–354, 372
CorelCENTRAL Calendar, 6, 317–337
    alarms, 322
    assigning tasks to events, 335–337
    changing calendar view, 319–320
    completing tasks, 334–335
    creating events, 320–326
    creating tasks, 332–334
    deleting events, 329
    deleting tasks, 337
    editing events, 326–329
    viewing, 318
CorelCENTRAL Memo, 6, 340–342
Create button, 11, 13, 17
Create Table dialog box, 84–85, 87–88
Create Table tool, 84–85
curve pointer, 309
curves, drawing in slides, 307–309
Custom filter, 194, 195–197
Custom QuickFilter dialog box, 196–197
cutting, 376

D

data area, 376
Data Chart Gallery, 286–287, 289–290
data, Paradox
    exporting, 256
    importing, 253–255
    publishing to Web pages, 249–251
    using in spreadsheets, 252
data, Quattro Pro
    aligning, 175–176
    charting, 203–215
    editing, 141–143
    entering, 138–140, 190–192
    filtering, 193–197
    formatting, 169–180
    grouping, 200–201
    manipulating, 189–201
    moving, 155–158
    selecting, 148–150
    sorting, 198–199
Data Sort dialog box, 198–199
data type, 376
databases
    concepts, 220–221
    creating, 222–242
    creating mailing labels, 244–248
    defined, 376
    records in, 220
    using data in spreadsheets, 252
dates
    changing for events, 328–329
    in documents, 118–119
Date/Time dialog box, 118–119
Day view, 319
Define Index dialog box, 129
Define Table of Contents dialog box, 125–126
Delete key, 41
Delete Structure/Content dialog box, 90–91
deleting
    calendar events, 329
    charts, 215
    columns, 153–154
    page breaks, 116
    rows, 153–154
    slides, 273–274

tasks, 337
text boxes in slides, 279
text in documents, 41
desktop environment, 4
dialog boxes
　About WordPerfect 9, 361–363
　Active Cells, 170–172, 179
　ASCII Delimiter Setup, 348
　Chart Series, 213–215
　Columns, 96–97, 108–109
　Create Table, 84–85, 87–88
　Custom QuickFilter, 196–197
　Data Sort, 198–199
　Date/Time, 118–119
　Define Index, 129
　Define Table of Contents, 125–126
　defined, 376
　Delete Structure/Content, 90–91
　Endnote Placement, 122–123
　Export Data, 256
　Field Mapping, 348–349
　Footnote/Endnote, 121, 122
　Functions, 166–167
　Generate, 126–127, 130
　Headers/Footers, 117
　Image Settings, 103–104
　Image Tools, 103, 104
　Import, 347–348
　Import Data, 109–110, 253–255
　Insert Columns/Rows, 89–90
　Insert Image, 100–101
　Line Spacing, 62–63
　Master Gallery, 280–281
　New Table, 223
　Open File, 18–19
　Page Setup, 112, 113, 114
　PerfectExpert, 11
　Person Properties, 344–345
　Print to, 363–365
　Properties for Table Format, 92–93
Repeat Event, 324–325
Save As, 23
Select Page Numbering Format, 119–120
Serial Number/PIN, 362
Series Properties, 290–293
Set Alarm, 322
Slide Properties, 294, 295–296
Spreadsheet Page Setup, 182–185
Startup Master Gallery, 262–263
Symbols, 53
Table Expert, 223–227
Table SpeedFormat, 94–95
dictionaries, adding words to, 77
Display button, 31
document window, 7
documents. *See also* pages; text
　closing, 25
　columns, 95–97, 376
　copying text in, 56–57
　correcting mistakes in, 41–42
　creating new, 10–17
　defined, 376
　deleting text in, 41
　editing text in, 38–41
　endnotes, 121–124, 376
　footers, 117–120, 376
　footnotes, 121–124, 376
　formatting, 47–69
　headers, 117–120, 377
　importing material from, 109–110
　indexes, 127–130
　inserting date/time, 118–119
　inserting graphics in, 100–101
　inserting text in, 38–39
　lists, 59–60
　Make It Fit feature, 106
　managing long documents, 111–131
　margins, 61–65, 112
　moving text in, 54–56, 58
　navigating within, 43–46

opening, 18–22
page breaks, 115–116, 378
page numbers, 119–120
printing, 24–25
resaving, 24
saving, 22–24, 379
selecting text in, 40
table of contents, 124–127
tables, 84–95, 379
working with, 9–25
drag-and-drop feature
   spreadsheets, 157–158, 209–211
   tables, 87–89
drawing tools, 297–312. *See also* graphics
   Bitmap Editor, 311–312
   creating action shapes, 310
   creating lines/curves, 307–309
   creating shapes, 300–307
   exploring, 298–299

E

Edit menu, WordPerfect, 72, 74
editing
   addresses, 346
   calendar events, 326–329
   cell contents, 142–143
   charts, 209–214
   document text, 38–41
   graphics, 102–104
   slide shows, 267, 271–284
   slides, 277
   spreadsheets, 147–158
   tasks, 334–337
Ellipse mouse pointer, 305–306
e-mail, 376
Endnote Placement dialog box, 122–123
endnotes, 121–124, 376
Enter key, 38
Event calendar, 318, 320
events, calendar
   assigning tasks to, 335–337
   creating, 320–323
   defined, 376
   deleting, 329
   editing, 326–329
   moving to different date, 328–329
   moving to different time, 323, 326–328
   recurring, 323–326
Excel, 180, 253, 254
Exit command, 7
exiting applications, 7–8
exiting PerfectExpert, 33
expansion controls, 29
experts. *See also* PerfectExpert
   Chart Expert, 204–207
   Form Expert, 229–232
   HTML Report Expert, 250–251
   Mailing Label Expert, 244–248
   Query Expert, 233–237
   Report Expert, 238–242
   Table Expert, 222–228
Export Data dialog box, 256
exporting data, 256

F

Field Mapping dialog box, 348–349
fields, 224–231, 376
File menu, 7, 10
files, 9–25, 376. *See also* documents; slides; spreadsheets
Fill Pattern palette, 301, 304–305
filled shapes, 304–307
fills, 305
filters, spreadsheet data, 193–197, 376
Find and Replace tool, 72–75
Find button, online help, 30
find function
   address books, 350–351
   documents, 72–73
   online help, 30–31

terms, 72–73
text, 72–73, 376
Font Face box, 48
fonts
   changing, 48
   changing color, 288–289
   changing size, 49
   defined, 376
   in mailing labels, 246
   in slides, 278, 288–289
   in spreadsheets, 176–178
   using QuickFont, 49
footers, document, 117–120, 376
Footnote/Endnote dialog box, 121, 122
footnotes, 121–124, 376
Foreground Fill Color palette, 304
Form Expert, 229–232
format, 376
Format menu, 62, 64
Format tool, 92–93
formatting
   cells, 172–173, 176–180
   charts, 212
   columns, Quattro Pro, 173–174
   columns, WordPerfect, 96–97
   documents, 47–69
   notebooks, 169–180
   numeric data, 170–173
   tables, 92–95
forms, 220, 229–232, 376
formula bar, 376
formulas, 160–165, 376, 379
Full document option, 25
Function Composer, 166
functions, 166–167, 377
Functions dialog box, 166–167

G

Generate dialog box, 126–127, 130
glossary, 375–379

grammar checking, 78–79
Grammar-As-You-Go, 78–79
graphics
   borders for, 102
   creating shapes, 300–307, 310
   drawing tools, 297–312
   editing, 102–104
   inserting in documents, 100–101
   rotating objects, 306–307
   sizing objects, 104
   wrapping text around, 105
graphs, 377
gridlines, 377

H

handles, 377
headers, document, 117–120, 377
Headers/Footers dialog box, 117
help, 27–33
   About WordPerfect, 361–363
   PerfectExpert, 31–33
   searching for answers in, 30–31
   starting online help, 28–30
Help menu, 28
Help Topics, 28
home directory, 101
home page mouse pointer, 310
horizontal scroll bar, 7, 137
How To button, 29
HTML, 249–251, 377
HTML Report Expert, 250–251
hyperlinks, 127, 130, 377

I

Image Settings dialog box, 103–104
Image Tools dialog box, 103, 104
images. *See* graphics
Import Data dialog box, 109–110, 253–255
Import dialog box, 347–348

INDEX 387

importing items
    addresses, 347–349
    material from documents, 109–110
    Paradox data, 253–255
Indent command, 64
indents, 63–65, 377
Index toolbar, 127–130
indexes, 127–130
input line, 136
Insert Columns/Rows dialog box, 89–90
Insert Image dialog box, 100–101
Insert menu, 53
installing WordPerfect Office 2000, 357–365
Internet. *See* Web
italicized text, 50–51

J

Justification button, 61
justify, 377

K

KDE (K Desktop Environment), 4, 377
key combinations, 377
keyboard, navigating with, 46
keyboard shortcuts. *See* shortcut keys
keywords, 30

L

labels, mailing, 244–248
landscape orientation, 113, 183, 184, 377
legend, 377
License Agreement, 5, 358–359
Line Color palette, 303
Line menu, 62
Line Shapes palette, 307, 309
Line Spacing dialog box, 62–63
Line Style palette, 308
lines
    color of, 303
    dashed, 308
    drawing in slides, 307–309
    freeform, 309
    spacing of, 62–63, 377
    style of, 377
    width of, 302
Linux, 5, 377
lists
    bulleted, documents, 59–60
    bulleted, slides, 272
    numbered, documents, 59–60

M

mail merge, 377
Mailing Label expert, 244–248
mailing labels, 244–248
Make It Fit feature, 106
margins
    documents, 61–65, 112
    spreadsheets, 182–183
Margins/Layout tab, 112
Master Gallery dialog box, 280–281
mathematical functions, 377
meeting entry, 377
memos, 340–342
menu bar, 7
Microsoft Excel, 180, 253, 254
mini-calendar, 333
Month view, 320
mouse pointer, 39, 40, 43–44

N

navigation
    documents, 43–46
    with keyboard, 46
    with scroll bars, 45–46
    with Shadow Cursor, 43–44
    slides, 265–266
    spreadsheets, 137, 143

navigation calendar, 318
New command, 10
New From Project command, 11
New Table dialog box, 223
Next Page browse control, 46
Next Page control, 29
Non Blanks filter, 194
notebooks, 169–180, 377
notes, Presentations, 282–284, 377
numbered lists, 59–60
Numbering button, 60
numbers
    in cells, 139
    decimal points, 170–171
    formatting numeric data, 170–173
    page numbering, 119–120
Numeric Format tab, 171, 172

O

objects. *See also* graphics
    defined, 378
    rotating, 306–307
    sizing, 104
    text wrap feature, 105
Office 2000. *See* WordPerfect Office 2000
online help. *See* help
Open button, 18, 19, 20
Open File dialog box, 18–19
operators, 160, 378
orientation, 378
outlines, 200–201, 378

P

Page Setup dialog box, 112, 113, 114
Page Setup settings, 112, 113, 114, 378
page view, 378
pages. *See also* documents; Web pages
    arranging text on, 61–65
    Make It Fit feature, 106
    margins, 61–65, 112
    numbering, 119–120
    orientation, 113, 183–184, 378
    page breaks, 115–116, 378
    size of, 114, 183–184
pane splitter, 136
paper orientation, 113, 378
paper size, 114
Paper Type tab, Quattro Pro, 184
Paradox, 217–257
    basics of, 219–242
    creating mailing labels, 244–248
    database concepts, 220–221
    database creation, 222–228
    environment, 222
    exporting data, 256
    forms, 220, 229–232
    importing data, 253–255
    publishing data to Web pages, 249–251
    queries, 221, 233–237
    records, 220
    reports, 221, 238–242
    shortcut keys, 373
    starting, 6
    tables, 220, 222–228
    using data in spreadsheets, 252
paradox command, 6
Paragraph menu, 64, 65
paragraphs
    indenting, 63–65
    line spacing of, 62–63
    selecting, 40
    text wrap and, 38
parenthesis ( ), 161
partitions, 234
pasting
    cells, 155–156
    defined, 378
    text, 54, 56, 57
PerfectExpert dialog box, 11

INDEX

PerfectExpert tool. *See also* experts
   creating shapes, 300–303
   creating slide shows, 264
   opening installed templates, 10–12
   opening online templates, 12–17
   starting, 31
   stopping, 33
   using, 31–33
Person Properties dialog box, 344–345
PIN Number, 362
plus sign (+), 29
portrait orientation, 113, 183, 378
Position list, 120, 129
Presentations, 259–313. *See also* slide shows; slides
   basics of, 261–270
   creating slide shows, 264
   printing in, 283–284
   QuickPlay feature, 269–270
   shortcut keys, 372
   Slide Editor. *See* Slide Editor
   Slide Outliner, 267, 274–275, 277
   Slide Sorter, 268–269, 273–274
   special effects, 285–296
   starting, 6, 262–263
   switching views, 265–270
presentations command, 6
Previous Page browse control, 46
Print button, 24, 25, 188
Print Margins tab, Quattro Pro, 183
Print Preview, Quattro Pro, 186–187
Print Scaling tab, Quattro Pro, 185
Print to dialog box, 363–365
printers, setting up, 363–365
printing
   audience notes, 284
   documents, 24–25
   slide shows, 283
   speaker notes, 284
   spreadsheets, 182–188

Project Viewer, 222
Prompt-As-You-Go, 82
properties, 378
Properties for Table Format dialog box, 92–93
property bar, 222
publishing data to Web, 249–251

Q

Quattro Pro, 133–216. *See also* cells; notebooks; spreadsheets
   autofill features, 190–192
   basics of, 135–145
   creating charts and graphs in, 203–215
   customizing workspace, 180
   filtering data, 193–197
   formatting data, 169–180
   formulas, 160–165
   functions, 166–167
   grouping data, 200–201
   manipulating data, 189–201
   moving data, 155–158
   operators, 160
   printing from, 182–188
   QuickFill, 191–192
   QuickFilter, 193–195
   QuickType, 190–191
   selecting data, 148–150
   shortcut keys, 371
   sorting data, 198–199
   starting, 6
quattropro command, 6
queries, 221, 233–237, 378
Query Expert, 233–237
QuickChart feature, 208
QuickCorrect, 79–81, 378
QuickFill, 191–192, 378
QuickFilter, 193–195
QuickFonts, 49
QuickFonts button, 48

QuickFormat, 172–173, 378
QuickPlay feature, 269–270
QuickTips, 378
QuickType, 190–191

R

range, 378
RealTime Preview feature, 48, 61
records, Paradox, 220
rectangle tools, 301–302
Redo button, 42
Redo function, 41–42, 378
reference, 378
registration, WordPerfect Office 2000, 361–363
relative addresses, 162–165
relative reference, 378
Repeat Event dialog box, 324–325
replacing text, 74–75, 378
Report Expert, 238–242
reports
    creating, 238–242
    described, 221
    publishing as HTML, 249–251
review questions
    Part I, Getting Started, 34
    Part II, Working with Words, 131
    Part III, Working with Data, 216
    Part IV, Working with Advanced Data, 257
    Part V, Working with Ideas, 313
    Part VI, Working with Time and People, 354
rows
    defined, 378
    deleting, 153–154
    grouping, 200
    headings, 136
    inserting, 150–152
    selecting, 149
    ungrouping, 201
Rows option, 90, 91
Ruler, displaying, 65

S

Save As command, 23
Save As dialog box, 23
Save button, 24
Save command, 23
saving documents, 22–24, 379
scroll bar slide, 45
scroll bars, 7, 45–46, 379
search function
    address books, 350–351
    documents, 72–73
    terms, 72–73
Search tab, Help menu, 30
Select Page Numbering Format dialog box, 119–120
semicolon (;), 256
Serial Number, 362
Serial Number/PIN dialog box, 362
Series Properties dialog box, 290–293
Set Alarm dialog box, 322
Shadow Cursor, 43–44
Shadow Cursor command, 43
Shadow palette, 303
shapes, creating in slides, 300–307, 310
sheet coordinates, 136
sheet coordinates box, 137
sheet tab, 136, 137, 143
sheets, 379
shortcut keys, 367–373
    common shortcuts, 368–369
    CorelCENTRAL, 372
    Paradox, 373
    Presentations, 372
    Quattro Pro, 371
    WordPerfect, 370
Show All filter, 194
Size tab, 113, 114

INDEX 391

rearranging, 274–275
sorting, 268–269
sound effects, 295–296
speaker notes, 282–283, 377
text in, 267, 276–279
transitions, 293–294
viewing, 265–270
SmartTools page, 13–14
sorting, 379
sound, for slides, 295–296
spacing, 62–63, 377
Spacing command, 62–63
Speaker Notes option, 282–283, 377
special characters, 52–54
special effects, presentations, 285–296
SpeedFormat tool, 94–95
Spell Checker, 77–78
spell checking
   Grammar-As-You-Go, 78–79
   Prompt-As-You-Go, 82
   QuickCorrect, 79–81
   Spell Checker, 77–78
   Spell-As-You-Go, 75–77
Spell-As-You-Go, 75–77, 379
Spreadsheet Page Setup dialog box, 182–185
spreadsheets. *See also* cells; notebooks; Quattro Pro
   aligning data, 175–176
   borders, 178–180
   cell addresses, 140, 144–145
   columns, 150, 152–154, 173–174
   editing, 141–143, 147–158
   elements of, 136
   entering data, 138–140, 190–192
   filtering data, 193–197, 376
   fonts, 176–178
   formatting, 169–180
   formulas, 160–165
   functions, 166–167
   grouping data, 200–201

   margins, 182–183
   multiple sheets, 143–145
   navigating, 137, 143
   outlining function, 200–201
   page orientation, 183–184
   page size, 183–184
   printing, 182–188
   rows, 149, 150–151, 153–154
   scaling, 184–185
   selecting cells, 138, 148–150
   selecting data, 148–150
   sorting data, 198–199
   using Paradox data in, 252
   vs. tables, 220
   zoom options, 187
standard bar, 222
Startup Master Gallery dialog box, 262–263
status bar, 7, 222, 379
status indicator, 136, 148
Subheading box, 128
Symbol command, 53
symbols, 52–54
Symbols dialog box, 53

T

Tab Control menu, 66
Tab key, 85, 88
Table Expert, 222–228
Table Expert dialog box, 223–227
table of contents, creating, 124–127
Table of Contents toolbar, 124–127
Table QuickCreate tool, 86–87
Table SpeedFormat dialog box, 94–95
tables
   defined, 379
   documents, 84–95
   slides, 286–289
   spreadsheets, 220–228
tabs, 65–69, 379

task attachment icon, 336, 337
tasks
   assigning to events, 335–337
   completing, 334–335
   creating, 318, 332–334
   deleting, 337
   displaying in online help, 39
   editing, 334–337
   viewing, 318
templates, 10–17, 379
text. *See also* documents; pages; words
   aligning, 61–62
   arranging on page, 61–65
   blocks of, 40
   capitalization of, 52
   in cells, 138
   changing case, 52
   changing font size, 49
   changing font type, 48
   copying, 56–57
   deleting, 41, 54, 55
   enhancing, 48–52
   finding, 72–73
   indenting, 63–65
   inserting, 38–39
   moving, 54–56, 58
   pasting, 54, 56, 57
   replacing, 74–75
   selecting, 40
   Shadow Cursor and, 43–44
   in slides, 267, 276–279
   typing with WordPerfect, 38
   wrapping around graphics, 105
text boxes, 107–109, 279, 379
text formatting bar, 222
time
   changing for events, 323, 326–328
   in documents, 118–119
tips

Slide Editor
   adding text to slides, 276
   changing font, 278
   changing slide designs, 280
   changing slide show designs, 280–281
   deleting text objects, 279
   editing slides, 276–279
   opening/viewing slides, 265–266, 267, 269
   printing slide shows, 283
   speaker notes, 282–283, 377
Slide Outliner, 267, 274–275, 277
Slide Properties dialog box, 294, 295–296
slide shows. *See also* Presentations; slides
   audience notes, 284
   changing design of, 280–281
   charts in, 289–293
   creating with PerfectExpert, 264
   editing, 267, 271–284
   playing, 269–270
   printing, 283
   QuickPlay feature, 269–270
   rearranging slides, 274–275
   speaker notes, 282–283, 377
   special effects, 285–296
   tables in, 286–289
Slide Sorter, 268–269, 273–274, 379
slides. *See also* Presentations; slide shows
   adding, 272
   adding text to, 276
   audience notes, 284
   bulleted lists, 272
   changing design of, 280
   defined, 379
   deleting, 273–274
   deleting text objects, 279
   drawing tools, 297–312
   editing slide text, 267, 277
   fonts, 278, 288–289
   navigating, 265–266

INDEX

CorelCENTRAL applications
   working with addresses, 347
   working with events, 321, 323
   working with tasks, 332, 334
Paradox
   creating mailing labels, 246
   working with partitions, 234
Presentations
   opening slides, 267, 269
   working with shapes, 302, 303, 306
program interface
   closing documents, 25
   exiting applications, 8
   opening documents, 18
   printing files, 24
   saving documents, 23, 24
   starting new documents, 10, 11
Quattro Pro
   changing cell addresses, 165
   changing spreadsheet paper size, 184
   entering data, 143
   grouping/ungrouping rows, 200, 201
   opening Active Cells dialog box, 170
   opening Data Sort dialog box, 198
   printing spreadsheets, 187, 188
   sizing columns/rows, 174
   status indicator, 148
   working with complex formulas, 161
WordPerfect
   displaying Ruler, 65
   finding/replacing terms, 72, 75
   indenting paragraphs, 64, 65
   inserting symbols, 53
   selecting words/paragraphs, 40
   working with graphics, 105
   working with tables, 84, 85
   working with tabs, 67
WordPerfect Office installation, 359
title bar, 7

Tool Palette, 298
toolbars, 7, 379
tools. *See also specific tools*
   drawing tools, 297–312
   writing tools, 71–82
Top 10 filter, 194
topic links, 30
topics, help, 28–32
transitions, slide, 293–294, 379
Typeover mode, 39
Typographic Symbols command, 53

U

underlined text, 50–51
Undo button, 42
Undo function, 41–42, 379
utilities. *See* tools

V

vertical scroll bar, 7, 137
View menu, 43

W

Web
   online templates available on, 12–14
   publishing data to Web pages, 249–251
Web browsers, 28, 30, 375
Web pages
   action shapes and, 310
   backgrounds, 250
   color in, 250
   defined, 379
   publishing data to, 249–251
Week view, 319
window control buttons, 7
Windows Emulator (WINE), 234
Windows-based systems, 20
WINE (Windows Emulator), 234
WordPerfect, 37–131

basics of, 37–46
correcting mistakes, 41–42
editing text in, 38–41
formatting documents, 47–69
shortcut keys, 370
starting, 6
typing text with, 38
WordPerfect 9 icon, 4
wordperfect command, 6
WordPerfect Office 2000
    exiting, 7–8
    exiting applications, 7–8
    exploring, 6–7
    help for, 27–33
    installing, 358–361
    introduction to, 3–8
    PIN Number, 362
    registering, 361–363
    Serial Number, 362
    setting up printer for, 363–365
    shortcut keys, 367–373
    starting, 4–6
WordPerfect Office 2000 menu, 4
WordPerfect Projects Online, 13–14
words. *See also* text

adding QuickCorrect entries, 79–80
deleting QuickCorrect entries, 81
finding, 72–73
replacing, 74–75
selecting, 40
working with Prompt-As-You-Go, 82
worksheets. *See* spreadsheets
World Wide Web, 379
Wrap Text dialog box, 105
writing tools, 71–82
    Find and Replace, 72–75
    Grammar-As-You-Go, 78–79
    Prompt-As-You-Go, 82
    QuickCorrect, 79–81
    Spell Checker, 77–78
    Spell-As-You-Go, 75–77

X

X Window systems, 4–5

Z

Zoom In button, 187
zooming, 187, 379